T0331862

Examining Fractal Image Processing and Analysis

Soumya Ranjan Nayak
Chitkara University, India

Jibitesh Mishra
College of Engineering and Technology, India

A volume in the Advances in
Computational Intelligence and
Robotics (ACIR) Book Series

Published in the United States of America by
    IGI Global
    Engineering Science Reference (an imprint of IGI Global)
    701 E. Chocolate Avenue
    Hershey PA, USA 17033
    Tel: 717-533-8845
    Fax: 717-533-8661
    E-mail: cust@igi-global.com
    Web site: http://www.igi-global.com

Library of Congress Cataloging-in-Publication Data

Names: Nayak, Soumya Ranjan, 1984- editor. | Mishra, Jibitesh, editor.
Title: Examining fractal image processing and analysis / Soumya Ranjan Nayak
    and Jibitesh Mishra, editors.
Description: Hershey PA : Engineering Science Reference, an imprint of IGI
    Global, [2020]
Identifiers: LCCN 2019015490| ISBN 9781799800668 (hardcover) | ISBN
    9781799800675 (softcover) | ISBN 9781799800682 (ebook)
Subjects: LCSH: Computer vision. | Image processing--Digital techniques. |
    Image analysis.
Classification: LCC TA1634 .E975 2020 | DDC 006.4/2--dc23 LC record available at https://lccn.
loc.gov/2019015490

This book is published in the IGI Global book series Advances in Computational Intelligence and Robotics (ACIR) (ISSN: 2327-0411; eISSN: 2327-042X)

British Cataloguing in Publication Data
A Cataloguing in Publication record for this book is available from the British Library.

For electronic access to this publication, please contact: eresources@igi-global.com.

Advances in Computational Intelligence and Robotics (ACIR) Book Series

ISSN:2327-0411
EISSN:2327-042X

Editor-in-Chief: Ivan Giannoccaro, University of Salento, Italy

MISSION

While intelligence is traditionally a term applied to humans and human cognition, technology has progressed in such a way to allow for the development of intelligent systems able to simulate many human traits. With this new era of simulated and artificial intelligence, much research is needed in order to continue to advance the field and also to evaluate the ethical and societal concerns of the existence of artificial life and machine learning.

The **Advances in Computational Intelligence and Robotics (ACIR) Book Series** encourages scholarly discourse on all topics pertaining to evolutionary computing, artificial life, computational intelligence, machine learning, and robotics. ACIR presents the latest research being conducted on diverse topics in intelligence technologies with the goal of advancing knowledge and applications in this rapidly evolving field.

COVERAGE

- Machine Learning
- Natural Language Processing
- Robotics
- Heuristics
- Automated Reasoning
- Pattern Recognition
- Computational Logic
- Artificial Life
- Agent technologies
- Algorithmic Learning

IGI Global is currently accepting manuscripts for publication within this series. To submit a proposal for a volume in this series, please contact our Acquisition Editors at Acquisitions@igi-global.com or visit: http://www.igi-global.com/publish/.

Titles in this Series

For a list of additional titles in this series, please visit:
https://www.igi-global.com/book-series/advances-computational-intelligence-robotics/73674

Edge Computing and Computational Intelligence Paradigms for the IoT
G. Nagarajan (Sathyabama Institute of Science and Technology, India) and R.I. Minu (SRM Institute of Science and Technology, India)
Engineering Science Reference • ©2019 • 347pp • H/C (ISBN: 9781522585558) • US $285.00

Semiotic Perspectives in Evolutionary Psychology, Artificial Intelligence, and the Study of Mind Emerging Research and Opportunities
Marcel Danesi (University of Toronto, Canada)
Information Science Reference • ©2019 • 205pp • H/C (ISBN: 9781522589242) • US $175.00

Handbook of Research on Human-Computer Interfaces and New Modes of Interactivity
Katherine Blashki (Victorian Institute of Technology, Australia) and Pedro Isaías (The University of Queensland, Australia)
Engineering Science Reference • ©2019 • 488pp • H/C (ISBN: 9781522590699) • US $275.00

Machine Learning and Cognitive Science Applications in Cyber Security
Muhammad Salman Khan (University of Manitoba, Canada)
Information Science Reference • ©2019 • 321pp • H/C (ISBN: 9781522581000) • US $235.00

Multi-Criteria Decision-Making Models for Website Evaluation
Kemal Vatansever (Alanya Alaaddin Keykubat University, Turkey) and Yakup Akgül (Alanya Alaaddin Keykubat University, Turkey)
Engineering Science Reference • ©2019 • 254pp • H/C (ISBN: 9781522582380) • US $185.00

Handbook of Research on Deep Learning Innovations and Trends
Aboul Ella Hassanien (Cairo University, Egypt) Ashraf Darwish (Helwan University, Egypt) and Chiranji Lal Chowdhary (VIT University, India)
Engineering Science Reference • ©2019 • 355pp • H/C (ISBN: 9781522578628) • US $295.00

For an entire list of titles in this series, please visit:
https://www.igi-global.com/book-series/advances-computational-intelligence-robotics/73674

701 East Chocolate Avenue, Hershey, PA 17033, USA
Tel: 717-533-8845 x100 • Fax: 717-533-8661
E-Mail: cust@igi-global.com • www.igi-global.com

Table of Contents

Chapter 12

Chapter 13

Detailed Table of Contents

Chapter 1

Kalyan Kumar Jena, Parala Maharaja Engineering College, India
Sasmita Mishra, Indira Gandhi Institute of Technology, India
Sarojananda Mishra, Indira Gandhi Institute of Technology, India

Research in the field of fractal image processing (FIP) has increased in the current era. Edge detection of fractal images can be considered as an important domain of research in FIP. Detecting edges in different fractal images accurate manner is a challenging problem in FIP. Several methods have introduced by different researchers to detect the edges of images. However, no method works suitably under all conditions. In this chapter, an edge detection method is proposed to detect the edges of gray scale and color fractal images. This method focuses on the quantitative combination of Canny, LoG, and Sobel (CLS) edge detection operators. The output of the proposed method is produced using matrix laboratory (MATLAB) R2015b and compared with the edge detection operators such as Sobel, Prewitt, Roberts, LoG, Canny, and mathematical morphological operator. The experimental outputs show that the proposed method performs better as compared to other traditional methods.

Chapter 2

Anandkumar R., Pondicherry Engineering College, India
Kalpana R., Pondicherry Engineering College, India

The tremendous development in the field of telecommunication and computer technologies leads to the preference of transferring information as a digital data. In this transformation of information, cryptography helps in encrypting/decrypting digital data, so that intruders will not be able to sniff the highly confidential information. Most information is transferred as a digital image, where image encryption is done by scrambling the original pixels of the image, and hence, the correlation between the original pixel and scrambled pixel differs leading to confusion to unauthorized accesses. Chaotic image encryption is one of the recent technologies in cryptosystems, where a pseudorandom and irregular key is used for encryption/decryption, as the key suffers a great change if some initial conditions are altered, leading to highly secured transmission in the network. In this chapter, a detailed survey is conducted on chaotic image encryption using fractal function, in which fractal key is used for encryption and decryption of an image.

Chapter 3

Pandian R., Sathyabama Institute of Science and Technology, India

Image compression algorithms are developed mainly for reduction of storage space, easier transmission, and reception. In this chapter, many image compression algorithms have been developed based on various combinations of transforms and encoding techniques. This research work mainly deals with the selection of optimum compression algorithms, suitable for medical images, based on the performance indices like PSNR and compression ratio. In order to find the effectiveness of the developed algorithms, characterization of the CT lung images are performed, before and after compression. The diagnosis of lung cancer is an important application for various medical imaging techniques. In this work, optimal texture features are identified for classification of lung cancer have also been incorporated as a case study. The texture features are extracted from the in CT lung images. BPN is trained to classify the features into normal and cancer.

Chapter 4

Tawheed Jan Shah, University of Kashmir, India
M. Tariq Banday, University of Kashmir, India

In this chapter, the performance of wavelet transform-based EZW coding and SPIHT coding technique have been evaluated and compared in terms of CR, PSNR, and MSE by applying them to similar color images in two standard resolutions. The application of these techniques on entire color images such as passport size photograph in which the region containing the face of a person is more significant than other regions results in equal loss of information content and less compression ratio. So, to achieve the high CRs and distribute the quality of the image unevenly, this chapter proposes the ROI coding technique. Compressing ROI portion using discrete wavelet transform with Huffman coding and NROI compressed with Huffman, EZW coding, SPIHT coding suggested effective compression at nearly no loss of quality in the ROI portion of the photograph. Further, higher CR and PSNR with lower MSE have been found in high-resolution photographs, thereby permitting the reduction of storage space, faster transmission on low bandwidth channels, and faster processing.

Image acquisition systems usually acquire images with distortions due to various factors associated with digitization processes. Poisson is one of the common types of noises present in the image, and it distorts the fine features. Hence, it is necessary to denoise the noisy image by smoothing it to extract the features with fine details. Among the denoising methods, anisotropic diffusion method provides more adequate results. In this chapter, the authors dealt with existing models such as Perona-Malik (PM), total variation, Tsai, Chao, Chao TFT, difference eigen value PM, adaptive PM, modified PM, and Maiseli models. The performances of the models were tested on synthetic image added with the Poisson noise. Quality metrics are used to quantify and to ensure the smoothness of the resultant images. However, in order to ensure the completeness of the denoising effect, the qualitative attributes such as sharpness, blurriness, blockiness, edge quality, and false contouring are considered on smoothened images. The analysis results are shown the completeness of the denoising effect of the models.

Uncompressed multimedia data such as images require huge storage space, processing power, transmission time, and bandwidth. In order to reduce the storage space, transmission time, and bandwidth, the uncompressed image data is compressed before its storage or transmission. This process not only permits a large number of images to be stored in a specified amount of storage space but also reduces the time required for them to be sent or download from the internet. In this chapter, the classification of an image on the basis of number of bits used to represent each pixel of the digital image and different types of image redundancies is presented. This chapter also introduced image compression and its classification into different lossless and lossy compression techniques along with their advantages and disadvantages. Further, discrete cosine transform, its properties, and the application of discrete cosine transform-based image compression method (i.e., JPEG compression model) along with its limitations are also discussed in detail.

Chapter 7

Rasmita Lenka, KIIT University (Deemed), India
Koustav Dutta, KIIT University (Deemed), India
Ashimananda Khandual, College of Engineering and Technology, India
Soumya Ranjan Nayak, Chitkara University, India

The chapter focuses on application of digital image processing and deep learning for analyzing the occurrence of malaria from the medical reports. This approach is helpful in quick identification of the disease from the preliminary tests which are carried out in a person affected by malaria. The combination of deep learning has made the process much advanced as the convolutional neural network is able to gain deeper insights from the medical images of the person. Since traditional methods are not able to detect malaria properly and quickly, by means of convolutional neural networks, the early detection of malaria has been possible, and thus, this process will open a new door in the world of medical science.

Chapter 8

Lakshmi Sarvani Videla, Koneru Lakshmaiah Education Foundation,
India
M. Ashok Kumar P, Koneru Lakshmaiah Education Foundation, India

The detection of person fatigue is one of the important tasks to detect drowsiness in the domain of image processing. Though lots of work has been carried out in this regard, there is a void of work shows the exact correctness. In this chapter, the main objective is to present an efficient approach that is a combination of both eye state detection and yawn in unconstrained environments. In the first proposed method, the face region and then eyes and mouth are detected. Histograms of Oriented Gradients (HOG) features are extracted from detected eyes. These features are fed to Support Vector Machine (SVM) classifier that classifies the eye state as closed or not closed. Distance between intensity changes in the mouth map is used to detect yawn. In second proposed method, off-the-shelf face detectors and facial landmark detectors are used to detect the features, and a novel eye and mouth metric is proposed. The eye results obtained are checked for consistency with yawn detection results in both the proposed methods. If any one of the results is indicating fatigue, the result is considered as fatigue. Second proposed method outperforms first method on two standard data sets.

Chapter 9

Cmak Zeelan Basha, Koneru Lakshmaiah Education Foundation, India
Azmira Krishna, Koneru Lakshmaiah Education Foundation, India
S. Siva Kumar, Koneru Lakshmaiah Education Foundation, India

Recognition of items in jumbled scenes is a basic test that has as of late been generally embraced by computer vision frameworks. This chapter proposes a novel technique how to distinguish a specific item in jumbled scenes. Given a reference picture of the article, a method for recognizing a particular article dependent on finding point correspondences between the reference and the objective picture is presented. It can distinguish objects in spite of a scale change or in-plane revolution. It is additionally strong to little measure of out-of-plane rotation and occlusion. This technique for article location works for things that show non-reiterating surface precedents, which offer rising to exceptional part coordinates. This method furthermore works honorably for reliably shaded articles or for things containing repeating structures. Note that this calculation is intended for recognizing a particular article.

Chapter 10

Abhisek Sethy, Koneru Lakshmaiah Education Foundation, India
Prashanta Kumar Patra, College of Engineering and Technology
Bhubaneswar, India

Offline handwritten recognition system for Odia characters has received attention in the last few years. Although the recent research showed that there has been lots of work reported in different language, there is limited research carried out in Odia character recognition. Most of Odia characters are round in nature, similar in orientation and size also, which increases the ambiguity among characters. This chapter has harnessed the rectangle histogram-oriented gradient (R-HOG) for feature extraction method along with the principal component analysis. This gradient-based approach has been able to produce relevant features of individual ones in to the proposed model and helps to achieve high recognition rate. After certain simulations, the respective analysis of classifier shows that SVM performed better than quadratic. Among them, SVM produces with 98.8% and QC produces 96.8%, respectively, as recognition rate. In addition to it, the authors have also performed the 10-fold cross-validation to make the system more robust.

This chapter describes a novel method to enhance degraded nighttime images by dehazing and color correction method. In the first part of this chapter, the authors focus on filtering process for low illumination images. Secondly, they propose an efficient dehazing model for removing haziness Thirdly, a color correction method proposed for color consistency approach. Removing nighttime haze technique is an important and necessary procedure to avoid ill-condition visibility of human eyes. Scattering and color distortion are two major problems of distortion in case of hazy image. To increase the visibility of the scene, the authors compute the preprocessing using WLS filter. Then the airlight component for the non-uniform illumination presents in nighttime scenes is improved by using a modified well-known dark-channel prior algorithm for removing nighttime haze, and then it uses α-automatic color equalization as post-processing for color correction over the entire image for getting a better enhanced output image free from haze with improved color constancy.

Image analysis is giving a huge breakthrough in every field of science and technology. The image is just a collection of pixels and light intensity. The image capturing was done in two ways: (1) by using infrared sensors and (2) by using radiography. The normal images are captured by using the infrared sensors. Radiography uses the various forms of a light family, such as x-ray, gamma rays, etc., to capture the image. The study of neuroimaging is one of the challenging research topics in the field of biomedical image processing. So, from this note, the motivation for this work is to analyze 3D images to detect Alzheimer's disease and compare the statistical results of the whole brain image data with standard doctor's results. The authors also provide a very short implementation for brain slicing and feature extraction using Freesurfer and OpenNeuro dataset.

    Kalyan Kumar Jena, Parala Maharaja Engineering College, India
    Sasmita Mishra, Indira Gandhi Institute of Technology, India
    Sarojananda Mishra, Indira Gandhi Institute of Technology, India

Research in the field of digital image processing (DIP) has increased in the current scenario. Edge detection of digital images is considered as an important area of research in DIP. Detecting edges in different digital images accurately is a challenging work in DIP. Different methods have been introduced by different researchers to detect the edges of images. However, no method works well under all conditions. In this chapter, an edge detection method is proposed to detect the edges of gray scale and color images. This method focuses on the combination of Canny, mathematical morphological, and Sobel (CMS) edge detection operators. The output of the proposed method is produced using matrix laboratory (MATLAB) R2015b and compared with Sobel, Prewitt, Roberts, Laplacian of Gaussian (LoG), Canny, and mathematical morphological edge detection operators. The experimental results show that the proposed method works better as compared to other existing methods in detecting the edges of images.

Preface

The influence and impact of digital images on modern society, science, technology and art are remarkable. Image processing has become such a critical component in contemporary science and technology without that many tasks would not even be attempted. Image analysis is one of the key components that have its implications on use of digital images. It is a truly interdisciplinary subject that draws from synergistic developments involving many disciplines and is used in medical imaging, microscopy, computer vision, geology and many other fields.

Gaining high-level understanding from digital images is a key requirement for computing. One aspect of study that is assisting with this advancement is fractal theory. This new science has gained momentum and popularity as it has become a key topic of research in the area of image analysis. This book has put thrust on this vital area.

This is a text for use in a first practical course in image processing and analysis, for final-year undergraduate or first-year post graduate students with a background in biomedical engineering, computer science, radiologic sciences or physics. Designed for readers who will become "end users" of digital image processing in various domains, it emphasizes the conceptual framework and the effective use of image processing tools and uses mathematics as a tool, minimizing the advanced mathematical development of other textbooks.

Featuring research on topics such as image compression, pattern matching, and artificial neural networks, this book is ideally designed for system engineers, computer engineers, professionals, academicians, researchers, and students seeking coverage on problem-oriented processing techniques and imaging technologies. The book is an essential reference source that discusses fractal theory applications and analysis, including box-counting analysis, multi-fractal analysis, 3D fractal analysis, and chaos theory, as well as recent trends in other soft computing techniques.

INSIDE THIS BOOK

In this regard, the first chapter of this book delivers the core concept of fractal image processing in application to edge detection. This Chapter focuses on the quantitative combination of canny, Log and soble edge detection operators are carefully studied.

The second chapter deal with chaos-based image encryption using fractal function, in which fractal key is used for encryption and decryption. On the basis of an empirical study, argues that fractal plays crucial role in empirical model of cryptography in digital domain with fractal key for engineering applications.

The third chapter, deal with the compression techniques on medical image analysis. This research work mainly deals with the selection of optimum compression algorithms based on the performance indices like PSNR and Compression ratio. The effectiveness of the developed algorithms is characterized in term of CT lung images before and after stage of compression technique. The optimal texture features are also studied for classification of Lung cancer has also been incorporated as a case study.

The fourth chapter, emphasizing on wavelet transform coding based on image compression techniques. The performance of wavelet transform based EZW coding, and SPIHT coding technique has been evaluated and compared in terms of CR, PSNR and MSE by applying them on similar color images in two standard resolutions in terms of ROI coding technique. Compressing ROI portion using discrete wavelet transform with Huffman coding and NROI compressed with Huffman, EZW coding, SPIHT coding.

The fifth chapter, referring a performance study based on image quality attributes on smoothened image obtained by anisotropic diffusion based models. The different models like Perona-Malik(PM), total variation, Tsai, Chao, Chao TFT, difference Eigen value PM, adaptive PM, modified PM and Maiseli are implemented. The performances of the models were tested on synthetic image are addressed. Quality metrics of the smoothness are presented. The de-noising effect, the qualitative attributes such as sharpness, blurriness, blockiness, edge quality, and false contouring are pointed out.

The sixth chapter, the classification of an image on the basis of number of bits used to represent each pixel of the digital image and different types of image redundancies is presented. This chapter also introduced Image Compression and its classification into different Lossless and Lossy Compression techniques along with their advantages and disadvantages. Further, discrete cosine transform, its properties and the application of image compression method (i.e., JPEG Compression Model) along with its limitations are also discussed in detail.

The seventh chapter focuses on medical image analysis for malaria with Deep learning for analysing the occurrence of Malaria from the Medical Reports. This approach is helpful in quick identification of the disease from the preliminary tests which are carried out in a person affected by malaria. The combination of Deep Learning has made the process much advanced as the Convolutional Neural Network is able to gain deeper insights from the medical images of the person.

The eighth chapter present an efficient approach that is combination of both eye state detection and yawn in unconstrained environment. In first analysis, the face region and then eyes and mouth are detected. Histograms of oriented gradient (HOG) features are extracted to detect eye closure. Distance between intensity changes in the mouth map is used to detect yawn. In second analysis, off the shelf face detectors and facial landmark detectors are used to detect the features and a novel eye and mouth metric is studied.

The ninth chapter deals with automatic article detection in a jumbled scene using point feature matching were successfully studied. Mainly it focuses how to distinguish a specific item in jumbled scenes, given a reference picture of the article based on finding point correspondences between the reference and the objective picture.

The tenth chapter R-HOG feature based off line character recognition were studied. The harnessed the Rectangle Histogram Oriented Gradient (R-HOG) for feature extraction method along with the Principal Component Analysis is thoroughly addressed in advantages to the pattern recognition applications.

The eleventh chapter describes a novel method to enhance degraded night time images by dehazing and color correction method. In the first part of this analysis, the filtering process was addressed for low illumination images and in second phase of analysis deal with dehazing model for removing haziness, and apart from this the color correction method are taken care for color consistency approach.

The twelfth chapter deal with biomedical 3D image analysis for Alzheimer's diseases detection. The implementation for brain slices and feature extraction using Freesurfer and OpenNeuro dataset also addressed.

In the last chapter, an algorithmic approach based on CMS edge detection technique was discussed. This article emphasizes adopting on the combination of Canny, mathematical morphological and Sobel (CMS) edge detection operators are presented.

CONCLUSION

This book is intended to give the recent trends on image analysis, 3D fractal analysis, chaos theory, texture analysis, color imaging, pattern recognition and to understand and study different application area. This book mainly focuses on stepwise discussion, exhaustive literature review, detailed analysis and discussion, rigorous experimentation result and application-oriented approaches.

Chapter 1
An Edge Detection Approach for Fractal Image Processing

Kalyan Kumar Jena
Parala Maharaja Engineering College, India

Sasmita Mishra
Indira Gandhi Institute of Technology, India

Sarojananda Mishra
Indira Gandhi Institute of Technology, India

ABSTRACT

Research in the field of fractal image processing (FIP) has increased in the current era. Edge detection of fractal images can be considered as an important domain of research in FIP. Detecting edges in different fractal images accurate manner is a challenging problem in FIP. Several methods have introduced by different researchers to detect the edges of images. However, no method works suitably under all conditions. In this chapter, an edge detection method is proposed to detect the edges of gray scale and color fractal images. This method focuses on the quantitative combination of Canny, LoG, and Sobel (CLS) edge detection operators. The output of the proposed method is produced using matrix laboratory (MATLAB) R2015b and compared with the edge detection operators such as Sobel, Prewitt, Roberts, LoG, Canny, and mathematical morphological operator. The experimental outputs show that the proposed method performs better as compared to other traditional methods.

DOI: 10.4018/978-1-7998-0066-8.ch001

INTRODUCTION

A fractal is a geometric shape (non regular) which has the equal degree of non regularity on every scale. It is considered as a fragmented or rough geometric structure which can be split into parts each of which is recognized as a reduced size replication of the whole. Several concepts and techniques of FIP are provided by Krantz et al. (1989), Uemura et al. (2000), Falconer (2004), Bassingthwaighte et al. (2013), Russ (2013), Nayak et al. (2015), Nayak et al. (2016), Nayak et al. (2018a), Nayak et al. (2018b), Nayak et al. (2018c), Nayak et al. (2018d), Nayak et al. (2018e), Nayak et al. (2018f), Nayak et al. (2018g), Nayak et al. (2019), Bhatnagar et al. (2019), Joardar et al. (2019), Kadam et al. (2019), Yin et al. (2019), Joshi et al. (2019), Li et al. (2019) and Padmavati et al. (2019). Fractals are considered as never ending patterns. These are referred to as infinitely complex patterns which are self similar across several scales. It is required to repeat a simple process again and again in an ongoing feedback loop in order to create the fractals. From mathematics point of view, a fractal is considered as a subset of Euclidean space for which the hausdorff dimension exceeds (strictly) the topological dimension. Fractals have the tendency to appear nearly equal at several levels. These provide identical patterns at increasingly small scales which are considered as unfolding symmetry or expanding symmetry. When the replication is same (exactly) at every scale, then it is referred to as affine self similar. On the basis of mathematical equations, these are normally nowhere differentiable. Generally, these are not limited to geometric patterns and also describe processes in time. Different techniques such as iterated function systems, L-systems, finite subdivision rules, etc. can be used to generate fractals. Fractal generating programs can be used to create fractal images. These can be used for modelling natural structures, image compression, analysis of medical diagnostic images, study of chaotic phenomenon, study of convergence of iterative processes, etc. Fractal geometry can be used to approximate several natural objects to a certain degree including mountain ranges, clouds, vegetables, coastlines, etc. These geometry concepts can be used to simulate as well as understand several objects in nature. Different methods or operators such as Sobel, Prewitt, Roberts, LoG, Canny, mathematical morphological operator, etc. can be used to detect the edges of fractal images. Several approaches, concepts as well as techniques are provided by Gonzalez et al. (2004), Gonzalez et al. (2007), Wang et al. (2016), Xin et al. (2012), Lahani et al. (2018), Othman et al. (2017), Podder et al. (2018), Shanmugavadivu et al. (2014), Wan et al. (2007), Wang (2007), Patel et al. (2011), Coleman et al. (2004), Huertas et al. (1986), Gupta et al. (2013), Chaple et al. (2014), Alshorman et al. (2018), Agrawal et al. (2018), Avots et al. (2018), Halder et al. (2019), Goel et al. (2013), Katiyar et al. (2014), Yu-qian et al. (2006), Giannarou et al. (2005), Scharcanski et al. (1997), Hemalatha et al. (2018) and Kumar et al. (2017) related to edge detection of several images.

The main contribution in this chapter is mentioned as follows:

1. A hybrid edge detection scheme is proposed in order to detect the edges of color and gray scale digital images using the quantitative combination of Canny, LoG and Sobel edge detection operators.
2. At first, Canny edge detector is applied in the original image. Afterwards, LoG operator is applied and then Sobel edge detector is applied to obtain the resultant image.
3. The results of the proposed edge detection method are produced using MATLAB R2015b and compared with Sobel, Prewitt, Roberts, LoG, Canny and Mathematical Morphological edge detection methods.

RELATED WORKS

Different methods or techniques have proposed by different researchers for the processing of fractal images. Some methods have focused in this section. Uemura et al. (2000) focuses on four methods to create a fractal dimension image and these methods are applied on brain MRI. The methods such as conventional, overlapping, symmetric and folded are used for estimating the fractal dimension. The methods such as conventional, overlapping and symmetric provide nearly same fractal dimension images. The folded method is used to attain the images. The brain surrounding structure can be removed by the help of the images (filtered) and can automatically identify the brain surface edge. The brain surface data can be used for several applications such as inter modal brain image registration, display of 3-D (three dimensional) surface, etc. Nayak et al. (2015) focuses on differential box counting technique to find a fractal dimension (uniform) for gray scale as well as color images. Nayak et al.(2016) presents an improved differential box counting technique to improve the accuracy by focusing on less fit error and to provide several fractal dimension at a time by focusing on least regression line and fractal dimension at every corresponding size of box. The presented method may be able to accurately capture the roughness and may provide better results consistently than other traditional methods. Nayak et al. (2018a) proposed a modified differential box counting method by the help of asymmetric triangle box grid partition. The presented approach is used for optimizing the accomplishment of the method by focusing on less fitting error in case of distinctive image, average fitting error in case of whole images and better precision box count through triangle box partition. It can solve under counting and over counting problem at a time. The presented method may provide less fit error and give better identification in case of scaled images than existing methods. Nayak et al. (2018b) presents a differential box counting method to accurately estimate the fractal dimension with less fitting error than existing methods such as original differential box counting, relative differential box counting, improved differential box counting, improved box counting. The presented method may perform better by focusing on less fitting error as compared to existing methods. Nayak et al. (2018c) presents an improved differential box counting algorithm by segmenting the box of grid into two patterns (asymmetric) in order to get greater precision box count and to estimate fractal dimension accurately by focusing on less computational time and less fit error than existing methods. Nayak et al. (2018d) presents a modified differential box counting method which addresses the issues such as lowest roughness variation, identical fractal dimension checked by decrementing or incrementing constant value to every intensity points, computational error in original differential box counting. On the basis of these issues, the presented method may perform better as compared to the existing methods. Nayak et al. (2018e) presents a new color fractal dimension estimation algorithm by the extension of original differential box counting algorithm and the implementation of maximum color Euclidean distance from every box block (non overlapping) of RGB components. The presented algorithm may capture the RGB color image surface roughness efficiently and the computational time of the presented method is comparatively less than the existing algorithms. This method may be more precise and more reliable method for color images. Nayak et al.(2018f) attempts to estimate the fractal dimension of RGB color images by the extension of differential box counting algorithm into a domain (color). Gradient images with known fractal dimension are generated with controlled images (experimentally) for validating this approach. The presented method may be more precise and efficient, and may take less time. Nayak et al. (2018g) focuses on ground truth study about fractal dimension of colors images having similar texture. Nayak et al. (2019) focuses on box counting mechanism and the improved algorithms associated with this mechanism, its working principle and the applications in medical image processing. Fractal dimension plays an important role for characterizing the irritated or complex objects available in nature. Classical Euclidian geometry may not able to analyze such complex objects accurately. Fractal dimension concept can be used for the processing of several images. Fractal dimension mechanism can work on self similarity theory. Fractal geometry can be applied in medical images for detecting the cancer cells in human body can also be applied in brain imaging to detect tumor, ECG signal, etc. Most of the researchers focus on box counting method for analyzing such complex structures. Joardar et al. (2019) proposed a feature extraction method on the basis of patch-wise fractal dimension (enhanced) for pose invariant face recognition. A fractal dimension computation technique based on improved differential box counting technique is used to extract the feature of human face thermal images. A Far Infrared imaging based human face database is used to test the accuracy, stability as well as robustness of the presented feature extraction technique. Bhatnagar et al. (2019) proposed a fusion framework for applications (night vision) such as vehicle navigation, pedestrian identification, supervision, etc. The presented framework is realized in the spatial domain. This work focuses on the concept of combination of low light vision and infrared imagery into an output for enhancing visual perception. This work also focuses on the idea of averaging all the origination images for obtaining an initial fused image. Afterwards, the fused image (initial) is improved by focusing the most important characteristics governed from the root mean square error and the fractal dimension of the visual as well as infrared images for obtaining the last fused image. The experiment shows that it may be better as compared to the traditional image fusion techniques by focusing on visual and significant evaluations.

PROPOSED METHODOLY

In this work, Canny, LoG and Sobel edge detection operators are used for detecting the edges of several fractal images. These operators are described as follows:

Canny Edge Detection Operator

Canny edge detection operator is described by Xin et al. (2012), Shanmugavadivu et al. (2014), Wang et al. (2016), Othman et al. (2017), Podder et al. (2018) and Lahani et al. (2018). This operator is known as one of the optimal edge detectors and it is most commonly used in practice. It detects edges based on specific criteria (parameters dependent) and it deals with multiple stage process. Here Gaussian filter is used for smoothening the image. A two dimensional first derivative operator is used on the smoothened image in order to focus the portion with high first spatial derivatives. In gradient magnitude image, edges rise with ridges. The algorithm for Canny edge detection process has the following steps shown below:

Step 1: Gaussian filter is applied for reducing the noise from image.

Step 2: Edges of the image are found out using appropriate edge detector. Sobel edge detector can be used for such purpose.

Step 3: Edge direction is found out using the formula $\theta = \tan^{-1}(SM_Y/SM_X)$ (SM_Y and SM_X are specified in Figure 2)

Step 4: Non-maxima suppression process is applied in order to suppress the pixel value which is not recognized to be an edge and it provides thin lines of edge.

Step 5: In order to remove streaking, hysteresis thresholding is used.

LoG Edge Detection Operator

Huertas et al. (1986), Coleman et al. (2004), Wan et al. (2007), Wang (2007) and Patel et al. (2011) describes about LoG edge detecton operator. It is a second order derivative operator and it focuses on zero crossings points in the image. It detects thin and sharp edges. It is a gradient based operator which focuses on both Gaussian as well as Laplacian operators. The Gaussian operator is used to reduce the noise and the Laplacian operator is used to identify the sharp edges. However, it may generate false edges and at the curved edges, the localization error may be severe. This edge detector is very sensitive to noise. It can use a single kernel M_{XY} of size 5×5 as mentioned in Figure 1 for edge detection of image. At first, the noise is reduced using Gaussian smooth filter and afterwards, the image is used for further processing. LoG is used to convolve the input image with LoG function. Then, it can detect the zero crossings in the filtered result in order to obtain the edges.

Sobel Edge Detection Operator

The mechanism of Sobel edge detection operator is described by Gupta et al. (2013), Chaple et al. (2014), Alshorman et al. (2018), Agrawal et al. (2018). This operator is considered as a gradient-based method. It applies a two dimensional spatial

Figure 1. LOG operator mask

0	0	-1	0	0
0	-1	-2	-1	0
-1	-2	16	-2	-1
0	-1	-2	-1	0
0	0	-1	0	0

M_{XY}

Figure 2. Sobel operator masks

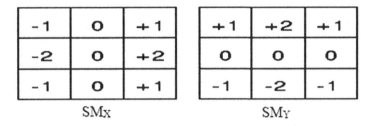

- 1	O	+ 1		+ 1	+2	+ 1
-2	O	+2		O	O	O
- 1	O	+ 1		- 1	-2	- 1

SM$_X$ SM$_Y$

gradient measure on image and focuses on high spatial frequency that leads to edges. Generally, It comprises of two 3×3 masks named as SM$_X$ and SM$_Y$ as shown in Figure 2, one for horizontal calculation (SM$_X$) and other for vertical calculation (SM$_Y$) for the detection of edges of an image. Here the gradient magnitude can be calculated as $((SM_X)^2+(SM_Y)^2)^{1/2}$ and the approximate gradient magnitude can be calculated as | SM$_X$ |+| SM$_Y$ |.

PROPOSED ALGORITHM

```
If(image I is grayscale)
I=imread('image');
G=rgb2gray(I);
[m,n]=size(G);

% Canny (C) of I is found

C=edge(G,'canny');
imshow(C);

% Black and White (BW) of I is found

BW = im2bw(G,0.4);
imshow(BW);

% Morphing (M) of BW image

M = bwmorph(BW,'remove');
imshow(M)
```

```
% Sobel (S) of I is found

S=edge(G,'sobel');
imshow(S);

% Prewitt (P) of I is found

P=edge(G,'prewitt');
imshow(P);

% Roberts (R) of I is found

R=edge(G,'Roberts');
imshow(R);

% LoG (LG) of I is found

LG=edge(G,'log');
imshow(LG);

% Generation of final C-L-S image

for i=1:m
     for j=1:n
          if C(i,j)==1
               CLSfinal(i,j)=C(i,j);
          else if LG(i,j)==1
               CLSfinal(i,j)=LG(i,j);
          else if S(i,j)==1
               CLSfinal(i,j)=S(i,j);
          else
               CLSfinal(i,j)=0;
          end
     end
end
```

```
else (for color image I)

% Canny (C) of I is found

C=edge(I,'canny');
imshow(C);

% Black and White (BW) of I is found

BW = im2bw(G,0.4);
imshow(BW);

% Morphing (M) of BW image

M = bwmorph(BW,'remove');
imshow(M)

% Sobel (S) of I is found

S=edge(G,'sobel');
imshow(S);

% Prewitt (P) of I is found

P=edge(G,'prewitt');
imshow(P);

% Roberts (R) of I is found

R=edge(G,'Roberts');
imshow(R);

% LoG (LG) of I is found

LG=edge(G,'log');
imshow(LG);
```

```
% Generation of final C-L-S image

for i=1:m
    for j=1:n
        if C(i,j)==1
            CLSfinal(i,j)=C(i,j);
        else if LG(i,j)==1
            CLSfinal(i,j)=LG(i,j);
        else if S(i,j)==1
            CLSfinal(i,j)=S(i,j);
        else
            CLSfinal(i,j)=0;
        end
    end
end
imshow(CLSfinal)
```

RESULTS AND DISCUSSION

The performance of the proposed method is analyzed using MATLAB R2015b. MATLAB is developed by MathWorks and it is considered as a numerical computing environment for the implementation of algorithms, plotting of graphs, analysis of data, design of user interfaces, processing of images and videos by the help of matrix manipulation mechanism, etc. In this chapter, several fractal images are taken from kaggle database for processing using the proposed method. The outputs of the proposed method are compared with the results of Sobel, Prewitt, Roberts, LoG, Canny and mathematical morphological edge detection methods. The experimental results are mentioned in Figure 3 to Figure 7.

Figure 3 to Figure 7 shows the outputs of Sobel, Prewitt, Roberts, LoG, Canny, mathematical morphological and the proposed method in (b), (c), (d), (e), (f), (g) and (h) respectively. From the results, it is observed (subjective method) that the proposed method provides better results (edges) for both gray scale and color images as compared to Sobel, Prewitt, Roberts, LoG, Canny, mathematical morphological edge detection methods. This method shows thick edges in some locations.

Figure 3. (a) Original Fractal image with size 400×400. (b) Result by applying Sobel edge detection operator. (c) Result by applying Prewitt edge detection operator. (d) Result by applying Roberts edge detection operator. (e) Result by applying LOG edge detection operator. (f) Result by applying Canny edge detection operator. (g) Result by applying Morphological operator. (h) Result by applying Proposed method.

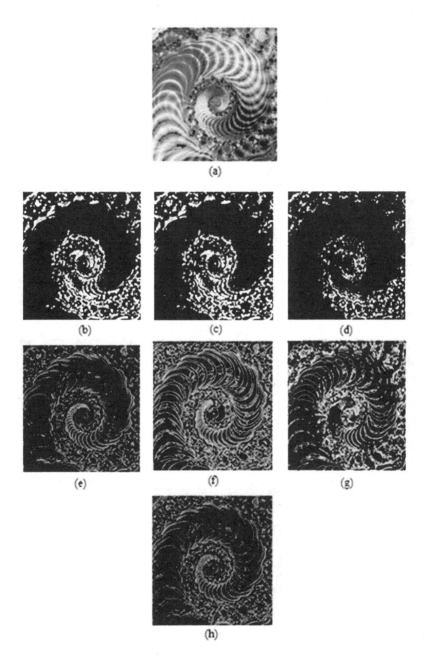

Figure 4. (a) Original Fractal image with size 400×400. (b) Result by applying Sobel edge detection operator. (c) Result by applying Prewitt edge detection operator. (d) Result by applying Roberts edge detection operator. (e) Result by applying LOG edge detection operator. (f) Result by applying Canny edge detection operator. (g) Result by applying Morphological operator. (h) Result by applying Proposed method.

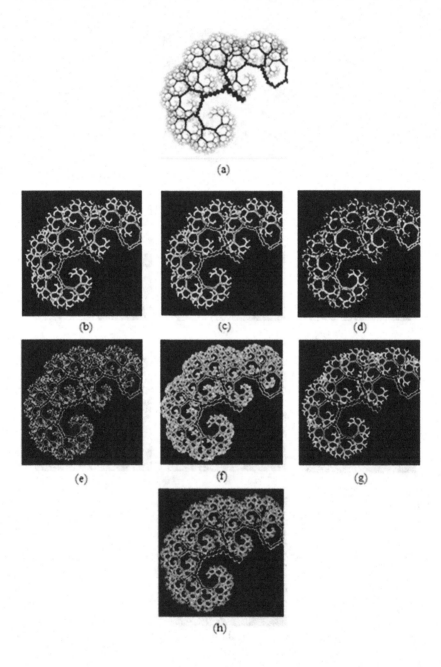

Figure 5. (a) Original Fractal image with size 225×225. (b) Result by applying Sobel edge detection operator. (c) Result by applying Prewitt edge detection operator. (d) Result by applying Roberts edge detection operator. (e) Result by applying LOG edge detection operator. (f) Result by applying Canny edge detection operator. (g) Result by applying mathematical morphological operator. (h) Result by applying Proposed method.

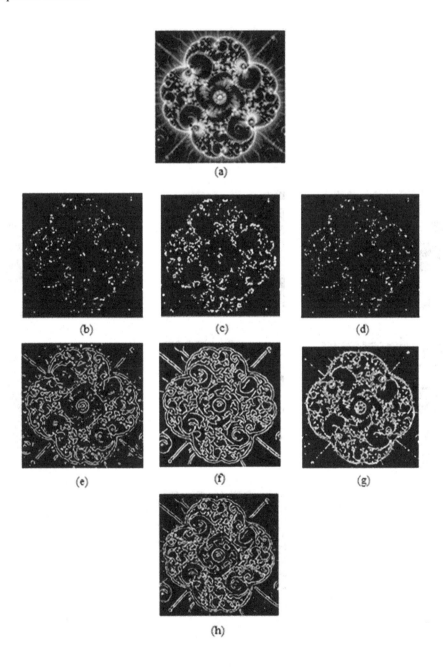

Figure 6. (a) Original Fractal image with size 400×400. (b) Result by applying Sobel edge detection operator. (c) Result by applying Prewitt edge detection operator. (d) Result by applying Roberts edge detection operator. (e) Result by applying LOG edge detection operator. (f) Result by applying Canny edge detection operator. (g) Result by applying mathematical morphological operator. (h) Result by applying Proposed method.

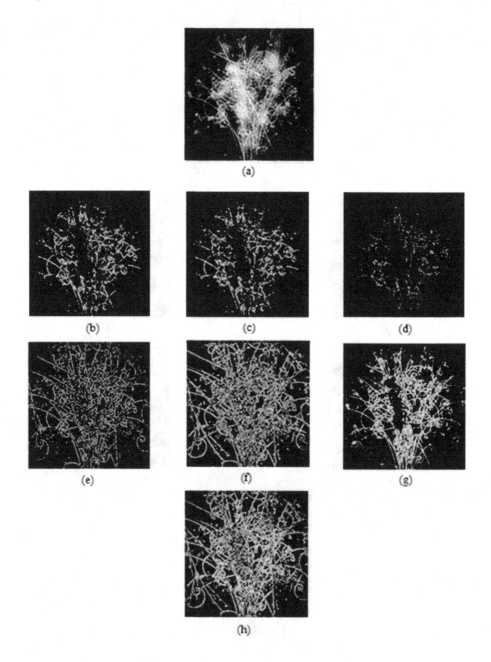

Figure 7. (a) Original Fractal image with size 400×400. (b) Result by applying Sobel edge detection operator. (c) Result by applying Prewitt edge detection operator. (d) Result by applying Roberts edge detection operator. (e) Result by applying LOG edge detection operator. (f) Result by applying Canny edge detection operator. (g) Result by applying mathematical morphological operator. (h) Result by applying Proposed method.

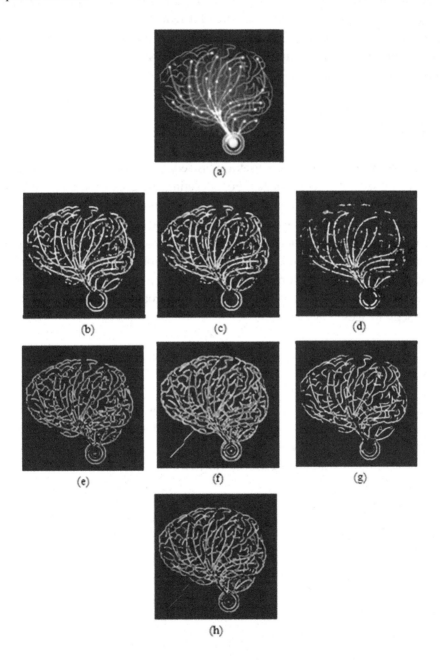

FUTURE RESEARCH DIRECTIONS

This chapter focuses on the processing of several fractal images. The fractal images are taken from kaggle database and processed using MATLAB R2015b for detecting the edges of fractal images. The results of proposed method are compared with Sobel, Prewitt, Roberts, LoG, Canny, mathematical morphological edge detection methods. We will carry our future research for reducing the thickness of edges in output images by using improved edge detection method and for developing an improved differential box counting technique with less fitting error for processing of several fractal images.

CONCLUSION

The method presented in this work uses a hybrid edge detection scheme for detecting the edges of several fractal images. For detecting the edges the combination of Canny, LoG and Sobel edge detectors are used. This method is easily implemented and is used for gray scale as well as color fractal images. From the analysis of the experimental results mentioned in Fig. 3 to Fig. 7, it is concluded that the proposed method shows edges prominently as compared to Sobel, Prewitt, Roberts, LoG, Canny, and mathematical morphological edge detection methods. This approach can be considered as a suitable edge detection approach for both gray scale and color fractal images.

ACKNOWLEDGMENT

We owe our deep gratitude to the department of Computer Science Engineering and Applications, Indira Gandhi Institute of Technology, Sarang (nodal centre of Utkal University, Bhubaneswar) for providing better research environment for the completion of our research work successfully.

REFERENCES

Agrawal, A., & Bhogal, R. K. (2018). Edge Detection Techniques in Dental Radiographs (Sobel, T1FLS & IT2FLS). In *International Conference on Communication, Networks and Computing* (pp. 411-421). Springer.

Alshorman, M. A., Junoh, A. K., Muhamad, W. Z. A. W., Zakaria, M. H., & Desa, A. M. (2018). Leukaemia's Cells Pattern Tracking Via Multi-phases Edge Detection Techniques. *Journal of Telecommunication, Electronic and Computer Engineering (JTEC), 10*(1-15), 33-37.

Avots, E., Arslan, H. S., Valgma, L., Gorbova, J., & Anbarjafari, G. (2018). A new kernel development algorithm for edge detection using singular value ratios. *Signal, Image and Video Processing*, 1–9.

Bhatnagar, G., & Wu, Q. J. (2019). A fractal dimension based framework for night vision fusion. *IEEE/CAA Journal of Automatica Sinica, 6*(1), 220-227.

Chaple, G., & Daruwala, R. D. (2014). Design of Sobel operator based image edge detection algorithm on FPGA. In *Communications and Signal Processing (ICCSP), 2014 International Conference on* (pp. 788-792). IEEE. 10.1109/ICCSP.2014.6949951

Coleman, S. A., Scotney, B. W., & Herron, M. G. (2004). A systematic design procedure for scalable near-circular Laplacian of Gaussian operators. In *Pattern Recognition, 2004. ICPR 2004. Proceedings of the 17th International Conference on* (*Vol. 1*, pp. 700-703). IEEE. 10.1109/ICPR.2004.1334275

Goel, S., Verma, A., & Kumar, N. (2013). Gray level enhancement to emphasize less dynamic region within image using genetic algorithm. In *Advance Computing Conference (IACC), 2013 IEEE 3rd International* (pp. 1171-1176). IEEE.

Gupta, S., & Mazumdar, S. G. (2013). Sobel edge detection algorithm. *International Journal of Computer Science and Management Research, 2*(2), 1578-1583.

Halder, A., Bhattacharya, P., & Kundu, A. (2019). Edge Detection Method Using Richardson's Extrapolation Formula. In *Soft Computing in Data Analytics* (pp. 727–733). Singapore: Springer. doi:10.1007/978-981-13-0514-6_69

Hemalatha, K., & Rani, K. U. (2018). Feature Extraction of Cervical Pap Smear Images Using Fuzzy Edge Detection Method. In *Data Engineering and Intelligent Computing* (pp. 83–90). Singapore: Springer. doi:10.1007/978-981-10-3223-3_8

Huertas, A., & Medioni, G. (1986). Detection of intensity changes with subpixel accuracy using Laplacian-Gaussian masks. *IEEE Transactions on Pattern Analysis and Machine Intelligence, PAMI-8*(5), 651–664. doi:10.1109/TPAMI.1986.4767838 PMID:21869362

Joardar, S., Sanyal, A., Sen, D., Sen, D., & Chatterjee, A. (2019). An Enhanced Fractal Dimension Based Feature Extraction for Thermal Face Recognition. In *Decision Science in Action* (pp. 217–226). Singapore: Springer. doi:10.1007/978-981-13-0860-4_16

Joshi, M., Agarwal, A. K., & Gupta, B. (2019). Fractal Image Compression and Its Techniques: A Review. In *Soft Computing: Theories and Applications* (pp. 235–243). Singapore: Springer. doi:10.1007/978-981-13-0589-4_22

Kadam, S., & Rathod, V. R. (2019). Medical Image Compression Using Wavelet-Based Fractal Quad Tree Combined with Huffman Coding. In *Third International Congress on Information and Communication Technology* (pp. 929-936). Springer.

Lahani, J., Sulaiman, H. A., Muniandy, R. K., & Bade, A. (2018). An Enhanced Edge Detection Method Based on Integration of Entropy—Canny Technique. *Advanced Science Letters, 24*(3), 1575–1578. doi:10.1166/asl.2018.11112

Li, X. X., Tian, D., He, C. H., & He, J. H. (2019). A fractal modification of the surface coverage model for an electrochemical arsenic sensor. *Electrochimica Acta, 296*, 491–493. doi:10.1016/j.electacta.2018.11.042

Nayak, S., Khandual, A., & Mishra, J. (2018g). Ground truth study on fractal dimension of color images of similar texture. *Journal of the Textile Institute, 109*(9), 1159–1167. doi:10.1080/00405000.2017.1418710

Nayak, S. R., & Mishra, J. (2018a). A modified triangle box-counting with precision in error fit. *Journal of Information and Optimization Sciences, 39*(1), 113–128. doi:10.1080/02522667.2017.1372155

Nayak, S. R., & Mishra, J. (2019). Analysis of Medical Images Using Fractal Geometry. In *Histopathological Image Analysis in Medical Decision Making* (pp. 181–201). IGI Global. doi:10.4018/978-1-5225-6316-7.ch008

Nayak, S. R., Mishra, J., & Jena, P. M. (2018b). Fractal Dimension of GrayScale Images. In *Progress in Computing, Analytics and Networking* (pp. 225-234). Springer. doi:10.1007/978-981-10-7871-2_22

Nayak, S. R., Mishra, J., Khandual, A., & Palai, G. (2018f). Fractal dimension of RGB color images. *Optik (Stuttgart)*, *162*, 196–205. doi:10.1016/j.ijleo.2018.02.066

Nayak, S. R., Mishra, J., & Padhy, R. (2016). An improved algorithm to estimate the fractal dimension of gray scale images. In *2016 International Conference on Signal Processing, Communication, Power and Embedded System (SCOPES)* (pp. 1109-1114). IEEE. 10.1109/SCOPES.2016.7955614

Nayak, S. R., Mishra, J., & Padhy, R. (2018c). A New Extended Differential Box-Counting Method by Adopting Unequal Partitioning of Grid for Estimation of Fractal Dimension of Grayscale Images. In *Computational Signal Processing and Analysis* (pp. 45–57). Singapore: Springer. doi:10.1007/978-981-10-8354-9_5

Nayak, S. R., Mishra, J., & Palai, G. (2018d). A modified approach to estimate fractal dimension of gray scale images. *Optik (Stuttgart)*, *161*, 136–145. doi:10.1016/j.ijleo.2018.02.024

Nayak, S. R., Mishra, J., & Palai, G. (2018e). An extended DBC approach by using maximum Euclidian distance for fractal dimension of color images. *Optik (Stuttgart)*, *166*, 110–115. doi:10.1016/j.ijleo.2018.03.106

Nayak, S. R., Ranganath, A., & Mishra, J. (2015). Analysing fractal dimension of color images. In *2015 International Conference on Computational Intelligence and Networks* (pp. 156-159). IEEE. 10.1109/CINE.2015.37

Othman, Z., & Abdullah, A. (2017). An Adaptive Threshold Based On Multiple Resolution Levels for Canny Edge Detection. In *International Conference of Reliable Information and Communication Technology* (pp. 316-323). Springer.

Padmavati, S., & Meshram, V. (2019). A Hardware Implementation of Fractal Quadtree Compression for Medical Images. In *Integrated Intelligent Computing, Communication and Security* (pp. 547–555). Singapore: Springer. doi:10.1007/978-981-10-8797-4_55

Patel, J., Patwardhan, J., Sankhe, K., & Kumbhare, R. (2011). Fuzzy inference based edge detection system using Sobel and Laplacian of Gaussian operators. In *Proceedings of the International Conference & Workshop on Emerging Trends in Technology* (pp. 694-697). ACM. 10.1145/1980022.1980171

Podder, P., Parvez, A. M. S., Yeasmin, M. N., & Khalil, M. I. (2018). Relative Performance Analysis of Edge Detection Techniques in Iris Recognition System. In *2018 International Conference on Current Trends towards Converging Technologies (ICCTCT)* (pp. 1-6). IEEE. 10.1109/ICCTCT.2018.8551023

Shanmugavadivu, P., & Kumar, A. (2014). Modified eight-directional canny for robust edge detection. In *Contemporary Computing and Informatics (IC3I), 2014 International Conference on* (pp. 751-756). IEEE. 10.1109/IC3I.2014.7019768

Uemura, K., Toyama, H., Baba, S., Kimura, Y., Senda, M., & Uchiyama, A. (2000). Generation of fractal dimension images and its application to automatic edge detection in brain MRI. *Computerized Medical Imaging and Graphics*, *24*(2), 73–85. doi:10.1016/S0895-6111(99)00045-2 PMID:10767587

Wan, J., He, X., & Shi, P. (2007). *An Iris Image Quality Assessment Method Based on Laplacian of Gaussian Operation*. MVA.

Wang, M., Jin, J. S., Jing, Y., Han, X., Gao, L., & Xiao, L. (2016). The Improved Canny Edge Detection Algorithm Based on an Anisotropic and Genetic Algorithm. In *Chinese Conference on Image and Graphics Technologies* (pp. 115-124). Springer. 10.1007/978-981-10-2260-9_14

Wang, X. (2007). Laplacian operator-based edge detectors. *IEEE Transactions on Pattern Analysis and Machine Intelligence*, *29*(5), 886–890. doi:10.1109/TPAMI.2007.1027 PMID:17356206

Xin, G., Ke, C., & Xiaoguang, H. (2012). An improved Canny edge detection algorithm for color image. In *Industrial Informatics (INDIN), 2012 10th IEEE International Conference on* (pp. 113-117). IEEE. 10.1109/INDIN.2012.6301061

Yin, L., Li, X., Zheng, W., Yin, Z., Song, L., Ge, L., & Zeng, Q. (2019). Fractal dimension analysis for seismicity spatial and temporal distribution in the circum-Pacific seismic belt. *Journal of Earth System Science*, *128*(1), 22. doi:10.100712040-018-1040-2

Yu-qian, Z., Wei-hua, G., Zhen-cheng, C., Jing-tian, T., & Ling-Yun, L. (2006). Medical images edge detection based on mathematical morphology. In *Engineering in Medicine and Biology Society, 2005. IEEE-EMBS 2005. 27th Annual International Conference of the* (pp. 6492-6495). IEEE.

ADDITIONAL READING

Bassingthwaighte, J. B., Liebovitch, L. S., & West, B. J. (2013). *Fractal physiology*. Springer.

Falconer, K. (2004). *Fractal geometry: mathematical foundations and applications*. John Wiley & Sons.

Giannarou, S., & Stathaki, T. (2005). Edge detection using quantitative combination of multiple operators. In Signal Processing Systems Design and Implementation, 2005. IEEE Workshop on (pp. 359-364). IEEE. 10.1109/SIPS.2005.1579893

Gonzalez, R. C., & Woods, R. E. (2007). Image processing. Digital image processing, 2.

Gonzalez, R. C., Woods, R. E., & Eddins, S. L. (2004). *Digital image processing using MATLAB* (Vol. 624). Upper Saddle River: Pearson-Prentice-Hall.

Katiyar, S. K., & Arun, P. V. (2014). Comparative analysis of common edge detection techniques in context of object extraction. arXiv preprint arXiv:1405.6132.

Krantz, S. G., & Mandelbrot, B. B. (1989). Fractal geometry. *The Mathematical Intelligencer*, *11*(4), 12–16. doi:10.1007/BF03025877

Kumar, S., Saxena, R., & Singh, K. (2017). Fractional Fourier transform and fractional-order calculus-based image edge detection. *Circuits, Systems, and Signal Processing*, *36*(4), 1493–1513. doi:10.100700034-016-0364-x

Russ, J. C. (2013). *Fractal surfaces*. Springer Science & Business Media.

Scharcanski, J., & Venetsanopoulos, A. N. (1997). Edge detection of color images using directional operators. *IEEE Transactions on Circuits and Systems for Video Technology*, *7*(2), 397–401. doi:10.1109/76.564116

KEY TERMS AND DEFINITIONS

Canny Operator: An edge detection operator that focuses on multistage algorithm for detecting edges in several images.

CLS: Canny, LoG, and Sobel.

Edge Detection: An image processing technique to find the objects boundaries within images.

Fractal Image Processing: Application of computer algorithms for performing image processing on several fractal images.

Fractal: A geometric shape (non-regular).

LoG Operator: An edge detection operator that focuses on zero crossings points in several images.

Mathematical Morphology: A technique to analyze and process geometrical structures.

Prewitt Operator: An edge detection operator that focuses on the computation of gradient approximation of the image intensity function.

Roberts Operator: An edge detection operator that focuses on approximation of image gradient using discrete differentiation operation.

Sobel Operator: An edge detection operator that focuses on two dimensional gradient measurements on several images and highlights the high spatial frequency regions which correspond to edges.

Chapter 2
A Review on Chaos–Based Image Encryption Using Fractal Function

Anandkumar R.
Pondicherry Engineering College, India

Kalpana R.
Pondicherry Engineering College, India

ABSTRACT

The tremendous development in the field of telecommunication and computer technologies leads to the preference of transferring information as a digital data. In this transformation of information, cryptography helps in encrypting/decrypting digital data, so that intruders will not be able to sniff the highly confidential information. Most information is transferred as a digital image, where image encryption is done by scrambling the original pixels of the image, and hence, the correlation between the original pixel and scrambled pixel differs leading to confusion to unauthorized accesses. Chaotic image encryption is one of the recent technologies in cryptosystems, where a pseudorandom and irregular key is used for encryption/decryption, as the key suffers a great change if some initial conditions are altered, leading to highly secured transmission in the network. In this chapter, a detailed survey is conducted on chaotic image encryption using fractal function, in which fractal key is used for encryption and decryption of an image.

DOI: 10.4018/978-1-7998-0066-8.ch002

INTRODUCTION

Encryption of images transferred through an open medium, can be very easily hacked by unauthorized users and is vulnerable to unexpected changes in the image leading to the breech of confidential information. Various procedures are being proposed till now, in order to protect the confidentiality of the image based information from intruders. All techniques encompass the vital criteria mentioned in the following section:

- **Low Correlation:** The original image and the encrypted image should not correlate can be preferably so zero, so that the attackers will not be able to predict the encrypted image (Kumari et al., 2017).
- **Large Key Size:** The larger the key size, there will be very less probability for brute force attack (Kumari et al., 2017).
- **Key Sensitivity:** When an intruder tries to manipulate the image pixel in order to decrypt the confidential image, that activity or any minute change, should lead to a completely different encrypted image (Kumari et al., 2017).
- **Less Time-Complexity:** The whole image encryption/decryption methodology should consume very less time, as the performance may degrade if the methodology has higher time (Kumari et al., 2017).
- There are more than 15 image encryption techniques, which preserves the image from unintended users as well as, encompassing the above discussed criteria. The following are the image-based encryption algorithm:
  ◦ Vigene`re Cipher
  ◦ Data Encryption Standard (DES)
  ◦ International Data Encryption Algorithm (IDEA)
  ◦ Blowfish
  ◦ Visual Cryptography
  ◦ RC4, RC5, RC6
  ◦ Triple Data Encryption Standard (TDES)
  ◦ Advanced Encryption Standard (AES)
  ◦ Scheme Based on Intertwining Chaotic Maps
  ◦ Scheme Based on Chaotic Function Using Linear Congruence's
  ◦ Scheme Based on Mixed Transform Logistic Maps
  ◦ Scheme Based on Peter De Jong Chaotic Map and RC4 Stream Cipher
  ◦ Scheme Based on Chaotic Map and Vigene`re Scheme

Performance analysis was done on all 15 image algorithms wherein correlation, key size, key sensitivity and time complexity were taken as performance evaluators. Table 1 depicts the performance measure of the above presented image encryption algorithms (Kumari et al., 2017).

From Table 1, it will be obvious that chaotic method of image encryption is found to have high encryption scenario, proving low correlation between original and encrypted image, the key space is also very large and a small change to the key value will result in a highly scrambled image leading to strong opposition against unauthorized access and the total time taken for encryption and decryption is also very low.

CHAOS BASED ENCRYPTION

The word "Chaos" carries a meaning of unpredictable behavior of a particular system taken into consideration. As discussed in the earlier sections, image based confidential information is being sent to a public network by my money-making sectors namely Military, Medical fields etc. In order to protect the image from the

Table 1. Performance evaluation of image encryption methods

Performance evaluator/Image encryption methods	Correlation	Key size	Key sensitivity	Time Complexity
Vigene`re	High	reasonable	Low	least
DES	Moderate	Low	High	high
IDEA	Moderate	Low	High	High
Blowfish	Moderate	Low	High	Moderate
Visual	Very low	moderate	Least	Least
RC4	Very low	reasonable	High	Least
RC5	moderate	reasonable	High	High
RC6	moderate	reasonable	High	High
TDES	High	reasonable	Low	High
AES	Moderate	Moderate	High	Low
Chaotic Maps	Very low	Moderate	High	Low
Chaotic function	Very low	Moderate	High	High
Logistic maps	Very low	Moderate	High	Moderate
Chaotic map and RC4	Very low	Maximum	High	Moderate
Chaotic map &Vigene're	Very low	Maximum	High	Least

hands of hackers, several image encryption techniques are being applied, so that it will be difficult for the network sniffers to crack the information hidden behind the image. From section 1, we had summarized that chaos based image encryption is one of the best image encryption algorithms, as the change in the secret key in order to diffuse the original image, will lead to a completely different image pixels leading to a unsuccessful attempt to any type of network attacks. The following Figure 1 depicts the flow of chaotic image encryption scheme (Fadhel et al., 2017).

In chaos-based image encryption, the pixels of the image are scrambled using the secret key, which is highly sensitive to change, with very large key-space and the time to encode and decode is also least. Hence, the resultant image pixel will have very less correlation with the original pixel, which makes the chaos based encryption to be used prevalently in all image based encryption. The above discussion can be clearly understood from Figure 1.

Chaos Based Image Encryption Methods

Image scrambling method is based on chaotic mapping in which the image is scrambled by taking its sensitivity to initial condition as a control parameter. Here pairs of pixels points will be widely distributed, which is then mingled with other pixel point, to achieve confidentiality. This method is being widely used as it has simple design and also achieves higher efficiency (Dong et al., 2010).

Multiple chaotic systems is a combination of both Lorenz and Rossler chaotic system, in which the sensitivity is based on 6 variables, which results in a larger key space, more sensitivity and less time complexity (Alsafasfeh et al., 2011).

Lorenz chaotic system equation:

$$x = \sigma\left(y - x\right)$$
$$y = rx - y - xz \qquad\qquad (1)$$
$$z = xz - \beta z$$

Figure 1. Chaos-based image encryption representation

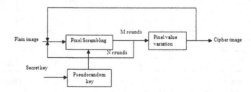

In Equation 1, σ, r, β are subjective factors which should be greater than 0. In Lorenz equation, x, y, z is the variables with higher sensitivity (Alsafasfeh et al., 2011).

Rossler chaotic system:

$$x = -y - z$$
$$y = x + ay \tag{2}$$
$$z = b + z(x - c)$$

In Equation 2, a, b, c are the arbitrary factors, where a=b and c > 0. This equation has one quadratic equation, where a change in x, y, z inputs in not proportional to the outcome. This makes Rossler system stronger than Lorenz system (Alsafasfeh et al., 2011).

Multiple chaotic systems:

$$x = \sigma\left(y - x\right) - y - z$$
$$y = rx - y - 20xz + x + ay \tag{3}$$
$$z = 5xy - bz + s + x\left(z - c\right)$$

The Equation 3 has 2 new factors b, s and the initial condition has 6 sensitive parameters making the proposed system more efficient than individual chaotic systems.

In cross chaotic map logistic map and Chebyshev maps are used in which a gray scale substitution method is used, which randomly changes the pixel values based on encryption matrix. After pixel substitution, row rotation and column rotation technique is performed, which makes cross chaotic map more protected and practicable (Wang et al., 2008).

Chen, Lu and Henon chaotic systems are another chaotic image encryption method used widely in all image-based network transactions (Anandkumar et al., 2019).

In Chen image encryption method the positions of the pixels are shuffled and the grey of the pixels are changed. From the obtained shuffled pixels, a secret key is encrypted to obtain a highly confidential image representation. Chen method is very highly resistant to brute force attack and has larger key space. The Chen's equation is as follows (Anandkumar et al., 2019; Guan et al., 2005):

$$\frac{dx}{dt} = a\left(y - x\right)$$

$$\frac{dy}{dt} = \left(c - a\right)x - xz + cy \qquad\qquad (4)$$

$$\frac{dz}{dt} = xy - bz$$

In the above Equation 4, a, b, c is the system attractors, where -a -b +c is always less than zero, where (a, b, c) = (35, 8, and 28). The image of the above-mentioned equation with the defined a, b, c values has the following image when experimented in Matlab is shown in Figure 2 (Guan et al., 2005).

From Figure 2, it is understood that, the orbit has higher starting value, making z>0, and as z value decreases, the orbit forms an elliptical shape in x-y plane and the ±c value makes the origin to take a spiral shape in (y-x) or (x-z) plane. Thus a

Figure 2. DSP execution

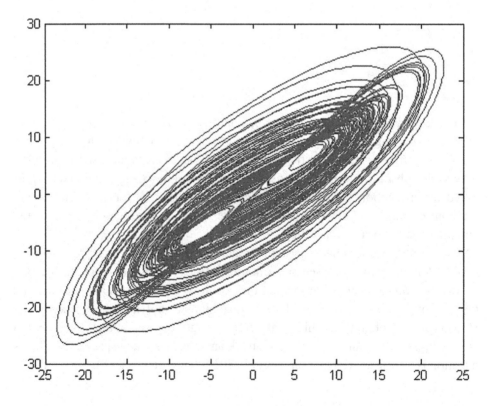

small change in initial value makes the orbit to encounter different shapes, leading to unstable behavior, achieving high level encryption.

Lu Systems

The Lu system has the following equation:

$$\frac{dx}{dt} = a\left(y - x\right)$$
$$\frac{dy}{dt} = -xz + cy \tag{5}$$
$$\frac{dz}{dt} = xy - bz$$

The Lu Equation 5, has a chaotic attractor where $(a, b, c) = (36, 3, 20)$, in which the initial conditions are obtained by mapping the external keys to the image pixels resulting in chaotic signal, which is masked by encrypting the chaotic signals (Fei et al., 2005).

Figure 3 depicts the Digital Signal Processing implementation using Matlab for Lu system, where the origin with the initial condition is neither sporadic nor convergent.

Henon System

In Henon system (Wei-Bin et al., 2009; Anandkumar et al., 2018) the positions of the image pixels are shuffled by using cat map method. The Henon map for the specified image is obtained from the following equation:

$$x_{i+2} = 1 - ax^2_{I+1} + bx_i \tag{6}$$

where a=0.3 and b $\in$ [1.07, 1.4], for which the system becomes chaotic. Here a, b, x_0, x_1 represents the secret key. After the generation of Henon map, a transform matrix of the pixel value from the Henon map is done in order to change the pixel value of shuffled image and the Henon mapped pixel value.

Figure 4 presents the knowledge that control parameters have same values, with a slight change in initial values, leading to a non-periodical shape of the pixels, of the picture taken into account (Anandkumar et al., 2019).

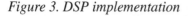

Figure 3. DSP implementation

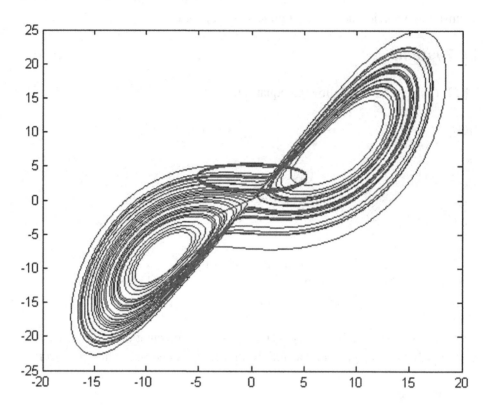

Chaos and Fractals in Image Encryption

In previous sections, many chaos based image encryption sets were discussed, where real numbers were applied in the quadratic equations and functions. A small change in the initial condition resulted in unpredicted behavior of the system, leading hackers to unstable position. This is the main theme behind chaos theory. Let us assume that instead of simple real numbers, complex numbers were applied. Even very simple functions, when iterated repeatedly might lead to a very complex cipher image, where decryption by intruders becomes a very challenging task. Thus, chaos based image encryption had a switch over to fractal functions, which has correlation to near zero, large key space and high key sensitivity. Both public and private key is used as a fractal key, which is followed by changing the pixel values and interchanging the pixel positions based on grey scale value to achieve more secure image transmission across public networks. Another merit of fractal key is that, as the key has complex numbers, the number of guesses made by hackers will be a long process, leading to shrieked key size and large key space.

Figure 4. Matlab implementation for Henon Map

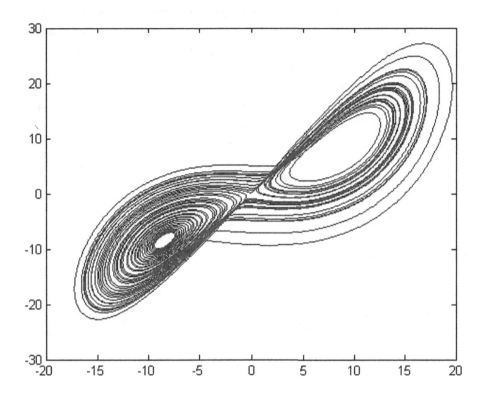

Gaston Julia and Benoit Mandelbrot gave direction to fractal based image encryption. Julia took complex functional iterations and introduced Julia sets to the world. Mandelbrot experimented with very difficult and perturbed functional iterations for producing a more secure image encryption scheme, Mandelbrot sets, giving a very tough situation to the hackers and intruders. The following sections discuss briefly about Julia sets and Mandelbrot sets and emphasize the importance of fractal sets (Agarwal, 2017; Cederberg, 2001).

Julia Sets

Consider the following quadratic equation:

$$Q_c = (Z^2 + C) \tag{7}$$

In the above Equation 7, Q_c is the function, for which Julia set has to be defined, Z is a complex value and C is the complex constant. Substitute a complex value, say Z_1. After applying that, a new value will be obtained, say X_0 which is then substituted for next iteration of the function in C. Like the same procedure has to be repeated, to produce the orbit of Z_0. The iteration has to be performed till the orbit behavior can be identified in a long run. The orbits that are bounded in complex plane should be marked as black dots and the orbits that move away to infinity should be marked as colored dots (White) (Cederberg, 2001).

It is depicted that, the boundary between black dots and white dots is called Julia sets and the boundary and the interior of the boundary are called filled Julia sets. Thus Julia sets encompasses many shapes, some shapes have a connection, and some shapes have distorted connection, making it a highly resistant algorithm against hackers (Radwan et al., 2015).

Mandelbrot Sets

Mandelbrot set is obtained from generalization of Julia sets. The obtained Julia sets can be connected or disconnected. If the Julia sets has connectedness property, then the sets correspond to Mandelbrot set. Consider the following quadratic equation

$Q_c=(Z^2+C)$

Substitute C value for the equation above, with different complex value for every iteration for various critical points Z. The Julia set is said to be connected only if the critical points does not move away to infinity. From the above observation, it is clear that, a Mandelbrot set has complex numbers in it, only of if the filled Julia set has 0 in it shows that Mandelbrot set lies within c-plane, only if $|C|<2$. If $|C|>2$, the orbit goes towards infinity and Mandelbrot set cannot be identified.

LITERATURE SURVEY ON CHAOS IMAGE ENCRYPTION USING FRACTAL SETS

Radwan et al. (2015) proposed, "Symmetric Encryption Algorithms Using Chaotic and Non Chaotic Generators: A Review", in which both chaotic and non-chaotic systems where compared along with substitution only phase, permutation only phase and both phases applied to each systems. For chaotic system Arnold's cat map and

Lorenz system was utilized for analysis and for non-chaotic systems Fractal sets and chess-based algorithms are used. Correlation coefficient, differential attack measures, Mean Square Error (MSE), Entropy, key sensitivity were used as performance measures, from which it was evident that combining both chaotic and non-chaotic system along with both substitution and permutation phases has higher security and less complexity when compared to other techniques.

Abd-El-Hafiz et al. (2014) presented, A fractal-based image encryption system, where multiple fractals images were used based on confusion and diffusion process leading a larger key size and higher sensitivity and zero correlation when compared to other techniques.

Agarwal et al. (2018) has proposed Secure Image Transmission Using Fractal and 2D-Chaotic Map in which a new 2D-Sine Tent composite map (2D-STCM), which is applied to superior fractal functions, in order to obtain chaotic key structure based on initial conditions. The chaotic key has larger space and it is very complex due to applied fractal sets and chaotic maps. This is then followed by confusion step, in which chaotic circular pixel shuffling (CCPS) is used to change the position of pixels in the plain image. And after that in diffusion stage, XOR operation is conducted in the shuffled pixel, and cipher image is acquired. The entire process carries out confusion and diffusion step three times, making the system more secure, robust and efficient than other systems.

Agarwal (2017) has proposed Symmetric Key Encryption using Iterated Fractal Functions, in which public keys are designed using superior Mandelbrot sets; known Mann iterated functions keeping few universal and confidential parameters on both sides. After exchanging open key between both parties, a private key which will be the same for both parties will be generated using Relative superior Julia sets known as, Ishikawa iterated fractal function. The chaotic nature of fractal sets makes the method more efficient with higher key sensitivity and very much stable against brute force attack. Agarwal, S et al(2017).

Rana et al. (2011) has presented A Generation of New Fractals for Sin Function, in which tangent function of type $\{\tan(Z^n)+C\}$ was used. Relative superior set, Ishikawa set is applied, which performs iteration producing new fractal images, which are chaotic in nature. The main concept here is connectivity of Julia set can be determined by Ishikawa iteration, which is not possible by other fractal functions (Rana et al., 2011).

Table 2. Comparison on experimental data

Reference	Techniques	Methods	Advantage	Disadvantage
Radwan, A.G et	Symmetric Encryption Algorithms Using Chaotic and Non Chaotic Generators: A Review	Arnold's cat map and Lorenz system, Fractal sets and chess-based algorithms	High security, speed	No image compression, No FGPA hardware design
Abd-El-Hafiz SK et al	A fractal-based image encryption system	Multiple fractal image	Larger key size, higher sensitivity and zero correlation, handles different image and same type of entropy.	Complex methodology when more enormous images are used for encryption
Shafali Agarwal	Secure Image Transmission Using Fractal and 2D-Chaotic Map	2D-Sine Tent composite map (2D-STCM), chaotic circular pixel shuffling (CCPS)	More secure, robust and efficient, large key space and key sensitivity is very high than all techniques.	Since confusion and diffusion is carried out three times, it has slightly high time complexity in spite of high level security and efficient performance.
Shafali Agarwal	Symmetric Key Encryption using Iterated Fractal Functions	Mann iterated fractal functions, Ishikawa iterated fractal function	Secure and reliable cryptosystem as fractal functions are chaotic in nature.	Key size compression is not achieved.
Rana.R et al	A Generation of New Fractals for Sin Function	Ishikawa fractional function	Determines connectivity of Julia sets, has sine and cosine properties	Mandelbrot set is not applied leading to inefficiency to secure more complex images

RESEARCH ISSUES

The chaos based image encryption paved way for a secure public network image transmission. The chaos based iteration has large key space, high key sensitivity and low time complexity. But only simple values can be applied as initial condition which leads to change in pixel position. After that, XOR operation is performed on the shuffled pixel image, to obtain a cipher image. In order to achieve security for more complex functions, fractals are applied to the functions, which will lead to more fractal images with different shapes, followed by confusion and diffusion stages. In fractals method, Julia set and Mandelbrot sets are applied to achieve the desired goal. Superior Mandelbrot sets are applied to functions known as, Mann fractal iteration and Relative superior Julia sets, applied to complex functions, known as Ishikawa fractal iteration. From the sections discussed above, it can concluded that fractal based chaotic image encryption, has more secure image encryption, larger key space, less correlation nearly equal to zero, when compared all other chaotic encryption methods.

REFERENCES

Abd-El-Hafiz, S. K., Radwan, A. G., Haleem, S. H. A., & Barakat, M. L. (2014). A fractal-based image encryption system. *IET Image Processing*, 8(12), 742–752.

Agarwal, S. (2017). Image encryption techniques using fractal function: A review. *International Journal of Computer Science and Information Technology*, 9(2), 53–68. doi:10.5121/ijcsit.2017.9205

Agarwal, S. (2017). Symmetric key encryption using iterated fractal functions. *International Journal of Computer Network and Information Security*, 9(4), 1–9. doi:10.5815/ijcnis.2017.04.01

Agarwal, S. (2018). Secure Image Transmission Using Fractal and 2D-Chaotic Map. *Journal of Imaging*, 4(1), 17.

Alsafasfeh, Q. H., & Arfoa, A. A. (2011). Image encryption based on the general approach for multiple chaotic systems. *J. Signal and Information Processing*, 2(3), 238–244. doi:10.4236/jsip.2011.23033

Anandkumar, R., & Kalpana, R. (2018, August). Analyzing of Chaos based Encryption with Lorenz and Henon Map. In *2018 2nd International Conference on I-SMAC (IoT in Social, Mobile, Analytics and Cloud)(I-SMAC) I-SMAC (IoT in Social, Mobile, Analytics and Cloud)(I-SMAC), 2018 2nd International Conference on* (pp. 204-208). IEEE.

Anandkumar, R., & Kalpana, R. (2019). A Survey on Chaos Based Encryption Technique. In *Enabling Technologies and Architectures for Next-Generation Networking Capabilities* (pp. 147–165). IGI Global. doi:10.4018/978-1-5225-6023-4.ch007

Cederberg, J. N. (2001). Chaos to Symmetry: An Introduction to Fractal Geometry. In *A Course in Modern Geometries* (pp. 315–387). New York, NY: Springer. doi:10.1007/978-1-4757-3490-4_5

Dong, Y., Liu, J., Zhu, C., & Wang, Y. (2010, July). Image encryption algorithm based on chaotic mapping. In *2010 3rd International Conference on Computer Science and Information Technology* (Vol. 1, pp. 289-291). IEEE.

Fadhel, S., Shafry, M., & Farook, O. (2017). Chaos Image Encryption Methods: A Survey Study. *Bulletin of Electrical Engineering and Informatics, 6*(1), 99–104.

Fei, P., Qiu, S. S., & Min, L. (2005, May). An image encryption algorithm based on mixed chaotic dynamic systems and external keys. In *Proceedings. 2005 International Conference on Communications, Circuits and Systems* (Vol. 2). IEEE.

Guan, Z. H., Huang, F., & Guan, W. (2005). Chaos-based image encryption algorithm. *Physics Letters. [Part A], 346*(1-3), 153–157. doi:10.1016/j.physleta.2005.08.006

Kumari, M., Gupta, S., & Sardana, P. (2017). A Survey of Image Encryption Algorithms. *3D Research, 8*(4), 37.

Radwan, A. G., AbdElHaleem, S. H., & Abd-El-Hafiz, S. K. (2016). Symmetric encryption algorithms using chaotic and non-chaotic generators: A review. *Journal of Advanced Research, 7*(2), 193–208. doi:10.1016/j.jare.2015.07.002 PMID:26966561

Rana, R., Chauhan, Y. S., & Negi, A. (2011). Generation of New Fractals for Sin Function. *Int. J. Comp. Tech. Appl., 2*(6), 1747–1754.

Risa. (n.d.). Retrieved from: http://risa.is.tokushima-u.ac.jp/~tetsushi/chen

Wang, L., Ye, Q., Xiao, Y., Zou, Y., & Zhang, B. (2008, May). An image encryption scheme based on cross chaotic map. In *2008 Congress on Image and Signal Processing* (Vol. 3, pp. 22-26). IEEE. doi:10.1109/CISP.2008.129

Wei-Bin, C., & Xin, Z. (2009, April). Image encryption algorithm based on Henon chaotic system. In *2009 International Conference on Image Analysis and Signal Processing* (pp. 94-97). IEEE. 10.1109/IASP.2009.5054653

KEY TERMS AND DEFINITIONS

Chaos Mapping: Chaotic map is an evolution function that shows some part of chaotic behavior. The chaotic mapping will be either discrete or continuous.

Chaos Theory: Chaos theory is the branch of mathematics deals with complicated linear dynamic systems.

Cryptography: Art of secret writing.

Decryption: Decryption is a process of converting cipher text to plain text.

Encryption: Encryption is process of converting a plain text to cipher text.

Chapter 3
Development of Algorithms for Medical Image Compression:
Compression Algorithms

Pandian R.
Sathyabama Institute of Science and Technology, India

ABSTRACT

Image compression algorithms are developed mainly for reduction of storage space, easier transmission, and reception. In this chapter, many image compression algorithms have been developed based on various combinations of transforms and encoding techniques. This research work mainly deals with the selection of optimum compression algorithms, suitable for medical images, based on the performance indices like PSNR and compression ratio. In order to find the effectiveness of the developed algorithms, characterization of the CT lung images are performed, before and after compression. The diagnosis of lung cancer is an important application for various medical imaging techniques. In this work, optimal texture features are identified for classification of lung cancer have also been incorporated as a case study. The texture features are extracted from the in CT lung images. BPN is trained to classify the features into normal and cancer.

DOI: 10.4018/978-1-7998-0066-8.ch003

INTRODUCTION

Image compression finds an extensive application in the field of medical image processing. Image storage problem is always encountering many practical applications. Image files contain considerable amount of redundant and irrelevant data and it is essential to propose suitable image compression algorithms which can be used to eliminate this. In this work, wavelet Transform based compression algorithms are developed for computer tomography image. Symlet based transformations have been proposed to transform the images and are encoded using the various encoding. The developed compression algorithms are evaluated in terms of Peak signal to noise Ration (PSNR), Compression ratio (CR), Means square error (MSE) and bits per pixel (BPP). The optimum compression algorithm is also found based, on the results obtained. so as to characterize the computed tomography (CT) image the features are extracted and it is proven that after compression, the CT images show its ability for identifying types of defects. The results are an indicator to the promising application of this for medical image compression schemes.

BASIC COMPRESSION TECHNIQUES

Image compression can be accomplished by the use of coding methods, spatial domain techniques and transform domain techniques (Vemuri et al. 2007). Coding methods are directly applied to images. General coding methods comprise of entropy coding techniques which include Huffman coding and arithmetic coding, run length coding and dictionary-based coding. Spatial domain methods which operate directly on the pixels of the image combine spatial domain algorithms and coding methods. Transform domain methods transform the image from its spatial domain representation to a different type of representation using well-known transforms.

REVIEW OF LITERATURE

Many researches applied various approaches in the field of medical image compression, in both lossless and lossy methods. Lossless compression is able to produce maximum compression ratio of 3:1 with a minimum loss of information. Since the digital images require more amount of space to store, the lossy compression is opted in order to remove insignificant information preserving every part of the relevant and important image information. More research works have been performed in teleradiology applications, to determine the degree of compression which maintains the diagnostic image quality (Ishigaki et al. 1990). MacMahon et al. (1991) proved that a ratio of 10:1 is sufficient for compressing the medical images. Cosman et al. (1994) proved that there is no significant loss of information for compression ratios up to 9:1. Lee et al. (1993), Goldberg (1994) and Perlmutter et al. (1997) pointed out that lossy compression techniques can be employed for medical images without much affecting the diagnostic content of images. The decompression results show no significant variation with the original for compression ratios up to 10:1 in case of medical images in the proposed work of Ando et al. (1999). Many researches (Slone et al. 2000, Skodras et al. 2001, Chen 2007 and Choong et al. 2007) proved that since, digital medical images occupy large amount of storage space, at least 10:1 compression ratio must be achieved. Kalyanpur et al. (2000) have proven the effect of Joint Photographic Experts Group (JPEG) and wavelet compression algorithms for medical images and satisfied without much loss of diagnostic ability upto10:1 compression. Persons et al. (2000) described the diagnostic accuracy and evaluated that compressed medical images with a compression ratio of 9:1, which will not result in image degradation. Saffor et al. (2001) evaluated the performance of JPEG and wavelet and found that the wavelet gave higher compression efficiency than JPEG without a compromise in image quality. Li et al. (2001) analyzed the effect of JPEG and wavelet compression and concluded that compression ratio up to 10:1 is satisfactory. Hui and Besar (2002) found the performance of JPEG2000 on medical images and showed that JPEG2000 is more effective, compared to JPEG when JPEG2000 images could retain more detail than a JPEG image. Both the types of compression (lossy and lossless), have been performed by Smutek (2005) and Seeram (2006). The lossless compression techniques produce best results with a high compression ratio of 3:1 and the lossy compression techniques with high compression ratios leads to distortion in decompressed image. The more advanced method for compressing medical images is JPEG2000 (Krishnan et al. 2005) which combines integer wavelet transform with Embedded Block Coding with Optimized Truncation (EBCOT). Asraf et al. (2006) estimated a compression technique, which is a hybrid of lossless and lossy techniques by means of neural network vector quantization and Huffman coding. This high complexity technique is experienced for medical images with compression ratio of 5 to10. Chen (2007) found a new algorithm for medical image compression that is based on set partitioning in hierarchical trees (SPIHT) algorithm. An 8 x 8 discrete cosine transform (DCT) approach is adopted to perform sub band decomposition. SPIHT is then employed to organize data. This is block-based technique and more difficulty is involved. The author concluded that for application in medical domain some adaptations are needed to eliminate blocking artifacts. Singh et al. (2007) obtained a technique for classification of DCT blocks into two categories, namely pure and complex, based on the variance in the block. Energy retained will be high if the image is decomposed to smaller number levels but compression obtained is less (Tahoces et al. 2008; Sadashivappa & Babu 2008). Dragan and Ivetic (2009) consideration that the issue is not whether to compress medical images using lossless or lossy techniques, but preferably which nature of compression can be used without compromising image quality. In this thesis, transform coding is adopted as it provides high compression. The next chapter Proposes the objectives and scope for medical images.

OBJECTIVE AND SCOPE

As per the literature summary, it is found that dedicated, sophisticated image compression algorithms are needed in storing the medical images. Hence, this research work aims to develop an optimum image compression algorithm. The detailed objectives of this research work are shown below.

IMAGE DATABASE

The image data for this research work is grouped as standard images, synthetic images, underwater images and medical images. Medical images include the Computer Tomography (CT) and Magnetic Resonance Imaging (MRI) are collected from sathyabama Institute of science and Technology, Chennai, Tamil Nadu. The images used in this work are categorized and tabulated in Tables 1, 2 and 3. Some sample of the image data is given below. The standard images such as Lena, cameraman and moon surface are collected from USC university signal and image processing institute of California (SIPI) Data base which is shown in Figure 1. The CT images are shown in Figure 2.

Figure 1. Standard images (512X512) TIFF

Figure 2. CT images of lung (512X512) DICOM

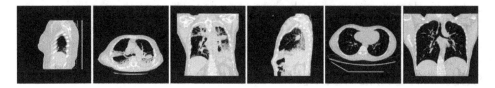

LOSSY COMPRESSION

In lossy image compression, the reconstructed image after compression is approximation of the original image. A lossy compression method is termed visually lossless when the loss of information caused by compression method is invisible for an observer. In general, a lossy compression is implemented using spatial domain encoding and transforms domain encoding methods.

TRANSFORMS OF IMAGES

Transform coding is a widely adopted method for image compression. Basic image compression scheme in this technique is implemented in the following order: decorrelation, quantization, and coding. DCT and DWT are the popular transforms used to decorrelate the pixels. The wavelet transform decomposes the image into different frequency sub bands, namely lower frequency sub bands and higher frequency sub bands, by which smooth variations and details of the image can be separated. Most of the energy is compacted into lower frequency sub bands. Most of the coefficients in higher frequency sub bands are small or zero and have a tendency to be grouped together and are also located in the same relative spatial location in the sub bands. Thus image compression methods that use wavelet transforms have been successful in providing high rates of compression while maintaining good image quality and are superior to DCT-based methods (Antonini et al. 1992, Manduca and Said 1996, Erickson et al. 1998 and Rani et al. 2009).In this work, discrete wavelet transform is used for transforming the image and is primarily used for decomposition of images. The effectiveness of wavelet in the compression is evaluated and also the effectiveness of different wavelets with various vanishing moments and various decomposition levels are analyzed based on the values of PSNR, Compression ratio, Means square error and bits per pixel. The optimum wavelet for Medical image is also found based on the results.

ENCODING

Encoding is performed in compression, for the reduction of the redundant data and elimination of the irrelevant data. The various encoding schemes such as Embedded Zero wavelet, (EZW), Set Partitioning In Hierarchical Trees(SPIHT),Spatial orientation Tree Wavelet(STW), Wavelet Difference Reduction(WDR) and Adaptively Scanned Wavelet Difference Reduction(ASWDR) are used and their effectiveness in the compression is evaluated based on the values of PSNR, Compression ratio, Means square error and bits per pixel. The optimum Encoding method is also found based on the results.

OVERVIEW OF ENCODING

EZW

The embedded zero tree wavelet algorithm (EZW) (Shapiro, 1993). The EZW is a easy, yet extremely effective, image compression algorithm, having the possessions that the bits in the bit stream are generated in order of significance, yielding a completely embedded code. The embedded code represents a sequence of binary decisions that discriminate an image from the "null" image. This algorithm applies a spatial orientation tree structure, which can be able to extract significant coefficients in wavelet domain.

SPIHT

This algorithm applies a spatial orientation tree structure, which can be able to extract significant coefficients in wavelet domain. The SPIHT (Said and Pearlman 1996) algorithm is unique in that it does not directly transmit the contents of the sets, the pixel values or the pixel coordinates.

The SPIHT coder includes a sequence of sorting and refinement passes applied with decreasing magnitude thresholds. In the sorting pass, the coefficients that exceed and equal to the current magnitude threshold are labeled significant and insignificant otherwise. When a coefficient is firstly labeled as significance, the sign of the coefficient is immediately outputted. If the sign of the significant coefficient is positive, SPIHT coder outputs "1". Conversely, it transmits "0" to the bit stream. When the insignificant nodes are coded, SPIHT coder scans the coefficient in the fixed order, which saves a lot of bits by partitioning the nodes in the subsets that contain many insignificant coefficients for the current magnitude threshold. After all coefficients are scanned in this sorting pass, SPITH coder starts to process the refinement pass.

STW

STW is basically the SPIHT algorithm; the only difference is that SPIHT is slightly more cautious in its organization of coding output. The only difference between STW and EZW is that STW uses a different approach to encoding the zero tree information. STW uses a state transition model. The locations of transformed values undergo state transitions, from one threshold to the next.

WDR

The term difference reduction is used to represent the way in which WDR encodes the locations of significant wavelet transform values, Although WDR will not produce a higher PSNR .The significance pass is the difference between WDR and the bit-plane encoding.In this work Standard images (tiff) are applied for Different types of mother Wavelets and Different Encoding Methods by varying vanishing moment and Decomposition Level which is tabulated in the Table 1 and optimum algorithm for Lossy is tabulated in Table 2. It is also evident that the rise in the number of vanishing moments leads to small loss of information. If the decomposition level is increased, the PSNR value gets decreased, irrespective of the wavelet type used for compression. All wavelets are performed well at decomposition level 1, which is found, in terms of PSNR value, CR and BPP.

Table 1. Lossy compression for Lena image

Encoding		PSNR	CR	BPP	MSE
SYM2 with level 1	SPIHT	44.2	2.86	17.2	2.3
	EZW	61.22	2.33	24.39	0.05
	STW	59.1	6.66	21.2	0.08
SYM2 with level2	SPIHT	42.01	2.7	15.27	4.09
	EZW	60.53	8.33	21.15	0.06
	STW	53.49	5.88	20.01	0.29
SYM2 with level3	SPIHT	40.13	2.7	15.27	4.09
	EZW	44.19	1.92	11.61	2.48
	STW	44.97	2.17	13.16	2.07
SYM2 with level4	SPIHT	36.69	1.22	4.39	13.94
	EZW	44.17	1.88	11.37	2.49
	STW	38.13	1.36	6.50	9.99
SYM3 with level1	SPIHT	39.48	2.32	29.69	7.33
	EZW	61.62	2.1	23.5	0.04
	STW	54.2	5.88	20.2	0.12
SYM3 with level2	SPIHT	41.28	2.63	14.92	4.84
	EZW	51.55	4.34	18.65	0.45
	STW	53.38	5.55	19.79	0.29
SYM3 with level3	SPIHT	39.29	1.54	8.59	7.66
	EZW	44.1	1.88	11.38	2.54
	STW	44.91	2.17	12.96	2.1
SYM3 with level4	SPIHT	36.62	1.2	4.22	14.17
	EZW	37.9	1.29	5.57	10.54
	STW	38.1	1.35	6.25	10.08
SYM4 with level1	SPIHT	43	2.7	16.2	3.2
	EZW	61.48	1.2	22.2	0.04
	STW	54.2	5.88	20.92	0.19
SYM4 with level2	SPIHT	41.35	2.63	15.11	4.77
	EZW	60.71	7.69	20.97	0.06
	STW	53.37	5.55	19.84	0.29
SYM4 with level3	SPIHT	39.85	1.54	8.56	6.73
	EZW	44.1	1.88	11.32	2.54
	STW	44.9	2.12	12.88	2.10
SYM4 with level4	SPIHT	36.22	1.2	4.18	15.53
	EZW	37.89	1.28	5.51	10.57
	STW	38.09	1.33	6.16	10.09
SYM5 with level1	SPIHT	42.2	2.56	15.3	4.4
	EZW	62.14	1.8	22.47	0.04
	STW	54.2	5.9	20.93	0.19

continued on following page

Table 1. Continued

Encoding		PSNR	CR	BPP	MSE
SYM5 with level2	SPIHT	41.59	2.5	14.81	4.51
	EZW	51.47	4.3	18.51	0.5
	STW	53.31	5.2	19.66	0.30
SYM5 with level3	SPIHT	40	1.5	8.51	6.49
	EZW	44.09	1.88	11.32	2.53
	STW	44.93	5.26	19.66	0.303
SYM5 with level4	SPIHT	36.74	1.2	4.14	13.78
	EZW	37.89	1.2	5.51	10.57
	STW	38.09	1.3	6.1	10.11
Coif 1 with level1	SPIHT	44.24	2.7	16.8	2.8
	EZW	61.26	2.32	23.8	0.09
	STW	59.01	6.66	21.2	1.2
Coif 1 with level2	SPIHT	41.3	2.7	15.22	4.82
	EZW	60.54	8.33	21.13	0.06
	STW	53.48	5.88	19.96	0.3
Coif 1 with level3	SPIHT	39.89	1.56	8.76	6.67
	EZW	51.6	3.8	17.70	0.45
	STW	44.97	2.19	13.09	2.07
Coif 1 with level4	SPIHT	36.7	1.22	4.36	13.89
	EZW	44.15	1.88	11.30	2.5
	STW	38.13	1.35	6.42	9.99
Coif 2 with level1	SPIHT	44.8	3.44	16.82	3.48
	EZW	60.9	10	25	0.03
	STW	59.12	6.66	21	0.06
Coif 2 with level2	SPIHT	41.41	2.63	15.07	4.69
	EZW	60.75	7.69	20.92	0.05
	STW	53.36	5.55	19.83	0.3
Coif 2 with level3	SPIHT	40.41	1.53	8.57	5.92
	EZW	51.44	3.66	17.46	0.47
	STW	44.88	2.16	12.88	2.11
Coif 2with level4	SPIHT	36.68	1.2	4.14	13.98
	EZW	37.89	1.28	5.44	10.57
	STW	38.08	1.33	6.13	10.08
Coif 3 with level1	SPIHT	44.2	3.33	16.12	3.49
	EZW	60.52	8.33	21.8	0.02
	STW	57.8	5.88	20.1	0.05
Coif 3 with level2	SPIHT	40.74	2.63	15.04	5.48
	EZW	60.86	7.69	20.89	0.05
	STW	53.33	5.55	19.78	0.30

continued on following page

Table 1. Continued

Encoding		PSNR	CR	BPP	MSE
	SPIHT	40.63	1.54	8.53	5.62
Coif 3 with level3	EZW	51.41	3.57	17.42	0.47
	STW	44.89	2.12	12.86	2.11
	SPIHT	36.26	1.2	4.1	15.38
Coif 3 with level4	EZW	37.87	1.28	5.39	10.62
	STW	38.08	1.33	6.1	10.12
	SPIHT	43.8	3.22	16.02	3.56
Coif 4with level1	EZW	60.75	8.33	21.2	0.02
	STW	57.2	5.88	20	0.2
	SPIHT	41.47	2.63	15.03	4.64
Coif 4with level2	EZW	60.98	7.69	20.93	0.05
	STW	53.33	5.55	19.83	0.3
	SPIHT	40.38	1.54	8.53	5.95
Coif 4with level3	EZW	51.39	3.7	17.45	0.47
	STW	44.86	2.12	12.86	2.12
	SPIHT	36.58	1.2	4.11	14.29
Coif 4with level4	EZW	37.86	1.28	5.41	10.66
	STW	38.06	1.33	6.1	10.17
	SPIHT	43.33	3.13	18.02	4.8
Bior 1.1 with level 1	EZW	86.02	9.09	25.02	0.03
	STW	60.34	7.14	20.07	0.02
	SPIHT	43.34	2.85	15.82	3.02
Bior 1.1 with level2	EZW	74.95	6.25	20.27	0.002
	STW	59.24	5.55	19.78	0.08
	SPIHT	40.3	1.63	9.46	6.08
Bior 1.1 with level3	EZW	52.9	3.7	17.54	0.33
	STW	47.15	2.3	14.02	1.25
	SPIHT	36.48	1.25	4.94	14.63
Bior 1.1 with level4	EZW	45.26	2.04	12.29	1.94
	STW	38.59	1.42	7.31	9.0
	SPIHT	42.14	3.03	17.05	5.01
Bior 1.3 with level1	EZW	86.02	9.09	25.02	0.03
	STW	61.02	7.14	21.08	0.02
	SPIHT	41.54	2.94	15.85	4.56
Bior 1.3 with level2	EZW	64.57	8.33	21.28	0.02
	STW	55.23	6.66	20.39	0.19
	SPIHT	40.35	1.64	9.49	6
Bior 1.3 with level3	EZW	52.10	4.16	18.26	0.41
	STW	46.08	2.43	14.18	1.61

continued on following page

Table 1. Continued

Encoding		PSNR	CR	BPP	MSE
Bior 1.3 with level4	SPIHT	36.41	1.26	5.03	14.87
	EZW	44.79	2.04	12.44	2.16
	STW	38.42	1.44	7.5	9.4
Bior 1.5 with level1	SPIHT	41.02	2.94	16.81	5.58
	EZW	82.9	9.09	23.8	0.4
	STW	60.08	7.12	22.02	0.02
Bior 1.5 with level2	SPIHT	40.75	2.94	15.91	5.47
	EZW	63.83	9.09	21.48	0.03
	STW	54.85	6.66	20.53	0.21
Bior 1.5 with level3	SPIHT	39.71	1.66	9.5	6.96
	EZW	44.62	2.12	12.84	2.25
	STW	45.84	2.43	14.28	1.69
Bior 1.5 with level4	SPIHT	36.76	1.26	5.09	13.62
	EZW	38.07	1.38	6.91	10.14
	STW	38.35	1.44	7.66	9.5
Bior 4.4with level1	SPIHT	41.01	2.7	15.02	5.58
	EZW	81.8	9.09	22	.020
	STW	59.8	6.25	20.22	0.04
Bior 4.4 with level2	SPIHT	41.11	2.63	14.96	5.04
	EZW	60.54	7.14	20.78	0.06
	STW	53.24	5.55	19.72	0.31
Bior 4.4 with level3	SPIHT	40.73	1.53	8.46	5.49
	EZW	51.29	3.44	17.27	0.48
	STW	44.76	2.12	12.72	2.17
Bior 4.4with level4	SPIHT	36.52	1.19	4.04	14.5
	EZW	43.93	1.81	10.81	2.64
	STW	37.98	1.32	5.97	10.35
Bior 6.8 with level1	SPIHT	38.4	7.69	20.9	9.39
	EZW	80.8	8.33	21.08	0.02
	STW	59.2	6.25	20.13	0.04
Bior 6.8 with level2	SPIHT	41.44	2.63	14.92	4.66
	EZW	60.56	7.14	20.78	0.06
	STW	53.18	5.55	19.7	0.31
Bior 6.8 with level3	SPIHT	40.1	1.52	8.37	6.34
	EZW	43.93	1.85	11.09	2.63
	STW	44.75	2.08	12.69	2.17
Bior 6.8 with level4	SPIHT	36.36	1.19	4.02	15.03
	EZW	37.81	1.28	5.30	10.78
	STW	38.02	1.32	5.95	10.27

Table 2. Optimum lossy compression for all images

Type of Image	Type of Transform		Encoding	PSNR	CR	BPP	MSE
Standard Lena(TIFF)	DWT	Bior1.1 with Level 1	EZW	86.02	9	25.02	0.03
CT Normal Lung (DICOM)	DWT	Bior 1.1 with Level 1	EZW	59.92	4.76	6.08	0.06
CT Normal Brain (DICOM)	DWT	Bior 1.1 with level 1	SPIHT	40.78	2.3	4.65	5.43
CT of Brain with ageing (DICOM)	DWT	Bior 1.1 with level 1	EZW	37.8	1.26	5.07	10.8
CT Alzheimer (DICOM)	DWT	Bior 1.1 with Level 1	EZW	36.74	1.72	3.35	13.78
MRI of Normal Back bone (DICOM)	DWT	Symlet 2 with Level 1	EZW	59.52	2.7	5.08	0.07
MRI of Back bone with Disease (DICOM)	DWT	Symlet 2 with Level 1	EZW	58.73	2.7	5.16	0.09
Synthetic Image(TIFF)	DWT	Bior 1.1 with Level 1	EZW	28.72	1.25	4.87	87.12
Under water Image (TIFF)	DWT	Bior 1.1 with Level 1	EZW	35.35	1.6	9.16	18.98

Table 2 summarizes performance of compression methods for different imaging modalities. From the table, it can be inferred that CT Image is better compression with Biorthogonal 1.1 whereas MRI is better Compression with Symlet2.This leads to a conclusion that, the nature of the image plays a vital role in compression. The results also indicate that, the encoding the different pixels in various images reflect the quality of compression in a unique way.

LOSSLESS COMPRESSION TECHNIQUES

In lossless compression techniques, the reconstructed image after compression is identical to the original image. In general, lossless compression is implemented using coding methods. Entropy coding encodes the particular set of symbols with the smaller number of bits required to represent them using the probability of the symbols. Compression is obtained by assigning variable-size codes to symbols. Shorter codeword is assigned to more possible symbols. Huffman coding (Huffman 1952) and Arithmetic coding (Rissanen 1976, Witten et al.1987) are the most popular entropy coding methods. Lossless image compression techniques can be implemented using Huffman coding and Arithmetic coding. The effectiveness of Arithmetic and Huffman Encoding are analyzed based on the values of PSNR, Compression ratio, Means square error and bits per pixel. The optimum compression algorithm is also found based on the results. The values are tabulated in Table 3.

CHARACTERIZATION OF MEDICAL IMAGES

Feature Extraction

It is the process of acquiring higher level information of an image such as color, shape and Texture. It is one of the important characteristics used in identifying objects or Region of interest in an image. Texture, the pattern of information or array of the structure establish in an image, is a significant feature of many image types. In a general sense, texture refers to surface characteristics and appearance of Texture features can be extracted in several methods, using statistical, structural, and model-based and transform information, in which the most common way is using the Gray Level Co occurrence Matrix (GLCM). GLCM contains the second-order statistical information of spatial relationship of pixels of an image.

Table 3. Lossless compression for all image

Type of Image	Algorithm	PSNR	CR	BPP	MSE
Standard- Lena	Huffman Encoding	44.6	1.45	7.3	2.3
	Arithmetic Encoding	90.2	1.5	9	0.8
Standard - Camera man	Huffman Encoding	44.01	1.18	7.21	2.58
	Arithmetic Encoding	72.77	1.25	7.2	3.2
CT Cancer Lung	Huffman Encoding	56	1.28	7.12	3.54
	Arithmetic Encoding	82	1.35	8	1.82
CT Normal Lung	Huffman Encoding	54	1.59	6.43	3.2
	Arithmetic Encoding	80.2	1.82	8.5	2.23
MRI	Huffman Encoding	52	2.1	6.9	2.65
	Arithmetic Encoding	83	2.5	7.5	2.75
Underwater	Huffman Encoding	45	0.25	7.34	2.54
	Arithmetic Encoding	76.23	0.32	8.2	3.2
Synthetic	Huffman Encoding	47	0.28	7.45	2.54
	Arithmetic Encoding	77.25	0.38	8.25	3.28

The features, extracted from the images are tabulated in Table 4 and 5. In this work, the classification can be defined as the identification task to which a set of group the image falls, either normal or cancer affected. The decision making tasks of classification can be easily achieved by the employment of neural networks.

CLASSIFICATION OF IMAGES

The features, are given as the inputs of non linear neural networks, in order to classify them into groups or classes. To perform efficient feature extraction, the features must have lesser intra class variance. Hence, the main objective of this work is to identify and formulate the set of features, which must be distinct enough from each class. Further, the network will be trained to classify the corresponding images, which will be categorized as either normal or cancer affected one. The derived features, which are tabulated, give a wide difference between the normal and cancer images as well the proposed compression algorithms do not affect the values much.

Table 4. GLCM image feature extractions

Features	Before Compression	After Compression
Image entropy	5.65	5.84
Auto correlation	22.9	23.87
Contrast	0.47	0.52
Correlation	0.96	0.96
Cluster prominence	832.6	834.2
Cluster shade	115	114.76
Dissimilarity	0.2	0.25
Sum of square	23.7	24.01
Sum of average	7.92	8.58
Sum of variance	65.8	65.93
Information measure of correlation	0.67	0.68
INM	0.98	0.97
Energy	0.24	0.31
Maximum probability	0.41	0.36
Homogeneity	0.91	0.89

Table 5. GLCM image feature extractions of normal and cancer lung image

Features	Normal Lung	Cancer Lung
Image entropy	5.73	4.77
Auto correlation	21.56	7.94
Contrast	0.56	0.34
Correlation	0.93	0.95
Cluster prominence	535.46	648.78
Cluster shade	82.96	78.95
Dissimilarity	0.25	0.23
Sum of square	21.71	8.04
Sum of average	8.52	4.45
Sum of variance	61.93	19.47
Information measure of correlation	0.61	0.63
INM	0.97	0.98
Energy	0.31	0.28
Maximum probability	0.52	0.54
Homogeneity	0.91	0.89

COMPARISON

The GLCM features are extracted from the images, before and after compression. The values revealed that no significant loss of diagnostic ability due to compression. The Gray level Co occurrence matrix based features are extracted in this work, so as to characterize the lung CT images. The difference in between the normal image and cancer image, clearly reveal the ability of this method to classify the normal image from the cancer image. Thus, the compressed medical images can also be used for diagnosis.

CONCLUSION

In this work, an optimum method for Medical image compression is analyzed. The performance of proposed algorithm is compared with that of the corresponding similar algorithms in terms of Compression Ratio, Bits per pixel, PSNR, MSE and subjective quality.

CT Image is better compression with Biorthogonal 1.1 whereas MRI is better Compression with Symlet2.This leads to a conclusion that, the nature of the image plays a vital role in compression. The results also indicate that, the encoding the different pixels in various images reflect the quality of compression in a unique way. SPIHT provides better CR irrespective of images and EZW yields the best PSNR and helps us to retain the quality of images. While choosing an optimum algorithm for medical images, it is necessary to retain the information in the images in order to use the images for further characterization and further usage in diagnostics. In this work, the optimum algorithm is chosen as symlet 2 for MRI and Biorthogonal 1.1 for CT Image.

In order to improve the coding performance of Lossy image compression, a hybrid Compression scheme based on Set Partitioning in Hierarchical Trees (SPIHT) with Huffman Coding is proposed. To evaluate the effectiveness the GLCM features are extracted from CT images before and after compression.

In this work, the algorithms are developed for classify the bio medical images. The features are extracted from CT images of normal Lung and Cancer affected Lung is taken into the study. GLCM based features are very useful in identifying diseases, since the features are showing wide difference between the two classes. The BPN is employed to classify the images. The classification accuracy of the BPN classifier finds the proposed compression algorithms do not alter the information of images and it is retaining the quality of images.

MATLAB ™ tools are used to implement the Compression, Feature Extraction and classification algorithms.

ACKNOWLEDGMENT

The authors wish to thank Dr.B.Sheelarani, Director Research, Sathyabama University and Dr.B.Venkatraman, Associate Director, Indira Gandhi Center for Atomic Research, Kalpakkam, Government of India for the technical support provided by them.

REFERENCES

Antonini, M., Barlaud, M., Mathieu, P., & Daubechies, I. (1992). Image Coding Using Wavelet Transform. *IEEE Transactions on Image Processing, 1*(2), 205–220. doi:10.1109/83.136597 PMID:18296155

Ashraf, M., Gardner, L., & Nethercot, D. A. (2006). Compression strength of stainless steel cross-sections. *Journal of Constructional Steel Research, 62*(1), 105–115. doi:10.1016/j.jcsr.2005.04.010

Chen, Y.-Y. (2007). Medical image compression using DCT-based subband decomposition and modified SPIHT data organization. *International Journal of Medical Informatics, 76*(10), 717–725. doi:10.1016/j.ijmedinf.2006.07.002 PMID:16931130

Choong, M-K., Logeswaran, R., & Bister, M. (2007). Cost-effective handling of digital medical images in the telemedicine environment. *International Journal of Medical Informatics, 76*(9), 646-654.

Cosman, P. C., Gray, R. M., & Olshen, R. A. (1994). Evaluating quality of compressed medical images SNR, subjective rating, and diagnostic accuracy. *Proceedings of the IEEE, 82*(6), 919 – 932. 10.1109/5.286196

Davis, L., & Aggarwal, J. (1979). Texture analysis using generalized co-occurrence matrices. *IEEE Transactions on Pattern Analysis and Machine Intelligence, PAMI-1*(3), 251–259. doi:10.1109/TPAMI.1979.4766921 PMID:21868856

Dragan. (2009). An approach to DICOM extension for medical image streaming. DAAAM international scientific book, 25-35.

Erickson, B. J., Manduca, A., Palisson, P., Persons, K. R., Earnest, F. IV, Savcenko, V., & Hangiandreou, N. J. (1998). Wavelet compression of medical images. *Radiology, 206*(3), 599–607. doi:10.1148/radiology.206.3.9494473 PMID:9494473

Goldberg, M. A., Pivovarov, M., Mayo-Smith, W. W., Bhalla, M. P., Blickman, J. G., Bramson, R. T., ... Halpern, E. (1994). Applicationof wavelet compression to digitized radiographs. *AJR. American Journal of Roentgenology, 163*(2), 463–468. doi:10.2214/ajr.163.2.8037051 PMID:8037051

Huffman, D. A. (1952). A Method for the Construction of Minimum-Redundancy Codes. *Proceedings of the IRE, 40*, 1098-1101. 10.1109/JRPROC.1952.273898

Ishigaki, Sakuma, Ikeda, Itoh, Suzuki, & Iwa. (1990). Clinical evaluation of irreversible image compression: analysis of chest imaging with computed radiography. *Journal of Radiology, 175*(3).

Kalyanpur, A., Neklesa, V. P., Taylor, C. R., Daftary, A. R., & Brink, J. A. (2000). Evaluation of JPEG and Wavelet Compression of Body CT Images for Direct Digital Teleradiologic Transmission 1. *Radiology, 217*(3), 772–779. doi:10.1148/radiology.217.3.r00nv22772 PMID:11110942

Lee, H., Kim, Y., Rowberg, A., & Riskin, E. A. (1993). Statistical distributions of DCT coefficients and their application to an interframe compression algorithm for 3-D medical images. *IEEE Transactions on Medical Imaging, 12*(3), 478–485. doi:10.1109/42.241875 PMID:18218440

MacMahon, H. (1991). *Radiology, Data compression: effect on diagnostic accuracy in digital chest radiography*. Academic Press.

Perlmutter, S. M., Cosman, P. C., Gray, R. M., Olshen, R. A., Ikeda, D., Adams, C. N., ... Daniel, B. L. (1997). Image quality in lossy compressed digital mammograms. *Signal Processing, 59*(2), 189–210. doi:10.1016/S0165-1684(97)00046-7

Persons all People, Among Young. (2000). A Report of the Surgeon General.

Rani & Bansal, R K. (2009). Comparison of JPEG and SPIHT image compression algorithms using objective quality measures. In *Proc. IEEE International Multimedia Signal Processing and Communication Technologies*, (pp. 90-93). IEEE.

Rissanen, J. J. (1976). Generalized Kraft Inequality and Arithmetic Coding. *IBM Journal of Research and Development, 20*(3), 198–203. doi:10.1147/rd.203.0198

Saffor, E., Ramli, A., & Kh, N. (2001). A comparative study of image compression between JPEG and wavelet. *Malaysian Journal of Computer Science, 14*, 39–45.

Said, A., & Pearlman, W. A. (1996). A new fast and efficient image codec based on Set Partitioning in Hierarchical Trees. *IEEE Transcation Circuits System Video Tech., 6*(3), 1–16.

Seeram, E. (2006). Irreversible compression in digital radiology. A literature review. *Radiography, 12*(1), 45–59. doi:10.1016/j.radi.2005.04.002

Singh, S., & Verma, H. K. (2007). DWT–DCT hybrid scheme for medical image compression. *Journal of Medical Engineering & Technology, 31*(2), 109–122. doi:10.1080/03091900500412650 PMID:17365435

Slone, R. M., Foos, D. H., Whiting, B. R., Muka, E., Rubin, D. A., Pilgram, T. K., ... Hendrickson, D. D. (2000). Assessment of Visually Lossless Irreversible Image Compression:Comparison of Three Methods by Using an Image-Comparison Workstation 1. *Radiology, 215*(2), 543–553. doi:10.1148/radiology.215.2.r00ap47543 PMID:10796938

Smutek, D. (2005). Quality measurement of lossy compression in medical imaging. *Prague Medical Report, 106*(1), 5–26. PMID:16007906

Vetterli, M., & Herley, C. (1992). Wavelets and filter banks: Theory and design. *IEEE Transactions on Signal Processing, 40*(9), pp2207–pp2232. doi:10.1109/78.157221

Witten, R. (1987). *Arithmetic coding revisited in Data Compression. DCC '95 Proceedings.*

Xin, L. (2001). Edge-directed prediction for lossless compression of natural images. *IEEE Transactions on Image Processing, 10*(6), 813–817. doi:10.1109/83.923277

KEY TERMS AND DEFINITIONS

BPP - Bits per Pixels:
CR - Compression Ratio:
CT - Computed Tomography:
DWT - Discrete Wavelet Transform:
DCT - Discrete cosine Transform:
EZW - Embedded Zero trees of Wavelet transforms:
GLCM - Gray-level co-occurrence matrix:
MSE - Mean Square Error:
PSNR - Peak Signal to Noise Ratio:
SPIHT - Set partitioning in hierarchical trees:
STW - Spatial Orientation Tree Wavelet:
WDR - Wavelet difference reduction:
ASWDR - Adaptively Scanned Wavelet Difference Reduction:

Chapter 4
Empirical Performance Analysis of Wavelet Transform Coding–Based Image Compression Techniques

Tawheed Jan Shah
University of Kashmir, India

M. Tariq Banday
University of Kashmir, India

ABSTRACT

In this chapter, the performance of wavelet transform-based EZW coding and SPIHT coding technique have been evaluated and compared in terms of CR, PSNR, and MSE by applying them to similar color images in two standard resolutions. The application of these techniques on entire color images such as passport size photograph in which the region containing the face of a person is more significant than other regions results in equal loss of information content and less compression ratio. So, to achieve the high CRs and distribute the quality of the image unevenly, this chapter proposes the ROI coding technique. Compressing ROI portion using discrete wavelet transform with Huffman coding and NROI compressed with Huffman, EZW coding, SPIHT coding suggested effective compression at nearly no loss of quality in the ROI portion of the photograph. Further, higher CR and PSNR with lower MSE have been found in high-resolution photographs, thereby permitting the reduction of storage space, faster transmission on low bandwidth channels, and faster processing.

DOI: 10.4018/978-1-7998-0066-8.ch004

INTRODUCTION

Wavelet-Based Image Compression

Wavelets were introduced as a signal processing tool in the late 1980s. Since then considerable attention has been given on the application of wavelets to Image compression (Woods & ONeil, 1986). Wavelet image coding follows a well-understood standard transform coding prototype (Lewis & Knowles, 1992). Foremost, the wavelet transform is applied on an image then the wavelet coefficients are quantized and later coded by applying lossless coding on the quantized coefficients. However, this transform gives a multi-resolution and multi-scale representation of the image. The wavelet transform uses wavelets of fixed energy to examine the transient, time-variant signals. A Wavelet is thus defined as an irregular mathematical function having limited duration effectively. The word 'wavelet' is used because it integrates to zero (Zhao et al., 2004).

One of the most crucial advantages of the wavelet is its ability to analyze the localized area of a large signal (Schelkens et al., 1999). Small wavelet can be used to isolate the fine details of the signal, and the large wavelet can identify the coarse details. Assume the sine wave generated in the real world by a noisy switch or power fluctuation with a small discontinuity which is hardly noticeable as shown in Figure 1. However, with the help of the wavelet coefficient plot, the exact location of the discontinuity can be found.

The wavelet transform (WT) of a signal is its time-frequency representation, and this transform does not change the information content of the signal. It is computed independently for different segments of the signal in time-domain at different frequencies. It gives good frequency resolution and poor time resolution at lower frequencies while at higher frequencies, it gives good time resolution and poor frequency resolution. The WT was developed to overcome the shortcomings

Figure 1. Sine wave with a small discontinuity

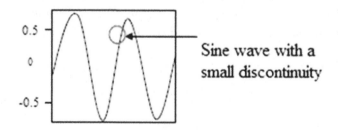

of STFT (Sifuzzaman et al., 2009). The basis sine and wavelet waveform are shown in Figure 2.

It can be seen intuitively that wavelet waveform might analyze the sharply changing signal better than a sine waveform, just as a fork handles some foods better than a spoon.

There are two types of Wavelet Transforms namely, Continous wavelet transform (CWT) and discrete wavelet transform and are explained below:

Continuous Wavelet Transform

The CWT is defined as the sum over all time of signal multiplied by dilated, translated versions of the wavelet function.

$$C\left(S,P\right)= \int_{-\infty}^{+\infty} f\left(t\right)\Psi\left(S,P,t\right)dt \;....$$ (1)

Where 'S' and 'P' represent the scale and position respectively. The result of the CWT given in Equation (1) is a series of wavelet coefficients 'C' which are the functions of S and P. Multiplying each wavelet coefficient of Equation (1) by properly dilated and translated wavelet gives the basic wavelets of the unique signal. Such basic wavelets of different scales and positions are shown in Figure 3.

The wavelet transform involves projecting a signal onto a complete set of translated and stretched versions of a mother wavelet Ψ (t). Assume that Ψ(t) has compact time-based and spectral support, upon which the set of basis functions can be defined. The basis set of wavelets is generated from the mother wavelet and is defined by Equation (2).

Figure 2. Basis sine and wavelet waveforms (Kanth, 2013)

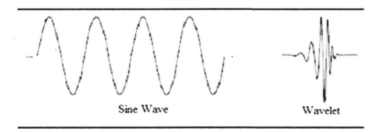

59

Figure 3. Continuous wavelets of different scales and positions (Kumar, 2011)

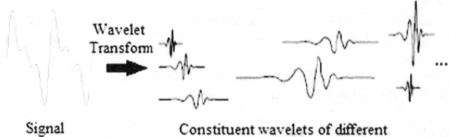

$$\Psi_{a,b}\left(t\right) = \frac{1}{\sqrt{a}}\,\Psi\left(\frac{t-b}{a}\right);\;\; a,b \in R\,\text{and}\,a > 0 \dots \tag{2}$$

where 'a' reflects the scale of a particular basis function such that its large and small values, offer low frequencies and high frequencies respectively and 'b' identify its translation along the time axis. Additionally, the term 1/a find a use for normalization. The mathematical expression for the one-dimensional wavelet transform of a function (signal) x(t) is given by Equation: (3).

$$w_f\left(a,b\right) = \int_{-\infty}^{+\infty} x\left(t\right)\Psi_{a,b}\left(t\right)dt \dots \tag{3}$$

And the inverse one-dimensional WT to reconstruct x(t) from w_f(a,b) is represented by Equation: (4).

$$x\left(t\right) = \frac{1}{C}\iint_{-\infty}^{+\infty} w_f\left(a,b\right)\Psi_{a,b}\left(t\right)db\,\frac{da}{a^2} \dots \tag{4}$$

where

$$C = \int_{-\infty}^{+\infty} \frac{\left|\Psi\left(\omega\right)\right|^2}{\omega}\,d\omega < \infty \dots \tag{5}$$

where $\Psi(t)$ is the mother wavelet and $\Psi(\omega)$ its Fourier transform. If both a, b are non-discrete variables and x(t) is also a Continous function, then $w_r(a,b)$ is called the CWT. Further, the value of C is required to be finite, which directs to one of the requisite properties of mother wavelet (Chowdhury & Khatun, 2012). If C is finite, then x(t) =0, to avoid a singularity in the integral, and thus x(t) must have zero mean. Mathematically, this condition is stated by Equation: (6).

$$\int_{-\infty}^{+\infty} \Psi\left(t\right) dt = 0 \dots \tag{6}$$

This is known as the admissibility condition. The other main requirement is that $\Psi(t)$ must be confined to a finite duration expressed by Equation (7).

$$\int_{-\infty}^{+\infty} \left|\Psi\left(t\right)\right|^2 dt < \infty \dots \tag{7}$$

The scaled versions of $\Psi(t)$ are represented in Figure 4.

Discrete Wavelet Transform

The continuous signals need to be converted into the digital one because these signals are ultimately processed by a digital computing machine. Therefore, it is prudent to define the discrete version of the CWT (Kumar, 2011). In order to define the CWT

Figure 4. Scaled versions of the mother wavelet

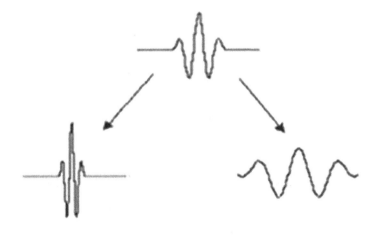

in terms of discrete values of dilation parameter 'a' and translation parameter 'b' instead of being continuous, make a and b discrete using Equation: (5),

$$a = a_0^m, \quad \text{and} \quad b = nb_0 a_0^m \ldots \tag{8}$$

where 'm' and 'n' are integers. On substituting the new values of 'a' and b given by Equation (8) in Equation (2), the discrete wavelets can be represented by Equation (9) as below:

$$\Psi_{m,n}(t) = a_0^{-\frac{m}{2}} \Psi\left(a_0^{-m} t - nb_0\right) \ldots \tag{9}$$

The values of a_0 and b_0 can be selected by numerous options. The option $a_0=2$ & $b_0=1$ gives $a=2^m$ & $b=n2^m$, and this corresponds to discretization of 'a' and 'b' in such a way that the sampling intervals, as well as the successive discrete values of a and b, vary by a factor of 2. This mode of sampling is commonly known as Dyadic decomposition. By using $a_0=2$ & $b_0=1$ in Equation (9), the discrete wavelets which constitute a family of orthonormal basis functions can be represented as given in Equation (10):

$$\Psi_{m,n}(t) = 2^{-\frac{m}{2}} \Psi\left(a_0^{-m} t - n\right) \ldots \tag{10}$$

Therefore, in general, the wavelet coefficients for the function x(t) are given by

$$C_{m,n}(x) = a_0^{-\frac{m}{2}} \int x(t) \Psi\left(a_0^{-m} t - nb_0\right) \ldots \tag{11}$$

and consequently, the wavelet coefficients can be derived for Dyadic Decomposition as

$$C_{m,n}(x) = 2^{-\frac{m}{2}} \int x(t) \Psi\left(a_0^{-m} t - nb_0\right) dt \ldots \tag{12}$$

The signal x(t) can, therefore, be reconstructed in the form of discrete wavelet coefficients as

$$x(t) = \sum_{m=-\infty}^{\infty} \sum_{n=-\infty}^{\infty} C_{m,n}(x) \Psi_{m,n}(t) \ldots \tag{13}$$

The transform coefficient given by Equation (11) is known as the wavelet series. This wavelet series is similar to the Fourier series because the input function x(t) is still a continuous function whereas the transform coefficients are discrete. The series given by Equation (11) is often called as the Discrete Time Wavelet Transform. When the translation and dilation parameters, as well as the input signal x(t), are in discrete form, the transformation is commonly referred as the discrete wavelet transform of the signal x(t). The generation and calculation of DWT is well suited to the digital computers because it involves only the multiplication and addition processes. DWT is being more and more used for compression of images due to the fact that it offers many advantages like progressive transmission by pixel accuracy and resolution, robustness to bit-errors, superior low bit-rate performance, ROI coding, etc.

MULTI-RESOLUTION CONCEPT AND ANALYSIS

Mallat (1989) introduced the wavelet decomposition based multi-resolution representation of signals. The multi-resolution method represents the signal (image) with a set of wavelet coefficients, each of which gives information about the frequency as well as location of the input signal. The DWT is used to perform the multi-resolution analysis of signals; therefore it decomposes a signal into sub-bands with different frequencies. As compared to the higher frequency sub-bands, the lower frequency sub-bands provide finer frequency resolution and coarser time resolution (Vaidyanathan, 1993). The resolution, which gives the amount of detailed information in the signal (image), is determined by the filtering operation and the scale is determined by the sampling rate. However, there are two operations concerned with this sampling rate; one is the Up-Sampling, and the other is the Down-Sampling. In case of up-sampling, the interpolator or up-sampler takes a signal X(n) and increase the number of its samples by a factor of 2 (Whittaker, 1915) as shown in Figure 5.

While as in down-sampling, the decimator decreases the number of samples of the input signal by the same factor. It is shown in Figure 6 below.

Figure 5. Up-sampler

Figure 6. Down-sampler

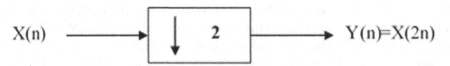

Now to determine the amount of detailed information in the signal, a filter bank is used. This filter bank consists of Analysis Bank and Synthesis Bank as shown in Figure 7.

Analysis Bank: The analysis bank consists of a low pass filter (LPF) and a high pass filter (HPF). LPF and HPF separates the input signal into frequency bands. When the signal is passed through these two filters, four sub-bands are produced which are represented as LL, HL, LH, & HH and are shown in Figure 8. This constitutes the first decomposition level and represents the finer scale of the expansion coefficients (Smith & Eddins, 1990). Such a successive low pass and high pass filtering of the discrete time signal for three levels of decomposition is represented in Figure 8 and is known as the Mallat-tree decomposition or Mallat Algorithm.

Since DWT describes the image as a sum of basic functions, i.e., wavelets into a set of high pass and low pass coefficients. The output from the LPF and the HPF gives the approximated and the detailed coefficients respectively, and each of the outputs are down sampled by a factor of 2. The block diagram of 1-D DWT for first level of wavelet decomposition is shown in Figure 9.

At each decomposition level, the two half band filters double the number of coefficients but the decimator down samples it by a factor of 2. This decimation by two halves the time resolution, as the entire signal is now represented by only half the number of samples with no loss of information. This process is called as sub-band coding. The process of filtering and down sampling is continued until the desired decomposition level is reached. The maximum number of desired decomposition levels is determined by the length of the original input signal. Thus, DWT of the original input image is obtained by concatenating the approximated coefficients and the detailed coefficients, starting from the last level of decomposition.

Figure 7. Filter bank

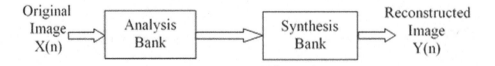

Figure 8. Finer and coarser scale wavelet coefficients (Deshlahra, 2013)

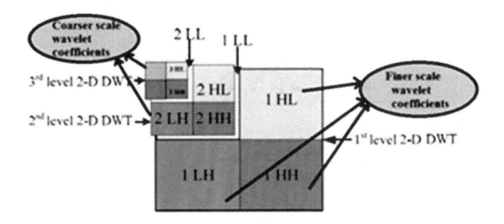

Figure 9. Block diagram of 1-D DWT for one level wavelet decomposition

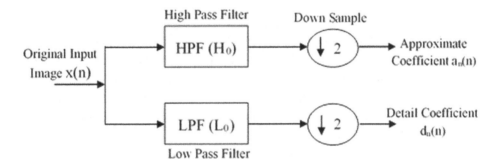

Also, the block diagram of the 2-D DWT for first level of wavelet decomposition is shown in Figure 10.

In 2-D DWT, the original input image is given to set of both HPF(H_0) and LPF(L_0). The outputs of LPF(L_0) and HPF(H_0) are then down sampled by 2, same as in case of 1-D DWT (Sriram & Thiyagarajans, 2012). As already shown in Figure 8, the four sets of coefficients HH, HL, LH, LL are obtained. The first letter represents the row transform and the second letter represents the column transform. The letter H means high pass signal and L means low pass signal. Hence, HL signal contains vertical elements. Similarly, LH and HH contain horizontal and diagonal elements respectively.

Figure 10. Block diagram of 2-D DWT for one level of wavelet decomposition

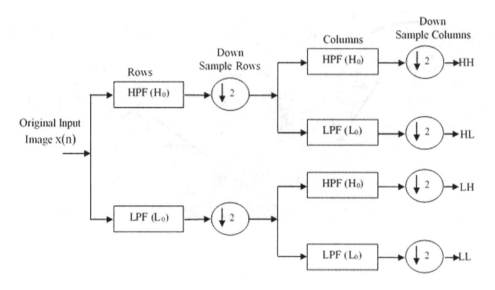

Synthesis Bank: It is the inverse of the analysis process. In case of forward DWT, the first step involved is the filtering and then decimation of the original input signal as already shown in Figure 9 and Figure 10 but in case of inverse DWT, first the up-sampling of the wavelet coefficients is done which is later followed by filtering. The block diagram for reconstruction of the 2-D inverse DWT from the combination of the approximated and the detailed coefficients is shown in Figure 11.

Besides, the perfect reconstruction of the original signal is possible only when the analysis and the synthesis filters satisfy certain conditions. Let $L_a(Z)$ and $H_a(Z)$ be the low pass analysis and high pass analysis filters, and the $L_s(Z)$ and $H_s(Z)$ be the low pass synthesis and the high pass synthesis. These filters must satisfy the given below conditions:

$$L_a(-Z)L_s(Z)+H_a(-Z)H_s(Z)=0 \ .... \tag{14}$$

$$L_a(Z)L_s(Z)+H_a(Z)H_s(Z)=2Z^{-d} \ .... \tag{15}$$

The conditions given in Equation (14) and Equation (15), implies that the reconstruction of the input signal is aliasing-free and the amplitude distortion has amplitude of one. Also, it is observed that, if the analysis and the synthesis filters are exchanged the perfect reconstruction doesn't change.

Figure 11. Block diagram for reconstruction of 2-D DWT

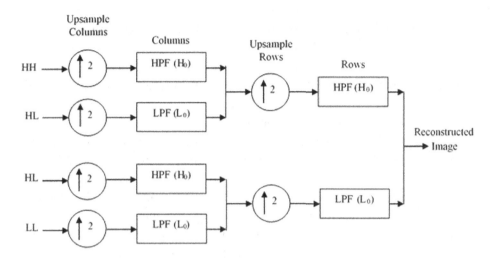

CLASSIFICATION OF WAVELETS

Wavelets are broadly classified into two types: (a) Orthogonal, and (b) Bi-orthogonal. Depending upon the characteristics and applications any of the two can be used.

Orthogonal Wavelets

Orthogonal wavelet filters are defined as those filters in which the forward wavelet filters and its associated inverse wavelet filters are of the same length but are not symmetric. The $HPF(H_0)$ and the $LPF(L_0)$ are associated to each other by Equation (16).

$$H_0(Z)=Z^{-N}L_0(-Z^{-1}) \dots \tag{16}$$

The coefficients of these orthogonal filters are real numbers and are alternated flip of each other. The alternating flip offers double-shift Orthogonality between the HPF's and the LPF's i.e.

$$\Sigma L[K]H[K-2]=0, \text{ where } K,1 \in Z \dots \tag{17}$$

The filters which satisfy the Equation (16) are called as the Conjugate Mirror Filters (CMF) (Sprljan et al., 2005).

Bi-Orthogonal Wavelets

Bi-orthogonal wavelet filters are defined as those filters in which the associated WT is invertible but not necessarily orthogonal. The HPF can be either symmetric or anti-symmetric, but the LPF is always symmetric. The coefficients of these types of filters are either real numbers or integers. For the perfect reconstruction of the signal, these filter banks has all even and odd length filters. The two analysis filters can be one symmetric and the other anti-symmetric with even length or symmetric with odd length. Also, the two sets of analysis and synthesis filters must be dual.

There are several basic functions that can be employed for achieving the Wavelet Transformation. Since the mother wavelet produces all wavelet functions used in the transformation through translation and scaling, it determines the characteristics of the resulting WT. Therefore, the details of the particular application must be taken into account, and the proper mother wavelet should be chosen to use the WT effectively. Some of the commonly used wavelet functions are shown in Figure 12.

The wavelet shown by Figure 12(a) is one of the oldest compactly supported and simplest wavelet proposed by famous mathematician Alfred Haar, in 1909. Therefore, any discussions on wavelets start with this basic wavelet. Haar wavelet is discontinuous and resembles to a step function. The Haar mother wavelet function is described by Equation (18).

Figure 12. Wavelet families (a) Haar (b) Daubechies2 (c) Coiflet1 (d) Symlet2 (e) Meyer (f) Morlet (g) Mexican Hat (Olkkonen, 2011)

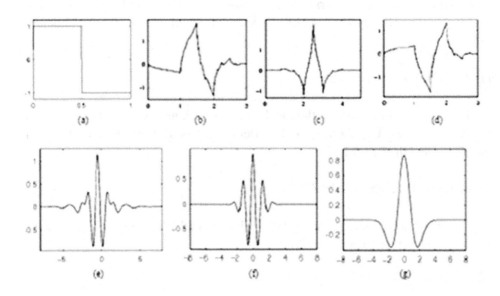

$$\Psi\left(t\right) = \begin{cases} 1 & 0 \leq t < 0.5 \\ -1 & 0.5 \leq t < 1 \dots \\ 0 & \text{otherwise} \end{cases} \quad (18)$$

also, its scaling function is expressed in Equation (19)

$$\phi\left(t\right) = \begin{cases} 1 & 0 \leq t < 1 \\ 0 & \text{otherwise} \end{cases} \dots \quad (19)$$

The Haar wavelet is the only wavelet which is both orthogonal and symmetric. The popular family of wavelets called the Daubechies wavelets (Daubechies, 1990; Daubechies, 1992), named after its inventor Ingrid Daubechies represent the foundation of wavelet signal processing. The names of the wavelets of this family are written as dbN, where db is the surname of the wavelet and N is the order. Daubechies wavelet of the order of 2 (db2) is shown in Figure 12(b). Another family of wavelets is the Coiflets (Coif1-Coif5), built by Daubechies at the request of R. Coifman. The wavelet function here has 2N instants equal to zero, and the scaling function has 2N-1 instants equal to zero. These two functions have a support of length 6N-1. The Symlets (Sym2-Sym8), projected by Daubechies as improvements to the db family are approximately symmetrical wavelets. The properties of both the db and the Sym wavelet family are similar. The Meyer (Meyer, 1993), Morlet and Mexican Hat are symmetric in shape. The Haar, Daubechies, Coiflets, Symlets and Meyer wavelets are capable of perfect reconstruction of the signal.

EMBEDDED ZERO TREE WAVELET CODING (EZW) TECHNIQUE

EZW coding, familiarized by J. M. Shapiro in 1993 (Usevitch, 2001) is considered as one of the effective and powerful wavelet-based image compression algorithm. EZW coding technique laid the foundation of wavelet based coders and provides excellent performance for the compression of still images at low bit rates as compared to the block based DCT algorithm. It is sometimes also called Embedded Coder because the compression process stops when a desired bit rate is reached. The EZW algorithm is dependent on four principle concepts:

1. DWT.
2. Estimation of the lack of significant information across scales.
3. Successive-approximation quantization.
4. Universal data compression using lossless coding such as Huffman coding, adaptive arithematic coding.

At low bit rates, the value of the most of the wavelet coefficients is either zeros or around to zero. This is because the natural images have a low pass spectrum in general. Therefore, it is very important to represent the low frequency wavelet coefficients accurately in any high quality coding scheme. Furthermore, in a dyadic wavelet decomposition, the wavelet transformed coefficients from different sub-bands can be considered as a tree(quad-tree) with highest magnitude and lowest frequency coefficient at the root node and the four children coefficients of each parent node being the spatially related coefficients in the corresponding previous sub-band as shown in Figure 13. The operation can be recursively applied on the four children coefficients and so on. In this manner, there is a high probability that the coefficient values of one or more trees are either zero or very close to zero, such trees are called zero-trees.

Wavelet coefficients are scanned in such a way that no child node is scanned before its parent node. Figure 14 and Figure 15 shows the scanning order for 3-levels of wavelet decomposition and the flow chart of the EZW algorithm respectively. Quad-tree based EZW coding technique uses the statistical properties of the trees in order to reduce the storage space required for storing the spatial locations of the important coefficients. A Wavelet coefficient is considered important if its value is above a certain threshold and is unimportant if the value is below the threshold.

Figure 13. Parent-children dependencies between wavelet coefficients in Sub-bands as quad tree

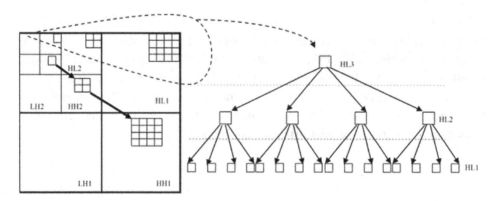

Figure 14. Scanning order for 3-levels of wavelet decomposition

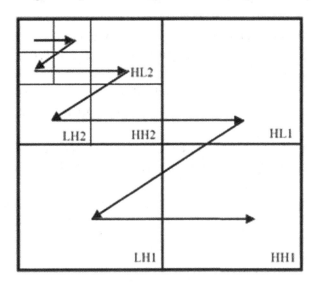

Figure 15. Flow Chart of EZW algorithm

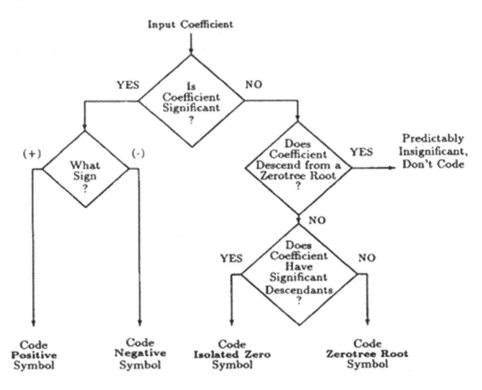

EZW coding uses four symbols to represent the wavelet coefficients:

1. **Zero-Tree Root (ZTR):** If the magnitude of the wavelet coefficient of a tree and all its descendants is less than a threshold value say, T, then the coefficient is called a zero-tree root.
2. **Isolated Zero (IZ):** If the magnitude of the wavelet coefficient of a tree is zero and some of its descendants are significant, then the coefficient is called an isolated zero.
3. **Positive Significant Coefficient**: If the magnitude of the coefficient is positive as well as significant at the threshold T, then the coefficient is called positive significant coefficient.
4. **Negative Significant Coefficient**: If the magnitude of the coefficient is negative as well as significant at the threshold T, then the coefficient is called negative significant coefficient.

Each of the symbols defined above may be represented by two binary bits. Therefore, fully embedded code representing a series of binary decisions is produced from the bit stream produced by EZW algorithms (Strang & Nguyen, 1996). On the other hand, the decoder, reconstructs the image by gradually updating the values of each coefficient in a tree. The encoder and the decoder are always synchronized to each other. EZW compression algorithm does not require any training tables, codebooks or any prior information about the image. The following main steps are involved in this algorithm:

1. **Initialization**: Set the threshold 'T' to the smallest power of '2' that is greater than $\max(m, n)\ |c(m,n)|/2$, where $c(m, n)$ are the wavelet coefficients.
2. **Significance Map Coding**: Scan all the coefficients in a predefined way and output a symbol when $|c(m, n)|>2$. When the decoder inputs this symbol, it sets $c(m, n) = \pm1.5T$.
3. **Refinement Pass or Subordinate Pass**: It refines each important coefficient by transferring one more bit of its binary representation. When the decoder receives this, it increments the current coefficient value by $\pm0.25T$.
4. Set $T=T/2$, and repeat step 2, if more iterations are required (Raja & Suruliandi, 2010).

SET PARTITIONING IN HIERARCHICAL TREES (SPIHT) CODING TECHNIQUE

SPIHT was developed by Said and Pearlman in 1996 (Said & Pearlman, 1996). The terms "Hierarchical Trees" and "Set partitioning" refers to the quad-trees and the way by which the quad-trees divide up and partition the WT values at a given threshold respectively. The basic difference between EZW and SPIHT is that SPIHT coding technique not only exploits the correlations of wavelet coefficients across the different sub-bands but also within the same band. The correlated wavelet coefficients are then grouped into trees called Spatial Orientation Trees (SOTs). SPIHT coding technique examines each tree and then divides the tree into one of three coefficient location lists namely the List of Insignificant Pixels (LIP), List of Insignificant Sets (LIS), and List of significant Pixels (LSP). The LIP and LIS contain the coordinates of pixels found to be insignificant and information about trees that have all the constituent entries insignificant at current threshold while the list of significant pixels contain the coordinates of pixels which are found to be significant at current threshold respectively.

The SPIHT algorithm involves three steps: Initialization, Sorting Pass and Refinement Pass.

1. **Initialization**: Initialize the LIP, LSP, LIS table and determine the number of magnitude refinement passes (n) from the maximum magnitude of the DWT coefficients which is given by

$$n = [\text{Log}_2 (\text{max}|(i,j)|)] \dots \qquad (20)$$

where $\text{max}|(i,j)|$ is the maximum magnitude of the wavelet coefficient at location(i,j). Then calculate the maximum threshold $T=2^n$.

2. In sorting pass, a significance test for each pixel in the LIP against the current threshold is performed. If the value of the coefficient at location (i,j) is significant(i.e., $>2^n$), then the symbol '1' and the sign bit is sent out. The coordinate is removed from the LIP and added to the LSP end of the table.

3. If the value of the coefficient at location (i,j) is insignificant(i.e., $<2^n$), then the symbol '0' is sent out. The coordinate is not removed from the LIP it is leftover for subsequent testing at a lower bit level.

4. All coefficients that are less than the set of insignificant coefficients is isolated to LIS, and bit '0' is sent out.

5.   During the magnitude refinement pass, each entry in the LSP except those which are added during the sorting pass, are encoded for n^{th} most significant bit.

6.   For the next scan, the threshold value is halved and the value of 'n' is decremented by '1' and then sorting, and refinement stages are repeated until n=0, or target bit-rate is achieved.

The decoder steps are exactly reverse of the steps followed in case of the encoder. SPIHT coding technique provides better image quality especially for color images, compact output bit-stream, simple quantization algorithm, less complexity, low power consumption, and an intensive, progressive transmission capability. SPIHT coder is restricted to images having pixel resolution of power '2' and needs a huge amount of memory because of number of lists. SPIHT Coder also has complex memory management as the list nodes are added, deleted, or moved from one list to another. Further, the list sizes can't be pre-allocated.

RELATED RESEARCH AND APPLICATION OF IMAGE COMPRESSION USING EZW AND SPIHT CODING TECHNIQUES

Nagamani and Ananth (2011) proposed an image compression technique for high resolution, grayscale satellite urban images. The proposed technique used DWT together with EZW and SPIHT coding techniques in order to achieve high Compression Ratio (CR) and better image quality. The CR and peak signal to noise ratio (PSNR) determined using EZW and SPIHT coding have been compared to each other for same set of images. The results obtained showed the possibility to achieve higher CR and PSNR (approximately CR of 8 and PSNR of 29.20) for SPIHT coding compared to EZW coding (approximately CR of 1.07 and PSNR of 13.07) for applications related to urban satellite imagery.

Tao et al.)2013) surveyed multimedia compression and transmission techniques to analyze them for energy efficiency in resource-constrained platform in terms of compression efficiency, memory requirement, and computational load. For image compression, three important techniques JPEG, JPEG2000, and SPIHT have been discussed. It was concluded that SPIHT is the best choice for energy-efficient compression algorithms due to its ability to provide higher compression ratio with low complexity. JPEG2000 achieved higher CR, which mean better quality than SPHIT. However, complexity of JPEG2000 tier-1 and tier-2 operations caused intensive, complex coding, higher computational load, and more energy consumption for resource-constrained systems.

Singh et al. (2012) evaluated DWT-EZW and DWT-SPIHT compression algorithms, based on parameters such as decomposition level, CR, PSNR, and compressed size. The results showed that DWT-SPIHT compression technique provided better image quality, PSNR value and compression ratio in comparison to the DWT-EZW technique.

Singh and Singh (2011) proposed an effective image compression technique for Lossy Virtual Human Spine image. Two image compression techniques viz; EZW and SPIHT using different wavelet filters has been compared on the basis of CR, PSNR, mean square error (MSE) and bits per pixel (BPP) values. Experimental results showed that PSNR in SPIHT increased by a factor of 13-15% as compared to the EZW technique. Additionally, SPIHT produced a fully embedded bit stream and offered better image quality at low bit rates than EZW.

EZW and SPIHT encoding techniques based Colored image compression has been undertaken using MATLAB (R2014a) on Windows 10, 64-bit OS, with Intel Core i3 processor having, 2GB RAM. Compression of two same colored images with standard pixel resolutions of 512x512 pixels and 256x256 pixels has been done by using SPIHT and EZW coding techniques. In order to compress the BMP formatted colored image, the image is separated into three channels; Red, Green and Blue channel. Then on each channel DWT is applied which converts the 2-D time domain signal into the frequency domain. The DWT of input image is achieved by using the Haar wavelet. After DWT, encoding using SPIHT and EZW techniques is performed separately. Further, the final compressed output image is achieved by combining the three distinctly compressed channels. Table 1, Table 2, Table 3, and Table 4 shows the input and output parameters for the two images.

The results are examined, compared and discussed.

To attain high CR and good quality of the reconstructed image, compression of both above-mentioned images has been commenced with different values of BPP. In case of SPIHT encoding, the range for BPP remained from 0.1499 (with 10 iterations) to 2.1466 (with 15 iterations) for 256x256 pixels image and 0.038 (with 10 iterations) to 1.2339 (with 15 iterations) for 512x512 pixels image. These values in case of EZW remained from 0.4561 (with 10 iterations) to 4.5082 (with 15 iterations) and 0.1268 (with 10 iterations) to 3.5512 (with 15 iterations) respectively for 256x256 and 512x512 pixels image. The whole image has been compressed for all of the above-mentioned values of BPP. CR, PSNR, and MSE, were calculated for the two techniques discussed above. PSNR vs. BPP of 512x512 pixels image and 256x256 pixels image are shown in Figure 16 (a) and Figure 16 (b).

For 512x512 pixels image, both SPIHT and EZW showed PSNR above 35dB while as the BPP varied from 0.038 to 3.5512. Higher CR of 16.4851 has been obtained using SPIHT technique. Highest PSNR of 49.9057 has been obtained using EZW technique. For 256x256 pixels image, SPIHT and EZW both showed

Table 1. Input and output parameters for 512x512 image using EZW

Wavelet Used Haar	Technique Used EZW			Output Parameters				
Number of Iterations & BPP	RED channel (BPP)	Green channel (BPP)	Blue Channel (BPP)	Average BPP	MSE	PSNR	C_R	Output File Size (Kb)
I(10) BPP=0.1268	0.35	0.26	0.13	0.2467	12.7138	37.0880	15.1396	51949
I(11) BPP=0.2712	0.64	0.49	0.27	0.4667	7.2424	39.5320	11.1812	70340
I (12) BPP=0.5290	1.04	0.85	0.53	0.8067	3.6620	42.4937	8.6051	91398
I (13) BPP=0.9500	1.58	1.48	0.95	1.3367	1.9736	45.1783	6.4163	122577
I (14) BPP=1.8059	2.48	2.90	1.81	2.3967	1.1109	47.6740	4.5787	171769
I (15) BPP=3.5512	3.67	4.19	3.55	3.8033	0.6645	49.9057	4.0963	192000

Table 2. Input and output parameters for 512x512 image using SPIHT

Wavelet Used Haar	Technique Used SPIHT			Output Parameters				
Number of Iterations & BPP	RED channel (BPP)	Green channel (BPP)	Blue Channel (BPP)	Average BPP	MSE	PSNR	CR	Output File Size (Kb)
I (10) BPP=0.038	0.23	0.17	0.04	0.1467	17.9538	35.5892	16.4851	47709
I (11) BPP=0.0884	0.41	0.32	0.09	0.2733	11.2306	37.6268	11.7589	66884
I (12) BPP=0.1897	0.66	0.54	0.19	0.4633	6.4281	40.0499	8.9424	87950
I (13) BPP=0.3525	0.99	0.99	0.35	0.7767	3.5273	42.6564	6.6822	117699
I (14) BPP=0.6257	1.63	1.97	0.63	1.4100	1.8647	45.4247	5.2420	150035
I (15) BPP=1.2339	2.82	3.23	1.23	2.4267	1.0414	47.9547	4.4816	175491

Table 3. Input and output parameters for 256x256 image using EZW

Wavelet Used Haar	Technique Used EZW			Output Parameters				
Number of Iterations & BPP	RED channel (BPP)	Green channel (BPP)	Blue Channel (BPP)	Average BPP	MSE	PSNR	C_R	Output File Size (Kb)
I (10) BPP=0.4561	1.04	0.81	0.46	0.7700	8.6102	38.7806	6.8412	28747
I (11) BPP=0.8628	1.61	1.30	0.86	1.2567	3.6200	42.5437	5.7151	34411
I (12) BPP=1.4216	2.26	1.92	1.42	1.8667	1.5518	46.2223	5.1027	38541
I (13) BPP=2.1464	3.00	2.79	2.15	2.6467	0.9394	48.4022	4.6229	42541
I (14) BPP=3.3167	3.74	3.86	3.32	3.6400	0.6968	49.7000	4.3522	45187
I (15) BPP=4.5082	3.74	3.86	4.51	4.0367	0.6328	50.1181	4.3172	45554

Table 4. Input and output parameters for 256x256 image using SPIHT

Wavelet Used Haar	Technique Used SPIHT			Output Parameters				
Number of Iterations & BPP	RED channel (BPP)	Green channel (BPP)	Blue Channel (BPP)	Average BPP	MSE	PSNR	C_R	Output File Size (Kb)
I (10) BPP=0.1499	0.66	0.53	0.15	0.4467	14.4617	36.5286	7.1707	27426
I (11) BPP=0.3167	1.01	0.82	0.32	0.7167	7.7260	39.2513	5.8587	33568
I (12) BPP=0.5792	1.40	1.19	0.58	1.0567	3.7554	42.3843	5.1760	37995
I (13) BPP=0.9132	1.84	1.77	0.91	1.5067	1.6996	45.8272	4.8162	40834
I (14) BPP=1.3639	2.68	2.86	1.36	2.3000	0.9605	48.3060	4.5484	43238
I (15) BPP=2.1466	2.68	2.86	2.15	2.5633	0.7246	49.5301	4.3996	44700

Figure 16. (a) PSNR Vs. BPP of 512x512 pixels image; (b) PSNR Vs. BPP of 256x256 pixels image

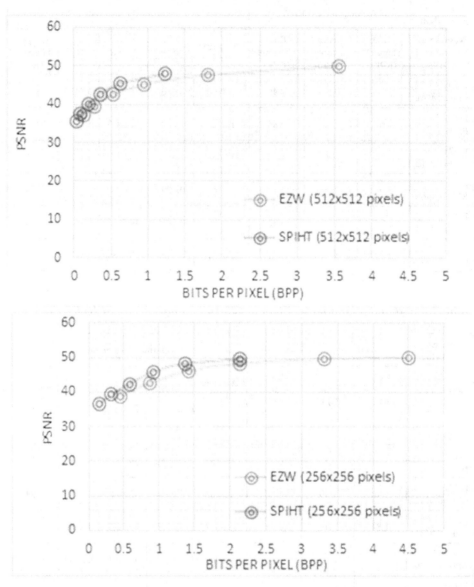

PSNR above 36dB while as the BPP varied from 0.1499 to 4.5082, which is higher than that for 512X512 pixels image. Higher CR of 7.1707 has been obtained using SPIHT technique. On observing the results, it is clear that SPIHT coding provides better image quality and higher CR using less BPP in comparison to the EZW coding techniques.

Figure 17(a) and 17(b) shows MSE vs. BPP of 512x512 and 256x256 pixels images. The MSE remained below 17.9538 for both techniques in case of 512x512 pixels image at 0.038 BPP while as in case of 256x256 pixels image; this value remained below 14.4617 at 0.1499 BPP. Further higher CR and MSE of 16.4851 and 17.9538 respectively, at 0.038 BPP for 512x512 pixels image has been found using SPIHT technique.

Figure 18(a) and 18(b) shows the comparison between 512x512 and 256x256 pixels image using SPIHT and EZW techniques respectively, on the basis of PSNR vs. BPP. For 512x512 pixels and 256 x256 pixels image compressed using SPIHT showed higher PSNR value of 47.9547 at 1.2339 BPP and 49.5301 at 2.1468 respectively. A higher CR of 16.4851 at 0.038 BPP was obtained for 512x512 pixels image using SPIHT as compared to the 256x256 pixel where a higher CR of 7.1707 at 0.1499 BPP was obtained.

For 512x512 pixels and 256x256 pixels image compressed using EZW showed higher PSNR value of 49.9057 at 3.5512BPP and 50.1811 at 4.5082 respectively. A higher CR of 15.1396 at 0.1268BPP has been obtained for 512x512 pixels image using EZW as compared to the 256x256 pixel where a higher CR of 6.8412 at 0.4561 BPP has been obtained. From the above-explained results, it is concluded that SPIHT and EZW for 512x512 pixels image shows outstanding performance in terms of CR.

Comparison of 512x512 and 256x256 pixels image using SPIHT and EZW on the basis of MSE Vs. BPP is shown in Figure 19(a) and 19(b). For 512x512 and 256x256 pixels image compressed using SPIHT showed a lower MSE value of 1.0414 at 1.2339 BPP and 0.7246 at 2.1466 respectively. While as for 512x512 and 256x256 pixels image compressed using EZW showed a lower MSE value of 0.6645 at 3.5512 BPP and 0.6328 at 4.5082 BPP respectively. Also, it is clear from the Figure 19(a) and 19(b) that SPIHT and EZW coding technique for 256x256 image showed outstanding performance in terms of MSE. In addition, high MSE and CR has been attained in 512x512 pixels image.

The application of DWT based SPIHT coding showed outstanding performance in terms of CR, PSNR, and MSE. In comparison to the EZW coding, SPIHT coding not only used less BPP but also provided reasonable image quality at higher CR's. The results show maximum CR's of 16.4851 using SPIHT and that of 7.1707 using EZW for 512x512 pixels and 256x256 pixels images respectively. For both of these approaches, PSNR remained above 35dB, which is sufficient for perceiving the image correctly by humans. In addition, SPIHT coding technique used less time during the execution process.

In addition, the application of lossless and lossy compression techniques on images introduce equal loss of information in the whole image which is not tolerable in certain types of images such as medical images, passport size photographs, etc One of the possible solutions to this problem may involve the coding of the image

Figure 17. (a) MSE Vs. BPP of 512x512 pixels image; (b) MSE Vs. BPP of 256x256 pixels image

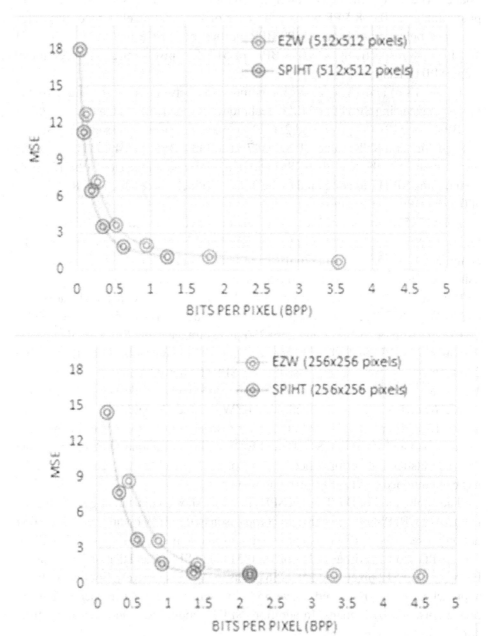

Figure 18. (a) Comparison of 512x512 pixels and 256x256 pixels image using SPIHT (PSNR Vs. BPP; (b) Comparison of 512x512 pixels and 256x256 pixels image using EZW (PSNR Vs. BPP)

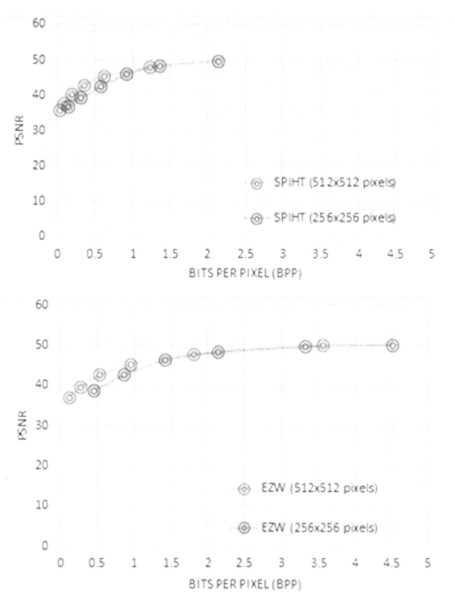

Figure 19. (a) Comparison of 512x512 pixels and 256x256 pixels image using SPIHT (MSE Vs. BPP); (b) Comparison of 512x512 pixels and 256x256 pixels image using EZW (MSE Vs. BPP)

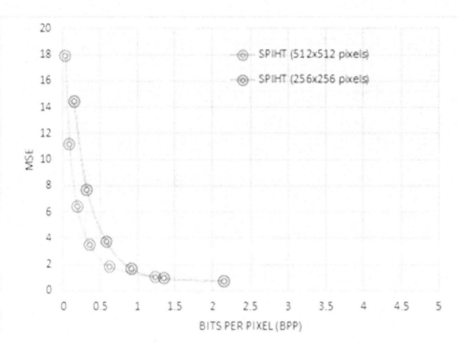

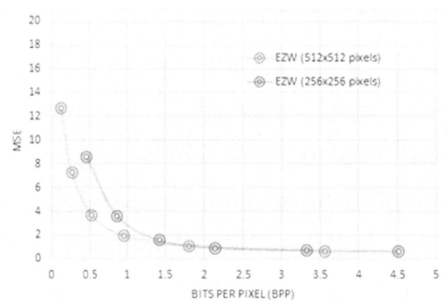

based on the feature extraction (Sayed, 2005) and another solution is the Region of Interest (ROI) Coding (Palanisamy & Samukutti, 2008) which is explained in the next section of this chapter.

ROI IMAGE COMPRESSION

The modern research in the field of image processing and human vision have shown that the human visual system (HVS) tends to focus on few preferred regions when viewing an image and thus motivated the concept of ROI coding (Stelmach et al., 1991). The various features that have been identified to effect visual attention include contrast (Stark et al., 1993) shape of the object (Mackworth & Morandi, 1967), size of the object (Findlay, 1980), location (Wise, 1984), color (Zmura, 1991), and context of a given image. Therefore, it is natural to exploit the characteristics of the human eye while designing the technical systems. Further, in some cases, the regions of importance may not remain same across applications. For example, in medical images, the diagnostically significant portions are regions of importance while as for passport size photographs, face is considered as the significant region. The significant region or the area of the image which attract the HVS attention more is known as the ROI or foreground and the insignificant region as non-region of interest (NROI). The other terms which are used in the literature for ROI include "object of interest" (Stough & Brodley, 2001), "focus of attention," "zone of interest," "preferential area" and "targets" (Giguet et al., 2001). Therefore loss of quality in the reconstruction of ROI after compression of such images is highly undesirable; however, some loss of information in the NROI can be accepted. Also, it has been observed that the NROI for these types of images occupy almost 50% or more of the image size. Therefore, NROI can be compressed by lossy algorithms while as ROI of the image can be left uncompressed or compressed through lossless or near lossless algorithms (Sridhar, 2008; Bharti et al., 2009). The technique that combines both lossless compression for ROI and lossy compression for NROI is known as the ROI coding and is the most frequently used image compression technique for the images having regions of different significance. Thus by means of ROI image coding technique, a high CR can be obtained, and the significant region can be preserved losslessly (Song, 2002; Bao & Ming, 2003) as compared to the stand alone lossless and lossy compression. At this stage, one question arises that if ROI is the only significant part in the image, then why to encode and transmit the NROI? NROI portions should be encoded because NROI portions are useful in the context of the region of interest such as to help the observer in identifying the position of the ROI. ROI coding usually supports progressive transmission by quality and thus helps to reduce the transmission time and storage cost to a great extent (Mohammed & Abd-Elhafiez, 2011). Finding the ROI of images, processing, storing or transmitting them with special consideration, besides having applications in image compression has also applications in telemedicine, channel coding, digital image archive, security, remote sensing and several other areas as well (Santa-Cruz et al., 1999).

Three steps are involved to develop any compression technique for ROI coding. In the first step, ROI is selected either dynamically or statically. The shape and size of the selected ROI can be regular or arbitrary and can be different for different observers and for different image classes. However, if the ROI is formed by a rectangle or circle, then the shape information is provided by coordinate points or radius and centre respectively (Chang et al., 2006). These regions are separated from one another. As a result, separate images containing ROI and NROI are created. Next step compresses the ROI image with some lossless or near lossless compression technique and the NROI with lossy compression technique. Finally, the two images are combined together to form the desired ROI coded image. A reverse process produces the decompressed image.

Advantages and Disadvantages of ROI Image Compression

ROI image compression technique offers a number of advantages over the standalone lossless and lossy image compression techniques. Some of them are listed below:

1. ROI compression technique allows fine control on the relative importance between ROI and NROI.
2. ROI image compression helps to preserve the ROI with higher visual quality as compared to the standalone lossy image compression techniques.
3. It helps to recover only the ROI first.
4. It offers higher CR's as compared to the standalone lossless image compression techniques but lower than standalone lossy compression techniques.
5. It helps to reduce the storage space and transmission time to a large extent as compared to the standalone lossless image compression techniques.

Related Research and Application of Image Compression Using ROI Coding Techniques

Various studies are carried out by prominent researches; however, some of the most relevant studies are presented in this sub-section of the chapter.

Jun Hou Li et al. used object segmentation to locate the facial region to which grayscale and projection were applied and proposed a color facial compression algorithm. The authors have done the analysis of minima and maxima in order to locate and extract the Facial features. To decrease the less valuable information in the final bit stream, background was set to zero. Finally, the ROI coding in JPEG2000 has been used to compress the facial region. The bit stream produced was compatible with the JPEG2000 standard.

Gerhard and Kinsner (1996) proposed WT for compression of passport images for subject recognition. The system included pre-processing to reduce insignificant information, thresholding of the wavelet-transformed coefficients, zero-tree coding of the coefficients, and arithmetic coding of the zero-tree code. At higher CR's, the authors employed post-processing to remove salt and pepper noise. As compared to the JPEG compression, the proposed system performed superior at CR's of above 40:1 resulting in better image quality. The images were acceptable for subject recognition.

Tropf and Chai (2005) proposed a method for efficient segmentation of passport images based on pixel difference. The face segmentation detects eyes and mouth to locate the facial region and compress it by using the ROI coding. The proposed work allowed decrease in the background redundancy and encoding time.

Kumar et al. (2011) applied ROI coding in telemedicine by using WT with lifting. The study used SPIHT. For each ROI in the image, an efficient ROI encoding scheme with diverse resolution has been proposed. By integrating all the encoded ROI image data, encoded background image and a header that contains the number of ROIs, co-ordinates, and resolutions of each ROI, the final encoded data has been formed. In the decoded image, the ROI data are located in their corresponding places, by using the co-ordinate details in the header. The experimental results showed that use of lifting wavelet transform and SPIHT attained high CR and quality of the ROI.

Optimum compression for passport size photographs is proposed by employing different types of compression methods compressing ROI and NROI within a photograph with different compression ratios. It is adequate to allot a lower bit rate to NROI in comparison to that of ROI because ROI has to be perceived with higher degree of accuracy than NROI. In the proposed method, the ROI in the photograph, i.e., the face of a person is selected automatically through a face detection algorithm, which is based on the color of the skin. The selected ROI may be rectangular or oval shaped; however, in this implementation a rectangular area has been chosen within the center of the image. The steps are shown in Figure 20.

Next, the input image is splited into two images, each corresponding to ROI and NROI portions. Source photograph is split into two by creating two masks, one for the ROI and other for the Non-ROI. The mask corresponding to the ROI contains

1's for all pixels belonging to the ROI and 0's for all pixels belonging to NROI and vice-versa. Separate ROI and NROI images are produced by performing AND operation between the source photograph and the two masks. The ROI image is then compressed using Huffman compression technique, and NROI is compressed using compression techniques such as Huffman, EZW or SPIHT with lower bit rates to achieve more compression. CR of both of the images is chosen carefully to achieve good quality of reconstruction of ROI and better overall CR. Finally, the two compressed images are merged together to produce the final compressed photograph.

Frontal view photos were collected from the Google and a Database of 100 Standard Indian Passport size images (50 Male and 50 Female) measuring 3.5cm x 3.5cm with pixel resolutions of 512 x 512 and 256 x 256 of a male and a female (Without hijab) plain background, without hats, glasses and other standard clothing was created and later used as sample photographs. For each passport photograph, the ROI, i.e., face of the person is detected based on the color of the skin, and later two separate images were created through masking, one corresponding to ROI and other NROI. For compression, DWT (Haar) with Huffman coding to ROI portion and Huffman, EZW and SPIHT coding to NROI portion but using different degrees of compression to two portions of the image have been used.

The compressed ROI and the NROI parts of the image are merged in the following ways:

M1: DWT based compression-using Huffman coding for both ROI and NROI merged into a JP2 file format;

M2: DWT based compression-using Huffman coding for ROI and EZW coding for NROI merged into a JP2 file format; and

M3: DWT based compression-using Huffman coding for ROI and SPIHT coding for NROI merged into a JP2 file format.

The results are analyzed, compared to each other, and discussed in the following section.

To achieve higher compression of the final image while maintaining high quality of the ROI and moderate to good quality of NROI, so that the image can be perceived by a human eye acceptably and visibly, compression of both ROI and NROI regions was commenced with different values of BPP. From the experimental results, it was found that for BPP an average value from 0.2141 to 0.2611 for 512x512 pixels photo and 0.3196 to 0.3787 for 256x256 pixels photo for ROI was adequate because the image at these values was correctly perceived. Likewise, for NROI these values for

Figure 20. ROI coding for passport photo compression

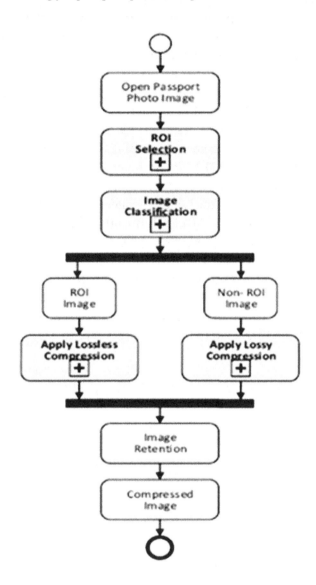

Huffman coding remained from 0.0892 to 0.1451 for 512x512 pixels photo and 0.1239 to 0.2050 for 256x256 pixels photos. In case of EZW encoding the range for BPP remained from 0.0194 (with 8 loops) to 0.6606 (with 14 loops) for 512x512 pixels photo and 0.1057 (with 8 loops) to 1.3171 (with 14 loops) for 256x256 pixels photo. These values in case of SPIHT remained from 0.0105 (with 8 loops) to 0.3496 (with 14 loops) and 0.0501 (with 8 loops) to 0.7106 (with 14 loops) respectively for 512x512 and 256x256 pixels photos. ROI and NROI portions of the photo were compressed for all of the above-mentioned ranges of values of BPP. The ROI and NROI portions were merged together to form the final compressed photo. PSNR, MSE, and CR were calculated for all the approaches to compression discussed in above section (M1, M2, and M3). A study employing services of 10 fellow scholars conducted to evaluate the best value for BPP for ROI and NROI portions of the image. It was found that compression using 0.2398 BPP for 512x512 pixels photo for ROI portion and 0.1121 BPP (Huffman), 0.1411 BPP (with 11 loops for EZW) and 0.0745 BPP (with 11 loops for SPIHT) gave best human perception of the final compressed photo. Likewise, these values for 256x256 pixels photo for ROI remained 0.3522 BPP, 0.1527 BPP (Huffman), 0.4652 BPP (with 11 loops for EZW) and 0.2414 BPP (with 11 loops for SPIHT).

Figure 21 and 22 shows, CR Vs. PSNR of 512x512 pixels and 256x256 pixels photos obtained in three approaches across different values of BPP for ROI while using optimum value of BPP for NROI.

For 512x512 pixels photo, all three approaches showed PSNR above 34 dB while as the CR varied from 13.0923 to 16.4323. Highest CR of 16.4323 has been obtained

Figure 21. CR vs. PSNR of 512 x 512, BPP varying for ROI

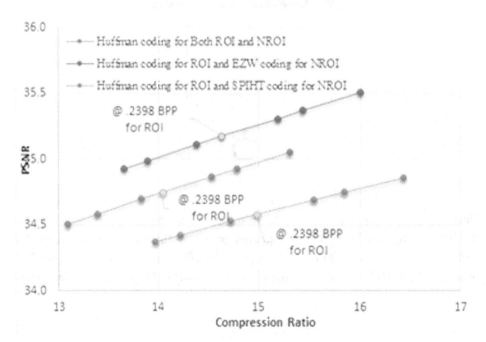

Figure 22. CR vs. PSNR of 256x256, BPP varying for ROI

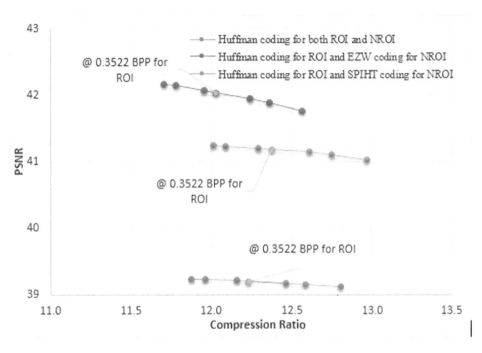

in approach M3. Highest PSNR of 35.5082 has been obtained in approach M2. For best human perception, i.e., compression of ROI at 0.2398 BPP determined earlier, either M2 or M3 might be used depending upon the tradeoff between the desired levels of compression, PSNR and visual quality of the image.

For 256x256 pixels photo, only approaches M2 and M3 showed PSNR above 44 dB while as the CR varied from 11.7075 to 12.9638, which is lower than that achieved for 512X512 pixels photo. Highest CR of 12.8045 and 12.9638 has been obtained in approaches M1 and M3 respectively. Highest PSNR of 42.1689 has been obtained in approach M2. For best human perception, i.e., compression of ROI at 0.3522 BPP determined earlier, approach M2 is ideal.

Figure 23 and 24 shows CR Vs. PSNR of 512x512 pixels and 256x256 pixels photos obtained in three approaches across different values of BPP for NROI while using optimum value of BPP for ROI. For 512x512 pixels photo, all the three approaches showed PSNR over 31 dB while as the CR varied from 11.9795 to 15.9920. However, approaches M2 and M3 outperformed M1 for optimum values of BPP for NROI.

Figure 23. CR vs. PSNR of 512x512, BPP varying for NROI

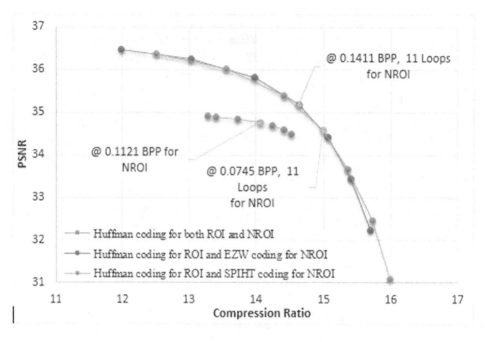

Figure 24. CR vs. PSNR of 256x256, BPP varying for NROI

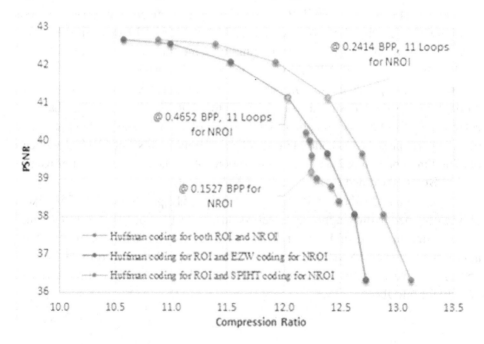

For 256x256 pixels photo, approaches M2 and M3 showed PSNR well above 40dB while as the CR varied from 10.5743 to 13.1240. Further, the visual quality and PSNR value of the final merged image, in case of approach M1 is low as compared to the approaches M2 and M3. But the performance of approaches M2 and M3 remained very close to each other and therefore either might be used.

Figure 25 and 26 shows CR Vs. PSNR of 512x512 pixels and 256x256 pixels photos obtained in three approaches across adequate ranges of BPP values (minimum, maximum and optimum) for ROI and NROI determined earlier to achieve the best human perception.

The use of minimum and maximum values of BPP for both ROI and NROI portions in approach M1 for 512x512 pixels photo showed no significant change in PSNR but CR changed by about 3.5. However, approaches M2 and M3 showed significant changes (about 4 dB in approach M2 and 5 dB in approach M3) in PSNR across minimum and maximum values of BPP. The CR in M2 approach changed from 11.3115 to 17.2876, and that in M3 approach changed from 11.7916 to 17.6427. PSNR remained well above 34 dB in all the approaches for optimum values of BPP for ROI and NROI with a CR between 14.0479 and 14.9831.

For minimum and maximum values of BPP for ROI and NROI portions in approaches M2 and M3 for 256x256 pixels photo, the performance remained nearly

Figure 25. CR vs. PSNR of 512x512, BPP minimum and maximum for both ROI and NROI

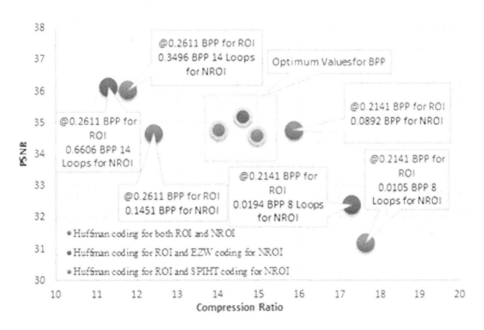

Figure 26. CR vs. PSNR of 256x256, BPP minimum and maximum for both ROI and NROI

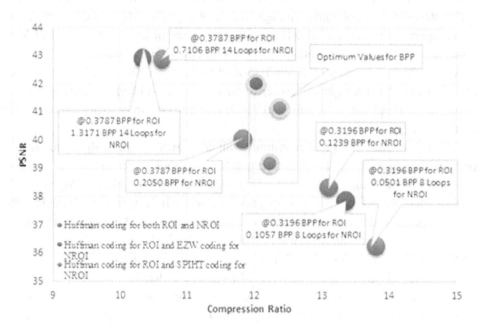

identical. However, for approach M1, there was a small change in both PSNR and CR. The PSNR for optimum values of BPP in case of M2 and M3 approaches remained above 41 dB and the compression ration above 12, which is slightly closer to maximum.

Figure 27, shows CR Vs. PSNR and Figure 28, shows CR Vs. MSE of 512x512 pixels and 256x256 pixels photos obtained in the three approaches across optimum values for BPP for ROI and NROI portions.

For the three worked approaches, on an average, the CR achieved for 512x512 pixels photo remained between 14.0479 and 14.9831, which is 119.68% of that achieved for 256x256 pixels photo. The PSNR for 512x512 pixels photo remained between 34.5846 and 35.1762, which is 85.86% of that achieved for 256x256 pixels photo.

The MSE in case of all approaches remained much lower for 256x256 pixels photo (around 15) in comparison to that of 512x512 pixels photo. The highest MSE (40.6346) with highest CR (about 15) for 512x512 pixels photo remained in approach M3. Lowest CR with lowest MSE has been found in 256x256 pixels photo.

Figure 27. Comparison of optimum results for 512x512 and 256x256 photographs (CR vs. PSNR)

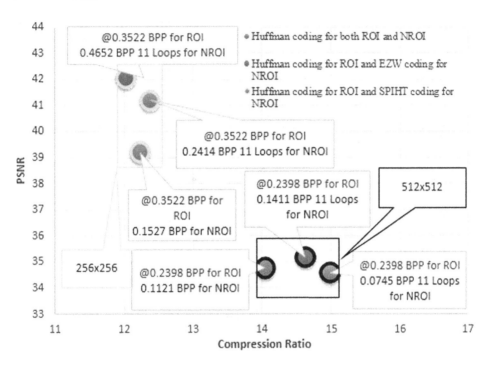

CONCLUSION AND FUTURE WORK

From this chapter, it is concluded that image compression techniques based on WT are more efficient as compared to other techniques. Wavelet based EZW and SPIHT coding techniques when used for compressing the image having standard pixel resolution of 512x512 and 256x256 showed not only better image quality at higher CR but also utilized lesser BPP. However, equal loss of quality occurred for the whole image which is not desirable for certain types of images like passport images, etc. This motivated for the design of more efficient technique which is known as the ROI coding technique. DWT based compression-using Huffman coding for ROI and EZW coding for NROI portions and DWT based compression-using Huffman coding for ROI and SPIHT coding for NROI portions presented marvelous performance in terms of MSE, PSNR and CR. For these approaches, PSNR remained well above 31-34 dB, which is considered minimum for perceiving the face correctly

Figure 28. Comparison of optimum results for 512x512 and 256x256 photographs (CR vs. MSE)

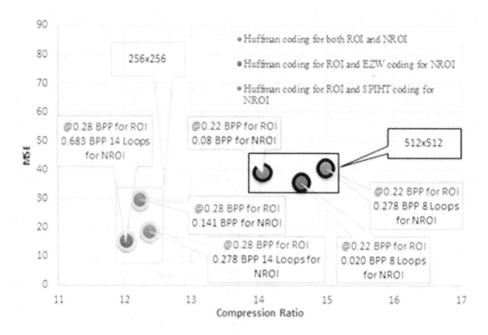

by humans. Encoding NROI with EZW showed slightly better performance than encoding NROI with SPIHT. Further, higher CR has been found in high-resolution photographs, thereby permitting the reduction of storage space, faster transmission on low bandwidth channels and faster processing without compromising on the quality of the ROI of the photograph.

The ROI Coding technique presented in this chapter can be applied to other images such as medical images, forensic images, etc., for obtaining higher quality of the ROI of the image as compared to the NROI. These images can also be watermarked for security purposes, and the effect of the compression on the watermark image can be examined. In this work, the ROI selection is done automatically, however; this selection can also be done interactively according to the one's choice and the effect of the area chosen, as ROI on the final compressed image can also be studied. Further, the work presented in this chapter can also be extended to the images containing multiple ROI's, where the different regions can be compressed using the different compression techniques already proposed in the above work.

REFERENCES

Bao, Z. L., & Ming, Z. (2003). ROI Coding Research Based on Residual Image. *Journal of Opto-Electronics Laser, 14*(1), 75–78.

Bharti, P., Gupta, S., & Bhatia, R. K. (2009). Comparative Analysis of Image Compression Techniques: A Case Study on Medical Images. *2009 International Conference on Advances in Recent Technologies in Communication and Computing*, 820–822. Retrieved from https://ieeexplore.ieee.org/document/5328178

Chen, Y. T., Tseng, D. C., & Chang, P. C. (2006). Wavelet-Based Image Compression with Polygon-Shaped Region of Interest. *LNCS 4319*, 878–887. Retrieved from https://link.springer.com/chapter/10.1007/11949534_88

Chowdhury, M. M. H., & Khatun, A. (2012). Image Compression Using Discrete Wavelet Transform. *International Journal of Computer Science Issues, 9*(1).

Cruz, D. S., Ebrahimi, T., Larsson, M., Askelof, J., & Christopoulos, C. A. (1999). *Region of Interest Coding in JPEG 2000 for Interactive Client/Server Applications. In IEEE 3rd Workshop on Multimedia Signal Processing* (pp. 389–394). Copenhagen, Denmark: MMSP. Retrieved from https://ieeexplore.ieee.org/document/793870

Daubechics, I. (1992). *Ten Lectures on Wavelets*. Society for Industrial and Applied Mathematics Philadelphia. doi:10.1137/1.9781611970104

Daubechies, I. (1990). The wavelet transform time-frequency localization and signal analysis. *IEEE Transformation and Information Theory, 36*(5), 961-1005. Retrieved from https://ieeexplore.ieee.org/document/57199

Deshlahra, A. (2013). *A Thesis on Analysis of Image Compression Methods Based On Transform and Fractal Coding*. Rourkela.

Findlay, J. M. (1980). The Visual Stimulus for Saccadic Eye Movements in Human Observers. *Perception, 9*(1), 7–21. doi:10.1068/p090007 PMID:7360616

Gerhard, D. B., & Kinsner, W. (1996). Lossy Compression of Head and Shoulder Images Using Zero-tree of Wavelet Coefficients. *IEEE Conference on Electrical and Computer Engineering*, 433-437. Retrieved from https://ieeexplore.ieee.org/document/548129

Giguet, D., Karam, L. J., & Abousleman, G. P. (2001). Very Low Bit-Rate Target Based Image Coding. *Proc. Asilomar Conf. on Signals, Systems, and Computers*, 778-782. 10.1109/ACSSC.2001.987030

Kanth, S. S. (2013). *Compression Efficiency for Combining Different Embedded Image Compression Techniques with Huffman Encoding. In 2013.* Melmaruvathur, India: International Conference on Communication and Signal Processing. Retrieved from https://ieeexplore.ieee.org/document/6577170

Kumar, S. (2011). *Thesis on Image compression based on improved SPIHT and region of interest.* Thapar University.

Kumar, T. M. P. R., & Latte, M. V. (2011). ROI Based Encoding of Medical Images: An Effective Scheme Using Lifting Wavelets and SPIHT for Telemedicine. *International Journal of Computer Theory and Engineering, 3*(3), 338-346. Doi:10.7763/IJCTE.2011.V3.329

Lewis, A. S., & Knowles, G. (1992). Image compression using the 2- D wavelet transform. *IEEE Transactions on Image Processing, 1*(2), 244–250. doi:10.1109/83.136601 PMID:18296159

Li, J. H., Cheng, Y., & Shi, H. (2013). Passport Photo Compression Technique with JPEG2000. *Proceedings of 2013 IEEE International Conference on Mechatronics and Automation.* Retrieved from https://ieeexplore.ieee.org/document/6618116

Mackworth, N. H., & Morandi, A. J. (1967). The Gaze Selects Informative Details Within Pictures. *Perception & Psychophysics, 2*(11), 547–552. doi:10.3758/BF03210264

Mallat, S. G. (1989). A Theory of multi-resolution Signal Decomposition: The Wavelet Representation. *IEEE Transactions on Pattern Analysis and Machine Intelligence, 11*(7), 674–693. doi:10.1109/34.192463

Meyer. (1993). Wavelets: their past and their future. *Progress in Wavelet Analysis and its Applications,* 9-18.

Mohammed, U. S., & Abd-Elhafiez, W. M. (2011). New Approaches for DCT Based Image Compression Using Region of Interest Scheme. *Applied Mathematics & Information Sciences, 5*(1), 29–43.

Nagamani, K., & Ananth, A. G. (2011). EZW and SPIHT Image Compression Techniques for High Resolution Satellite Imageries. *International Journal of Advanced Engineering Technology Computer Application, 2*(2), 82-86.

Olkkonen, H. (2011). *Discrete Wavelet Transforms- Bio-Medical Applications.* doi:10.5772/1818

Palanisamy, G., & Samukutti, A. (2008). Medical image compression using a novel embedded set partitioning significant and zero block coding. *The International Arab Journal of Information Technology*, 5(2), 132–139.

Raja, S. P., & Suruliandi, A. (2010). Performance Evaluation on EZW & WDR Image Compression Techniques. In 2010 international conference on communication control and computing technologies. Ramanathapuram, India: Academic Press. Retrieved from https://ieeexplore.ieee.org/abstract/document/5670757

Said, A., & Pearlman, W. A. (1996). A new, fast, and efficient image codec based on set partitioning in hierarchical trees. *IEEE Transactions on Circuits and Systems for Video Technology*, 6(3), 243–250. https://ieeexplore.ieee.org/document/499834. doi:10.1109/76.499834

Sayed, U. (2005). Image Coding Technique Based on Object-Feature Extraction. *Proceedings of (NRSC'2005)*.

Schelkens, P., Munteanu, A., & Cornelis, J. (1999). Wavelet-based compression of medical images: Protocols to improve resolution and quality scalability and region-of-interest coding. *Future Generation Computer Systems*, 15(2), 171–184. doi:10.1016/S0167-739X(98)00061-2

Sifuzzaman, M., Islam, M. R., & Ali, M. Z. (2009). Application of Wavelet Transform and its Advantages Compared to Fourier Transform. *Journal of Physical Sciences*, 13, 121-134.

Singh, P. N., Gupta, D., & Sharma, S. (2012). Performance Analysis of Embedded Zero Tree and Set Partitioning In Hierarchical Tree. *International Journal of Computer Technology & Applications*, 3, 572-577.

Singh, P., & Singh, P. (2011). Design and Implementation of EZW & SPIHT Image Coder for Virtual Image. *International Journal of Computer Science and Security, Kuala Lumpur, Malaysia*, 5(5), 433–442.

Smith, M. J. T., & Eddins, S. L. (1990). Analysis/synthesis techniques for sub-band image coding. *IEEE Trans. Acoustic, Speech, Signal Processing*, 1446–1456. Retrieved from https://ieeexplore.ieee.org/abstract/document/57579/similar#similar

Song, C. (2002). ROI Image Coding methods in JPEG2000. *TV Engineering*, 5, 15–18.

Sprljan, N., Grgic, S., & Grgic, M. (2005). Modified SPIHT algorithm for wavelet packet image coding. *Real-Time Imaging*, 11(5-6), 378–388. doi:10.1016/j.rti.2005.06.009

Sridhar, K. V. (2008). *Implementation of Prioritised ROI Coding for Medical Image Archiving using JPEG2000*. International Conference on Signals and Electronic Systems. Retrieved from https://ieeexplore.ieee.org/document/4673403

Sriram, B., & Thiyagarajans, S. (2012). Hybrid Transformation technique for image compression. *Journal of Theoretical and Applied Information Technology, 41*(2), 175-180.

Stark, L., Yamashita, I., Tharp, G., & Ngo, H. X. (1993). Search Patterns and Search Paths in Human Visual Search. In D. Brogan, A. Gale, & K. Carr (Eds.), *Visual Search 2* (pp. 37–58). London: Taylor and Francis.

Stelmach, L. B., Tam, W. J., & Hearty, P. J. (1991). Static and Dynamic Spatial Resolution in Image Coding: An Investigation of Eye Movements. *Proc. SPIE Human Vision, Visual Processing and Digital Display II, 1453*, 147-152. 10.1117/12.44351

Stough, T. M., & Brodley, C. E. (2001). Focusing Attention on Objects of Interest Using Multiple Matched Filters. *IEEE Transactions on Image Processing, 10*(3), 419–426. doi:10.1109/83.908516 PMID:18249631

Strang, G., & Nguyen, T. (1996). *Wavelets and Filter Banks*. Wellesley, MA: Wellesley Cambridge Press.

Tao, M., Hempel, M., Dongming, P., & Sharif, H. (2013). A survey of energy-efficient compression and communication techniques for multimedia in resource-constrained systems. *IEEE Communications Surveys and Tutorials, 15*(3), 963–972. doi:10.1109/SURV.2012.060912.00149

Tropf, A., & Chai, D. (2005). Region Segmentation for Facial Image Compression. *Proc. IEEE Communications and Signal Processing,* 1556-1560. Retrieved from https://ieeexplore.ieee.org/document/1689320

Usevitch, B. E. (2001). A Tutorial on Modern Lossy Wavelet Image Compression: Foundations of JPEG 2000. *IEEE Signal Processing Magazine, 18*(5), 22–35. doi:10.1109/79.952803

Vaidyanathan, P. (1993). *Multirate Systems and Filter Banks*. Prentice-Hall.

Whittaker, E. T. (1915). On the Functions which are Represented by the Expansions of Interpolation Theory. *Proceedings of the Royal Society of Edinburgh, 35*, 181–194. doi:10.1017/S0370164600017806

Wise, J. (1984). *Eye Movements While Viewing Commercial NTSC Format Television*. White Paper, SMPTE Psychophysics Committee.

Woods, J., & ONeil, S.D. (1986). Sub-band coding of images. *IEEE Transactions on Acoustics, Speech and Signal Processing, 34*(5), 1278-1288, https://ieeexplore.ieee.org/document/1164962

Zhao, J. H., Sun, W. J., Meng, Z., & Hao, Z. H. (2004). Wavelet transform characteristics and compression coding of remote sensing images. *Optics and Precision Engineering, 12*(2), 205–210.

Zmura, M. D. (1991). Color in Visual Search. *Vision Research, 31*(6), 951–966. doi:10.1016/0042-6989(91)90203-H PMID:1858326

KEY TERMS AND CONDITIONS

WT: Wavelet Transform
STFT: Short Time Fourier transform
CWT: Continous Wavelet Transform
DWT: Discrete Wavelet Transform
LPF: Low Pass Filter
HPF: High Pass Filter
EZW: Embedded Zero Tree Wavelet
SPIHT: Set Partitioning in Hierarchical Trees
CR: Compression Ratio
PSNR: Peak Signal to Noise Ratio
MSE: Mean Square Error
JPEG: Joint Photographic Experts Group
BPP: Bits Per Pixel
ROI: Region of Interest
NROI: Non-Region of Interest
HVS: Human Visual System

Chapter 5

A Performance Study of Image Quality Attributes on Smoothened Image Obtained by Anisotropic Diffusion–Based Models:
A Comparative Study and Performance Evaluation

Muthukumaran Malarvel
ⓘ https://orcid.org/0000-0002-7805-6472
Chitkara University, India

Sivakumar S.
Koneru Lakshmaiah Education Foundation, India

ABSTRACT

Image acquisition systems usually acquire images with distortions due to various factors associated with digitization processes. Poisson is one of the common types of noises present in the image, and it distorts the fine features. Hence, it is necessary to denoise the noisy image by smoothing it to extract the features with fine details. Among the denoising methods, anisotropic diffusion method provides more adequate results. In this chapter, the authors dealt with existing models such as Perona-Malik (PM), total variation, Tsai, Chao, Chao TFT, difference eigen value PM, adaptive PM, modified PM, and Maiseli models. The performances of the models were tested on synthetic image added with the Poisson noise. Quality metrics are used to quantify and to ensure the smoothness of the resultant images. However, in order to ensure t

DOI: 10.4018/978-1-7998-0066-8.ch005

he completeness of the denoising effect, the qualitative attributes such as sharpness, blurriness, blockiness, edge quality, and false contouring are considered on smoothened images. The analysis results are shown the completeness of the denoising effect of the models.

INTRODUCTION

Images are widely used in many application areas such as medical, industrial automation & inspections, defense, astronomy, satellite imaging, surface inspection, and forensic science to retrieve features for interpretation. The detection of features present in the image depends on the eminence of the image, which is related to few factors, such as low contrast, noise, different sizes of features, and the undetectable foregrounds and background (Mohan et al., 2014). The noisy image reduces the ability to extract the features such as fractal dimension, fractal geometry and textures with fine information (Soumya, et al., 2018A, 2018B, 2018C). Image noise could be formed during the acquisition and transmission particularly; the image is contaminated by Poisson noise.

Photon noise, also known as Poisson noise, which is a number of photons senses from the sensor and also uncertainty associated with the measurement of light. Poisson component accounts for the signal-dependent due to photon accumulation. In order to remove such noises, it is a challenging task without disturbing the features present in the image.

Wrong feature extraction directs the identification of inaccurate features. Moreover, preserving the feature information present in the Region of Interest (ROI) of the noisy image is considered as a severe problem during denoising and smoothing, and it is an essential for image understanding and analysis. In this regard, several edge-preserving techniques while applying denoising and smoothing have been proposed in recent years. Image denoising is often used before the image segmentation, analysis, and interpretation wherein the corrupted images need to improve for meaningful feature extraction.

The Performance of smoothing techniques on the noisy images also depends on the various distortions such as blur, sharpness, blockiness, edge quality and false contours. These distortions degrade the images and affect the image features present in them, even though the resultant images are much denoised and smoothened. It would be desirable to prevent the features from distortions during denoising and smoothing process, and also we consider the effect of these attributes on the smoothened image to quantify the smoothing process using some of the quality metrics.

In the denoising and smoothing approaches, nonlinear techniques such as nonlinear Gaussian filters, partial differential equation, anisotropic diffusion filter, nonlocal means and bilateral filters can provide a satisfactory result than linear methods (Mohan et al., 2014; Pal et al., 2015). Implementing the anisotropic diffusion for image enhancement, restoration, smoothing and edge detection was introduced by Perona and Malik also called as P-M Model (Perona et al., 1990).

LITERATURE SURVEY

Several researchers are motivated by Catte et. al. (1992) and Rudin et. al. (1992) methods to introduce new approaches till date. Catte et al. (1992) proposed a scheme that approaches to incorporating Gaussian filter prior each iteration of diffusion function in pre-denoising. This scheme has still problem with selection of a suitable value for σ parameter of the Gaussian filter. Nonlinear total variation (TV) based method was proposed by Rudin et al. (1992) which provides a better result on staircases using gradients alone.

Many improved anisotropic diffusion (AD) models with different enhancements based on image on local information have been approached for digital image processing. Chao et al. (2005, 2006, 2008 and 2010) approached AD based technique for removing noises, detection of defects and demonstrated them on astronomical images, sputtered glass, solar wafer, and surface images. Tsai et. al. (2005) formulated (TCAD) a method for detection of defects in sputtered glass where a non-negative reducing function is employed in the diffusion coefficient function. Further, Chao et. al. (2006) introduced an AD based method (CTAD) with incorporating the local variance information of gray-levels in the diffusion coefficient function to remove the noisy stars of the nebula image. Furthermore, an improved version of AD model Chao et. al. (2008) (CTAD-TFT) has been approached where weighted sharpening diffusion function was employed in the diffusion coefficient function for sharpened and smoothened the surface image of Thin Film Transistor Liquid Crystal Displays. A modified AD technique named CTD for an edge-preserving smoothing was proposed by Chao et. al. (2010). It employs both local gradient and gray-level normalized variance in diffusion coefficient function with the adaptive selection of threshold parameter.

A difference eigenvalue Perona-Malik (DEPM) model (Tian et al., 2011) was proposed for edge preserving while smoothing the noisy image. In order to measure image gradient magnitude, it employed difference eigenvalue as an edge indicator in the diffusion function. Guo et al. (2012) proposed an Adaptive Perona-Malik (APM) model and it segments the image into two parts using the edge indicator. In these parts, APM removes the noise and preserve the edge accordingly. Based on directional Laplacian,

Wang et al. (2013) introduced a Modified Perona-Malik (MPM) model to remove noise and preserving edges. MPM incorporated a weighted Laplacian in the diffusion function to diffuse image along the edge direction of the original image. Maiseli et. al. (2016) introduced an edge sensitive detector to preserve the edges of the feature in the image by implementing a diffusion-driven iterative method (MG).

Although a huge number of anisotropic based models have developed for image denoising and smoothing. In our study, we are inspired on the existing models that are developed for solving various problems on different domains, and these models performed well on their respective domains. However, these existing papers focused on the extraction of image features present in the experiment or test images, but it should be considered the other distortions such as sharpness, blurriness, blockiness, edge quality and false contours of the image during smoothing process. It is important to experiment and analyse the specific distortions occurs by the denoising models.

In this chapter, the existing models such as P-M, TV, TCAD, CTAD, CTAD-TFT, CTD, DEPM, APM, MPM and MG are assessed to identify the specific distortions occurs during the smoothing process. The performance of the existing models was evaluated using Standard Deviation (SD), Root Mean Square Error (RMSE), Signal-to-Noise Ratio (SNR), Peak Signal-to-Noise Ratio (PSNR), Entropy (E) and Mean Structural SIMilarity (MSSIM). Furthermore, the smoothened images are evaluated in terms of quality attributes such as sharpness, blurriness, blockiness, edge quality, and false contouring to ensure the completeness of the smoothing of the respective models.

ANISOTROPIC DIFFUSION MODELS

PM Model

A diffusion algorithm through a partial differential equation (PDE) can be removed image noise.

Perona et. al. (1990) introduced an anisotropic diffusion technique derived from heat equation

$$\begin{cases} \partial I_t(x,y) \big/ \partial t = div[c_t(|\nabla I|).\nabla I_t(x,y)] \\ \qquad I_{t=0} = I_o \end{cases} \tag{1}$$

where I_0 is the original image at time t, div is a divergence operator, $\nabla I_t(x,y)$ is image gradient and $c(\|\nabla\|)$ is diffusion coefficient.

Implementation of continuous anisotropic diffusion in Equation 1 is by using nearest neighbors of four directions and the Laplacian operator

$$I_{t+1}(x,y) = I_t(x,y) + \frac{1}{4}\sum_{i=1}^{4}\left[c_t^i(x,y) \cdot \nabla I_t^i(x,y)\right] \tag{2}$$

where $\nabla I_t^i(x,y)$, i=1,2,3 and 4, denote the four neighbors gradient in the north, south, east and west gradient directions, respectively.

$$\nabla I_t^1(x,y) = I_t(x,y-1) - I_t(x,y)$$
$$\nabla I_t^2(x,y) = I_t(x,y+1) - I_t(x,y)$$
$$\nabla I_t^3(x,y) = I_t(x+1,y) - I_t(x,y)$$
$$\nabla I_t^4(x,y) = I_t(x-1,y) - I_t(x,y)$$

$c_t^i(x,y)$ is the diffusion coefficient related with $\nabla I_t^i(x,y)$, and is deliberated as a function of the gradient $\nabla I_t^i(x,y)$ in the PM model $c_t^i(x,y) = g(\nabla I_t^i(x,y))$.

Two diffusion coefficient functions are used commonly is given by Perona-Malik as Equations 3 and 4

$$g\left(\nabla I\right) = \exp\left[-\left(\frac{|\nabla I|}{k}\right)^2\right] \tag{3}$$

$$g\left(\nabla I\right) = \frac{1}{1+\left(\frac{|\nabla I|}{k}\right)^2} \tag{4}$$

where k is a positive constant threshold value to regulator the denoising level.

TV Model

The Total variation (TV) (Rudin et al., 1992) model is a method based on the noise statistics present in an image. If the diffusion function is $c(s) = (\varepsilon + s^2)^{-\frac{1}{2}}$, then the total variation (TV) formulated as

$$
\begin{cases}
\dfrac{\partial I}{\partial t} = div\left[c\left(\left\|\nabla I\right\|, \varepsilon\right).\nabla I\right] \\[2mm]
c\left(\left\|\nabla I\right\|, \varepsilon\right) = \dfrac{1}{\sqrt{\varepsilon + \left\|\nabla I\right\|^2}}
\end{cases}
\tag{5}
$$

where $\varepsilon = 10^{-6}$.

Equation 4 was rewritten as

$$
g\left(\nabla I\right) = \dfrac{1}{\sqrt{1 + \left(\dfrac{|\nabla I|}{k}\right)^2}}
\tag{6}
$$

TCAD Model

Tsai et al. (2005) proposed a model based on AD for defect detection in sputtered surfaces with inhomogeneous textures, and it can be called TCAD. The mathematical representation of the model is denoted as

$$
g(\nabla I_t^i(x,y)) = \dfrac{1}{1 + \left(\dfrac{\left\|\nabla I_t^i(x,y)\right\|}{k(0)t^{-(1/3)}}\right)^2}
\tag{7}
$$

where k(0) is gradient magnitude average of the entire image and is calculated as below

$$
k(0) = \dfrac{1}{4MN} \sum_{i=1}^{4} \sum_{x=0}^{M-1} \sum_{y=0}^{N-1} \nabla I_t^i(x,y)
\tag{8}
$$

where MN is the image size.

CTAD Model

A modified Chao and Tsai AD named (CTAD) scheme was proposed (Chao et al., 2006) to removing spurious noisy stars in the astronomical images. The revised diffusion coefficient function of CTAD is

$$g(\nabla I, \sigma^2) = \frac{1}{1 + \left(\dfrac{\|\nabla I\|}{k.\sigma^2}\right)^2} \tag{9}$$

where σ^2 is the local variance of gray levels in a 3x3 neighborhood window. The local variance defined as

$$\sigma_t^2(x, y) = \frac{1}{9} \sum_{i=-1}^{1} \sum_{j=-1}^{1} (I_t(x+i, y+j) - \bar{I}_t(x, y))^2 \tag{10}$$

where $\bar{I}_t(x, y)$ is the gray level mean in the 3x3 window. (x,y) is the pixel coordinates at iteration t.

CTAD-TFT Model

The CTAD-TFT model (Chao et al., 2008) combines both the smoothing and sharpening processes in a single function. The sharpening diffusion coefficient function $v(\nabla I)$ is defined as

$$v(\nabla I) = \alpha \bullet [1 - g(\nabla I) \tag{11}$$

where α is the weight of sharpening coefficient function with $0 \leq \alpha \leq 1$. The diffusion coefficient function $g(\nabla I)$ is the same as that defined in Equation 4.

The modified diffusion model of CTAD-TFT id defined as

$$I_{t+1}(x, y) = I_t(x, y) + \frac{1}{4} \sum_{i=1}^{4} \left[g(\nabla I_t^{(i)}(x, y) - v(\nabla I_t^{(i)}(x, y) \right] \nabla I_t^{(i)}(x, y) \tag{12}$$

CTD Model

Chao et al. (2010) Diffusion model can preserve edges and feature details while diffusion process where incorporates both local gradient and normalized gray-level variance. The diffusion function is described as

$$g\left(\nabla I_t^i(x,y), \sigma_{t,N}^2(x,y)\right) = \cfrac{1}{1 + \left(\cfrac{\nabla I_t^i(x,y).\sigma_{t,N}^2(x,y)}{k}\right)^2} \tag{13}$$

The normalized variance is given by

$$\sigma_{t,N}^2(x,y) = 1 + \frac{\sigma_t^2(x,y) - Min\sigma_t^2}{Max\sigma_t^2 - Min\sigma_t^2}.254 \tag{14}$$

where $\sigma_t^2(x,y)$ is gray level variance at iteration t.

DEPM Model

A Difference Eigen value Perona-Malik (DEPM) model (Tian et al., 2011) calculated from the Hessian matrix which defined as

$$H = \begin{bmatrix} u_{xx} & u_{xy} \\ u_{xy} & u_{yy} \end{bmatrix}$$

Two Eigen values λ_1 and λ_2 are calculated for matrix H which is positive semi definite.

$$\lambda_1 = \frac{1}{2}\left[(u_{xx} + u_{yy}) + \sqrt{(u_{xx} - u_{yy})^2 + 4u_{xy}^2}\right] \tag{15}$$

$$\lambda_2 = \frac{1}{2}\left[(u_{xx} + u_{yy}) - \sqrt{(u_{xx} - u_{yy})^2 + 4u_{xy}^2}\right] \tag{16}$$

where $\lambda_1 \geq \lambda_2$. λ_1 and λ_2 is max and min local variation at a pixel. The difference eigenvalue edge indicator P(u) defined as

$$P(u) = (\lambda_1 - \lambda_2)\lambda_1 w(u(x,y)) \tag{17}$$

where $w(u(x,y))$ is a weighting factor. Its value is assessed from the gray-level variance. The defined equation is presented as

$$w(u(x,y)) = \theta \frac{\sigma_t^2(x,y) - \min\{\sigma_t^2\}}{\max\{\sigma_t^2\} - \min\{\sigma_t^2\}} \tag{18}$$

where $\min\{\sigma_t^2\}$ and $\max\{\sigma_t^2\}$ are represented as the minimum and maximum gray-level variances of u, respectively; θ, a constant. P(u) is integrated into the classical diffusion model using Equation 4 and the k value is estimated using normalized difference eigenvalue.

$$k = \exp(-\overline{P}(G * u)) \tag{19}$$

where G represents a Gaussian filter and $\overline{P}(G * u)$ is normalized various eigenvalue operator defined by $\overline{P}(G * u) = P(G * u) / P_{max}$, and Pmax is the maximum value of P(G*u).

APM Model

An Adaptive Perona-Malik (APM) was proposed by Guo et al. (2012) and it is based on the variable exponent. The mathematical equation of the model is presented as

$$\frac{\partial u}{\partial t} = div\left(\frac{\nabla u}{1 + (|\nabla u| / k)^{\alpha(x)}}\right) - \lambda(u - f), \quad (x,t) \in \Omega \times (0,T) \tag{20}$$

The edge indicator $\alpha(x)$ is chosen as follows:

$$\alpha\left(|\nabla G_\sigma * f|\right) = 2 - \frac{2}{1 + k|\nabla G_\sigma * f|^2} \tag{21}$$

or

$$\alpha\left(\left|\nabla G_{\sigma} * u\right|\right) = 2 - \frac{2}{1 + k\left|\nabla G_{\sigma} * u\right|^{2}} \tag{22}$$

where λ is a weight parameter that regulates the reliability between the smoothing image u and the noise image f.

MPM Model

The Modified Perona-Malik (MPM) model (Wang et al., 2013) is represented as follows

$$\frac{\partial u}{\partial t} = \vec{n} \; \nabla^{T}(c(\|\nabla u\|)\nabla u)\vec{n} + \alpha \cdot c(\|\nabla u\|)\nabla u \tag{23}$$

where $\vec{n}$ chosen by $(-I_{y}, I_{x})/\|\nabla I\|$ in the proposed MPM model, $\nabla^{T}(c(\|\nabla u\|)\nabla u)$ is the Hessian matrix and α is a small constant. The modified weight function c(.) presented as

$$c\left(\|\nabla I\|\right) = 1 / \sqrt{1 + \left(\|\nabla I\|\right)^{2}} \tag{24}$$

MG Model

A diffusion-driven edge detector was proposed by Maiseli et al. (2016) (MG) model. The diffusion equation of the MG model was presented as

$$\frac{\partial u}{\partial t} = div\left(\frac{1 + \dfrac{|\nabla u|}{k}}{1 + \left(\dfrac{|\nabla u|}{k}\right)^{2}} \nabla u\right) + \lambda(u - u_{0}) \tag{25}$$

where λ is a regularization parameter that creates an adjustment between denoising and original images. u_0 is the original image. The edge detector written as

$$\varphi(|\nabla u|) = \frac{1 + \dfrac{|\nabla u|}{k}}{1 + \left(\dfrac{|\nabla u|}{k}\right)^2} \tag{26}$$

where k is non-zero constant.

IMPLEMENTATION AND ANALYSIS

To study the performance of the various anisotropic diffusion based denoising models such as P-M, TV, TCAD, CTAD, CTAD-TFT, CTD, DEPM, APM, MPM and MG, a synthetic image is considered as a input image, in which a Poisson noises are added to it. All of these denoising models are implemented using .NET and Matlab platform.

The original synthetic image and Poisson noise added image are shown in Figure 1(a) and 1(b). The smoothened images obtained from the above mentioned denoising models are shown in Figure 2(a - j), respectively.

Figure 1. (a) Original image and (b) noise added image

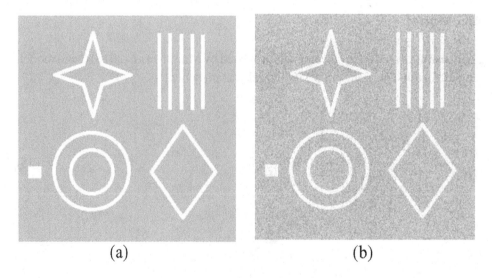

(a)   (b)

Figure 2. Smoothened images (a) Noisy image contaminated by Poisson noise; (b)-(k) smoothened images obtained by P-M, TV, TCAD, CTAD, CTAD-TFT, CTD, DEPM, APM, MPM and MG models, respectively.

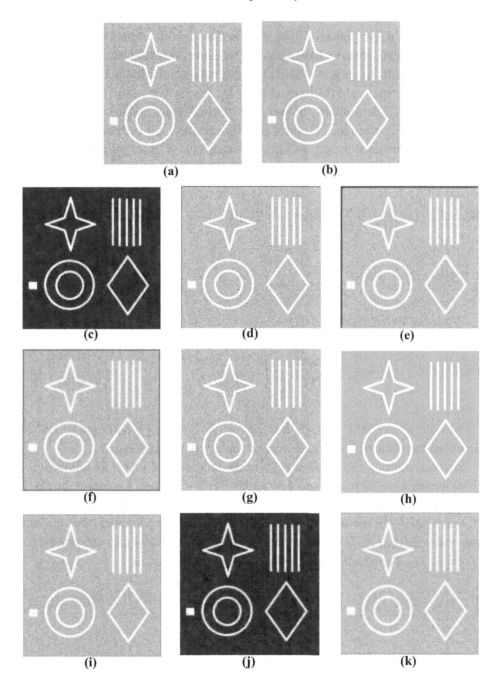

Quality Evaluation of Smoothened Images

Evaluation of Smoothness Using Measures

The qualities of the smoothened images are evaluated with original synthetic image by using quantitative metrics like Standard Deviation (SD), Root Mean Square Error (RMSE), Signal-to-Noise Ratio (SNR), Peak Signal-to-Noise Ratio (PSNR), Entropy (E) and Mean Structural SIMilarity (MSSIM) (Zahran et al., 2013).

The arithmetic dissimilarity between the original image and the denoised image known as MSE, determines the loss of image quality. For the original image as F(i,j) and the denoised image as G(i,j) with size M × N, Root Mean Square Error (RMSE) can be defined as

$$MSE(F,G) = \frac{1}{MN} \sum_{i=0}^{M-1} \sum_{j=0}^{N-1} \left[F(i,j) - G(i,j) \right]^2,$$

$$RMSE(F,G) = \sqrt{MSE} \tag{27}$$

While the PSNR is defined as:

$$PSNR(F,G) = 10 \log_{10} \left(\frac{255^2}{MSE(F,G)} \right) \tag{28}$$

A lower value of MSE indicates lesser error, and is directly proportional to PSNR. However, the value of PSNR and error are inversely proportional.

Shannon entropy (S_t) is calculated on the smoothened image as follows: in a given image, a spatial resolution $M \times N$ and bit level resolution b contains the pixels with gray values ranging from 0 to $L-1$, where L is the gray level of the pixel, namely, 2^b. Let $n(=M \cdot N)$ be the total number of pixels and n_i be the number of pixels with gray value $i \in [0, L-1]$. Then the normalized histogram of the image at iteration t is $H_i^{(t)} = n_i / n$. The Shannon entropy at iteration t is defined as

$$S_t = -\sum_{i=0}^{L-1} H_i \ln(H_i) \tag{29}$$

The entropy is a measure of the information of the image distortion content. In Eq. (29), the Shannon entropy is utilized to measure the entropy of the processed images, which illustrates and quantifies the variance or disorder of the smoothened images. Here, a lesser entropy value indicates lesser disorder.

In order to computing the similarity between images, MSSIM measure is calculated. SSIM is calculated between the two windows, F and G, of common window size $n{\times}n$. In this study, the common window size is set as 3×3. A higher value of MSSIM indicates that the resultant image has more similarity to the original image.

$$SSIM(F,G) = \frac{(2\mu_F\mu_G + c_1)(2\sigma_{FG} + c_2)}{(\mu_F^2 + \mu_G^2 + c_1)(\sigma_F^2 + \sigma_G^2 + c_2)} \qquad (30)$$

where μ_F is the average of F; μ_G is the average of G; σ_F^2 and σ_G^2 are the variance of F and G respectively; σ_{FG} is the covariance; c_1 and c_2 are stabilizing parameters, generally $c_1 = 0.05$ and $c_2 = 0.05$. Recall that the covariance between F and G is defined as

$$\sigma_{FG} = \frac{1}{L-1}\sum_{i=0}^{L-1}(F_i - \mu_F)(G_i - \mu_G)$$

Their mean SSIM is defined as

$$MSSIM(F,G) = \frac{1}{W}\sum_{j=1}^{W}SSIM(F_j,G_j) \qquad (31)$$

where W is number of local windows of size 3×3 in the image.

Table 1 list the evaluation measures of the smoothened images of the various models. The measures reveal that, DEPM model performs well in the synthetic image.

Table 1. Quality evaluation measures of smoothness

Models→ / Measures↓	P-M	TV	TCAD	CTAD	CTAD-TFT	CTD	DEPM	APM	MPM	MG
RMSE	3.6401	178.2595	13.5096	12.2390	7.9682	10.8151	0.8030	6.8253	149.88880	8.4836
PSNR	36.9085	4.7104	25.5180	26.3759	30.1036	27.4502	50.037	31.4483	4.6155	29.5592
E	2.7885	3.8837	4.3193	4.0252	3.6379	4.0354	0.6369	3.5295	4.1341	3.3693
MSSIM	0.8691	0.2944	0.0176	0.0877	0.5565	0.3377	0.9021	0.6765	0.2373	0.7592

Evaluation of Smoothness Using 2D Profiles

In order to evaluate the effectiveness of the smoothness, 2D intensity line profiles were compared on the smoothened images shown in Figure 2(b-k). The sample scans line shown in Figure 3. Two lines were taken for analysis where line1 (line 78) passing through the star and vertical lines objects, and line2 (line 207) passing through filled square box, circles and diamond objects. Figure 4 depicts the 2D scan line profiles of the smoothened images.

Evaluation of Sharpness and Blurriness

It is very important to quantify the sharpness and blurriness of the smoothened images. Excess blur in an image is a distortion and causes difficult for user to identify and classify the features in smoothened images. In this chapter, blur measure (BM) (Kanjar, 2013) employed for evaluation of sharpness and blurriness of the smoothened images. It is no-reference image quality measure is defined as

Given an image I, first step is to find the edge of the image using Sobel operator. Let E be a set containing all edge pixels in the image computed using Sobel operator. N_{xy} is a set of 8-neighbors of a pixel $I(x,y)$ where $I(x,y){\in}E$ and $I(x',y') \in N_{xy}$.

Figure 3. Sample scan line; first scan line at 78 and second scan line at 207

Figure 4. 2D scan line profiles; (a1-j1) Scan line at 78 of the smoothened images shown in Figure 2(b-k); (a2-j2) Scan line at 207 of the smoothened images shown in Figure 2(b-k)

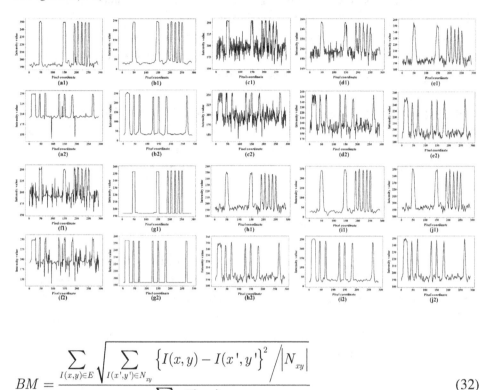

$$BM = \frac{\sum\limits_{I(x,y) \in E} \sqrt{\sum\limits_{I(x',y') \in N_{xy}} \{I(x,y) - I(x',y')\}^2 \Big/ \left| N_{xy} \right|}}{\sum\limits_{I(x,y) \in E} I(x,y)} \qquad (32)$$

A higher value of BM score means that there is higher change in intensity along the edges, which in turn means that image has higher sharpness, where as a lower value of BM score means smaller changes in intensity along the edges and means that blurriness is very high in the image. Table 2 lists the sharpness and blurriness measure of smoothened images. TV and MPM models yield higher sharpness than other models

Table 2. Evaluation measure of sharpness and blurriness of the smoothened images

Models→ Measure↓	P-M	TV	TCAD	CTAD	CTAD-TFT	CTD	DEPM	APM	MPM	MG
BM	0.1245	0.5804	0.1487	0.0825	0.0541	0.1467	0.1391	0.0695	0.5104	0.0352

Evaluation of Blockiness

Edges should be considered in a digital image, because it plays a major role for image brightness changes and discontinuities. For example, in the smoothing process, a particular block boundary produce an abrupt change of intensities across blocks, for the reason of sharp transients like edges represent high frequency component while long unchanging spaces correspond to low frequency component (Tang et. al. (2016)).

In order to measure the blockiness of the smoothened images, blockiness measure (BL) (Tang et al., 2016) employed for evaluation. Table 3 lists the value of BL. Higher value of BL indicates serious blockiness in the image. CTAD-TFT model provides lesser blockiness than others do. The DEPM has serious blockiness in the smoothened image.

Evaluation of Edge Quality

In the contour-texture model of images, the edges are the finest and informative part of the image. Therefore, ensuring the edge quality is the essential evaluation on the smoothened images. Pratt (1978) is a well-known measure to evaluate the quality of the edges preserved by existing smoothing models. This measure considered both the correctness of the edge location and absent/false alarm edges. The figure of merit (FoM) is defined as

$$FoM = \frac{1}{\max\{n_d, n_t\}} \sum_{i=1}^{n_d} \frac{1}{1 + a d_i^2}, \tag{33}$$

where n_d and n_i are the number of detected and ground-truth edge points, respectively, and d_i is the distance to the closest edge possible for the ith edge pixel detected. In this chapter, the binary edge image obtained from the Canny edge detector with various threshold values which is considered the ground-truth edge or reference image. The $\max\{n_d, n_i\}$ represents the number of false alarm edges or, conversely missing edges. Table 4 shows the values of Figure of Merit and False alarm.

Table 3. Evaluation measure of blockiness of the smoothened images

Model Measure	P-M	TV	TCAD	CTAD	CTAD-TFT	CTD	DEPM	APM	MPM	MG
BL	0.1629	0.1669	0.1095	0.1085	0.0498	0.1505	0.5277	0.1153	0.1633	0.1087

Table 4. Figure of merit

Model Measure	P-M	TV	TCAD	CTAD	CTAD-TFT	CTD	DEPM	APM	MPM	MG
FoM	0.9693	0.9710	0.9017	0.8412	0.8777	0.9624	0.9950	0.8484	0.9826	0.8679
False Alarm/ Missing edges	313	331	665	636	424	685	15	499	400	457

Evaluation of False Contour

Generally, false contours that are artifacts obtained in smooth regions during denoising process. Therefore, it should ensure the false contour present in the smoothened images. During the quantization process, digital images have a restricted number of intensity levels. False contours are show due to the insufficient number of intensity levels in the digital image. In this study, Weber ratio (Lee (2006)) R_w is employed to detect the presence of false contour f_w. The Weber ratio is defined as $R_w = \Delta I / I$, where ΔI represents the difference between the intensities of the foreground and the background, and I represents the illumination of the background.

The Weber ratio f_w is defined as

$$f_w = \frac{\frac{1}{MN}\left(\sum_{i=0}^{M-1}\sum_{j=0}^{N-1}\left|I_{ij} - \overline{m}\right|\right)}{\overline{m}} \tag{34}$$

where $M \times N$ is the local window sized 3×3. I_{ij} denotes the intensity value at center pixel of the $M \times N$ and $\overline{m}$ represents the mean intensity value of the $M \times N$. The calculation of the Weber ratio is explained in the following steps. (i) The smoothened image was composed of re-quantization, which is done by bit-depth reduction. The 8-bit depth smoothened image was re-quantized into 6-bit depth. (ii) A difference image was constructed by subtracting the re-quantized image from the input smoothened image. (iii) Evaluate the Weber ratio on the subtracted image. Table 5 shows the value of Weber ratio f_w for false contour. The lower value indicates that the lower false contour present in the smoothened image.

Table 5. Weber ratio

Model Measure	P-M	TV	TCAD	CTAD	CTAD-TFT	CTD	DEPM	APM	MPM	MG
f_w	0.0079	0.0162	0.0413	0.0194	0.0112	0.0252	0.0060	0.0078	0.0140	0.0058

CONCLUSION

In this chapter, anisotropic diffusion based denoising methods P-M, TV, TCAD, CTAD, CTAD-TFT, CTD, DEPM, APM, MPM and MG were implemented and analyzed their performance based on the quality attributes. The quality attributes of the smoothened images were evaluated using 2D intensity profiles, sharpness, blurriness, blockiness, edge quality, and false contours. Hence, the implemented anisotropic diffusion based models have their own specific domain and produce better performance and results on it. However, all of these existing models generate the either one or other distortions during smoothing process. In future direction, it is needed to improve or modify the denoising models by considering all the quality attribute factors for better preservation of image features and without loss of fine details.

REFERENCES

Catte, E., Lions, P. I., Morel, J. M., & Coll, T. (1992). Image selective smoothing and edge detection by nonlinear diffusion. *SIAM Journal on Numerical Analysis*, *29*(1), 182–193. doi:10.1137/0729012

Chao, S. M., & Tsai, D. M. (2006). Astronomical image restoration using an improved anisotropic diffusion. *Pattern Recognition Letters*, *27*(5), 335–344. doi:10.1016/j.patrec.2005.08.021

Chao, S. M., & Tsai, D. M. (2008). An anisotropic diffusion-based defect detection for low-contrast glass substrates. *Image and Vision Computing*, *26*(2), 187–200. doi:10.1016/j.imavis.2007.03.003

Chao, S. M., & Tsai, D. M. (2010). An improved anisotropic diffusion model for detail- and edge-preserving smoothing. *Pattern Recognition Letters*, *31*(13), 2012–2023. doi:10.1016/j.patrec.2010.06.004

De, K., & v, M. (2013). A new no-reference image quality measure for blurred images in spatial domain. *J. of Image and Graphics*, *1*(1), 39–42. doi:10.12720/joig.1.1.39-42

Guo, Z., Sun, J., Zhang, D., & Wu, B. (2012). Adaptive perona-malik model based on the variable exponent for image denoising. *IEEE Transactions on Image Processing*, *21*(3), 958–967. doi:10.1109/TIP.2011.2169272 PMID:21947525

Lee, J. W., Lim, B. R., Park, R.-H., Kim, J.-S., & Ahn, W. (2006). Two-stage false contour detection using directional contrast features and its application to adaptive false contour reduction. *IEEE Transactions on Consumer Electronics*, *52*, 179–188.

Maiseli, B. J., & Gao, H. (2016). Robust edge detector based on anisotropic diffusion-driven process. *Information Processing Letters*, *116*(5), 373–378. doi:10.1016/j.ipl.2015.12.003

Mohan, J., Krishnaveni, V., & Guo, Y. (2014). A survey on the magnetic resonance image denoising methods. *Biomedical Signal Processing and Control*, *9*, 56–69. doi:10.1016/j.bspc.2013.10.007

Pal, C., Chakrabarti, A., & Ghosh, R. (2015). A brief survey of recent edge-preserving smoothing algorithms on digital images. *Procedia Computer Science*, 1–40.

Perona, P., & Malik, J. (1990). Scale-Space and Edge Detection Using Anisotropic Diffusion. *IEEE Transactions on Pattern Analysis and Machine Intelligence*, *12*(7), 629–639. doi:10.1109/34.56205

Pratt, W. K. (1978). *Digital Image Processing*. New York: Wiley.

Rudin, L. I., Osher, S., & Fatemi, E. (1992). Nonlinear total variation based noise removal algorithms, Phys. *D Nonlinear Phenom.*, *60*(1-4), 259–268. doi:10.1016/0167-2789(92)90242-F

Soumya, R. N., Mishra, J., & Palai, G. (2018). A modified approach to estimate fractal dimension of gray scale Images. International Journal for Light and Electron Optics, 161, 136-145.

Soumya, R. N., & Mishra. J. (2018a). Fractal Dimension of Gray Scale images. Progress in Computing. *Analytics and Networking*, *710*, 225–234. doi:10.1007/978-981-10-7871-2_22

Soumya, R. N., & Mishra, J. (2018c). Analysis of Medical images using Fractal Geometry. In Histopathological Image Analysis in Medical Decision Making, (pp. 181-201). Academic Press.

Tang, C., & Wang, B. (2016). A no-reference adaptive blockiness measure for JPEG compressed images. *PLoS One*, *11*(11), 1–12. doi:10.1371/journal.pone.0165664 PMID:27832092

Tian, H., Cai, H., Lai, J. H., & Xu, X. (2011). Effective image noise removal based on difference eigenvalue. *18th IEEE Int. Conf. Image Process*, 3357–3360. 10.1109/ICIP.2011.6116392

Tsai, D. M., & Chao, S. M. (2005). An anisotropic diffusion-based defect detection for sputtered surfaces with inhomogeneous textures. *Image and Vision Computing*, *23*(3), 325–338. doi:10.1016/j.imavis.2004.09.003

Wang, Y. Q., Guo, J., Chen, W., & Zhang, W. (2013). Image denoising using modified Perona-Malik model based on directional Laplacian. *Signal Processing*, *93*(9), 2548–2558. doi:10.1016/j.sigpro.2013.02.020

Zahran, O., Kasban, H., El-Kordy, M., & El-Samie, F. E. A. (2013). Automatic weld defect identification from radiographic images. *NDT & E International*, *57*, 26–35. doi:10.1016/j.ndteint.2012.11.005

Chapter 6

A Review of Contemporary Image Compression Techniques and Standards

Tawheed Jan Shah

iD https://orcid.org/0000-0001-5587-9110
University of Kashmir, India

M. Tariq Banday

iD https://orcid.org/0000-0001-8504-5061
University of Kashmir, India

ABSTRACT

Uncompressed multimedia data such as images require huge storage space, processing power, transmission time, and bandwidth. In order to reduce the storage space, transmission time, and bandwidth, the uncompressed image data is compressed before its storage or transmission. This process not only permits a large number of images to be stored in a specified amount of storage space but also reduces the time required for them to be sent or download from the internet. In this chapter, the classification of an image on the basis of number of bits used to represent each pixel of the digital image and different types of image redundancies is presented. This chapter also introduced image compression and its classification into different lossless and lossy compression techniques along with their advantages and disadvantages. Further, discrete cosine transform, its properties, and the application of discrete cosine transform-based image compression method (i.e., JPEG compression model) along with its limitations are also discussed in detail.

DOI: 10.4018/978-1-7998-0066-8.ch006

INTRODUCTION

Images and Their Classification

Image is a visual representation of a subject usually a physical object. It may be two-dimensional(2-D) or three-dimensional(3-D) such as a statue and a photograph respectively. An image is actually a rectangular grid (Rao & Hwang, 1996) of basic picture element called dot or pixel arranged in M rows and N columns, originating from the upper left corner. The expression M x N is known as the resolution of the image. Each pixel in an image has a fixed size on a given display. Mathematically, "An image may be defined as a 2-D function f(x, y), where 'f' is the amplitude and (x, y) are spatial co-ordinates. The amplitude 'f' at any pair of co-ordinates (x, y) is called the intensity value of an image (Penebaker, & Mitchell, 1993). When the intensity and co-ordinate values are finite discrete quantities, the image is called as the "Digital Image". Since digital image is a regular arrangement of pixels so there exist certain relationships between them. Consider two pixels P(m, n) and Q(u, v) at co-ordinates (m, n) and (u,v) respectively. The distance between these two pixels is measured in order to find out how close these two pixels are and how they are related to each other. However, there are a number of ways to measure this distance, e.g. Euclidean distance, Chessboard distance and City-block distance. The Mathematical formula for calculating each of these distances is given as follows.

The Euclidean distance between two 2-D image points P(m, n) and Q(u, v) is defined as:

$$\sqrt{\left(m - u\right)^2 + \left(n - v\right)^2}. \tag{1}$$

The Chessboard distance between two 2-D image points P(m, n) and Q(u, v) can be calculated as follows:

$$\max(|m\text{-}n|, |n\text{-}v|) \tag{2}$$

For the above two 2-D pixels, the City-block distance is:

$$|m\text{-}u| + |n\text{-}v| \tag{3}$$

On the basis of number of bits used to represent each pixel of the digital image, these can be classified into three categories namely i) binary image, ii) grey scale Image, and iii) RGB or color image. Binary images are also called as Black and white images. This means each pixel is represented by a single bit. Since the number of bits per pixel i.e. n=1 in case of binary images, therefore the number of possible colors used to represent the image is $2^n = 2^1 = 2$. Typically, two colors used are black (0) and white (1 or 255) though any two colors can be used. A binary image is usually stored in computer memory as Bitmap. In grayscale images, 8-bits are used to represent each pixel (Rao & Yip, 1990). Therefore, the number of possible shades of gray is 256 ranging from 0 to 255. A pixel value of '0' and '255' represents the black and white color respectively. The values in between 0 to 255 are used for varying shades of gray. An RGB image is typically represented using 24 bits, 8 for red, 8 for green and 8 for blue. A 24-bit image thus yields a potential of 16.7 million color values. RGB images do not use a palette but requires three times more memory than black and white version of the same image with same size.

Image Redundancy

Redundancy and irrelevancy reduction are the two main components of image compression. The main aim of redundancy reduction is to remove duplication from the image signal and irrelevancy reduction omits parts of the image signal that is ignored by the Human Visual system (HVS). Redundancy is a main issue in image compression and its extent may vary from one image to another image. It is a mathematically quantifiable entity and therefore not an abstract concept. If N_o and N_c denote the number of information carrying units in the original and compressed images respectively, then the compression ratio (C_R) can be mathematically expressed as:

$$\left(C_R\right) = \frac{N_o}{N_c} \tag{4}$$

Also relative data redundancy (R_D) of the original image can be defined as

$$\left(R_D\right) = 1 - \frac{1}{C_R} \tag{5}$$

Three possibilities arise here:

1. If $N_o = N_c$, then $C_R = 1$ and hence $R_D = 0$ which implies that there is no redundancy between the pixels of the original image.
2. If $N_o \gg N_c$, then $C_R \to \infty$ and hence $R_D > 1$ which implies considerable amount of redundancy in the original image.

3.   If $N_o << N_c$, then $C_R > 0$ and thus $R_D \to -\infty$ which indicates that the original image contains less data than the compressed image.

Image redundancy can be broadly categorized into two types namely: i) statistical redundancy; and ii) psycho-visual redundancy. The first type of redundancy can further be categorized as inter-pixel redundancy and coding redundancy. The inter-pixel redundancy further consists of spatial redundancy and temporal redundancy.

Statistical Redundancy

This type of redundancy comprises of Inter-pixel redundancy and Coding redundancy. The former type of Redundancy is due to the correlation between neighboring pixels in an image. It means that the neighboring pixels are not statistically independent. The Inter-pixel correlation is referred as Inter-pixel Redundancy. Coding Redundancy is related with the representation of information (Wang et al., 2004). The information is represented in the form of codes.

Spatial Redundancy

Spatial redundancy represents the statistical correlation between neighboring pixels in an image. It is not necessary to represent each pixel in an image independently. It can also be predicted from its neighbors.

Temporal Redundancy

Temporal Redundancy is the statistical correlation between pixels from consecutive frames in a video sequence. Motion compensated predictive coding is employed to reduce temporal redundancy.

Psycho-Visual Redundancy

Psycho-visual redundancy is related with the features of the HVS. In the HVS, visual information is not perceived equally. Some information may be more important than other information. If less data is used to represent less important visual information, perception will not be affected. This implies that visual information is psycho-visually redundant and eliminating this type of redundancy leads to efficient compression.

IMAGE QUALITY MEASUREMENT

Quality measurement in case of a specific image compression technique is the measurement of closeness of the compressed image to an original image. This type of measurement is normally simple and straightforward task in case of lossless image compression system because the compressed image is same as the original image. However, a number of standard criteria such as C_R, execution time are employed for measuring the quality of an image in such a case. On the other hand, the task of image quality measurement is very much difficult in case of lossy image compression technique, as it is very difficult to describe the nature and extent of degradation in the reconstructed image. Since the reconstructed image is not same as the original image, therefore the two images are usually compared in order to find out the amount of distortion in the reconstructed image as compared to the original image. The significance of image quality measurement has been recognized for many years and the need for an exact quality measurement is more vital in the recent years due to the evolving multimedia applications (Cosman et al., 1996). There are basically two approaches for image quality assessment, the subjective and the objective approach.

Subjective Approach

In subjective approach, the decompressed image is presented to a group of viewers in order to rate it in comparison to its original. In fact, there are various procedures available for subjective quality assessment and each of them can be used depending upon the application (Timo et al., 1996). The two frequently used assessment methods are the rank-ordered and the quantitative ratio-scaling. In the rank-ordered method, decompressed images are accepted according to the degree of error or impairment and in the latter; values are first allotted to the given image quality parameters, and the results are then normalized. Since these methods of image quality measurement are dependent on the number of available observers and their eyesight therefore such subjective assessments are not only cumbersome and expensive, but also time consuming and hence are not usually preferred.

Objective Approach

Objective image quality measurement in case of a lossy compression technique involves the calculation of mathematical function that determines the information loss in a decompressed image. The objective approach not only facilitates the comparison of different coding techniques but also permits the design of new coding techniques. The two most commonly used objective quality measurements are Mean Square Error (MSE) and Peak Signal to Noise Ratio (PSNR). The MSE between the original image f(x,y) and decompressed image F(x,y) is given by Equation: (6).

$$\left(MSE\right) = \frac{1}{MN} \sum_{X=0}^{M-1} \sum_{Y=0}^{N-1} \left[f\left(x,y\right) - F\left(x,y\right) \right]^2 \tag{6}$$

where the two images f(x,y) and F(x,y) are MxN each.

Also the PSNR between the two images (Shi & Sun, 2000) is given by Equation: (7).

$$PSNR = 10 \log_{10} \left(\frac{255^2}{MSE} \right) dB \tag{7}$$

Higher value of PSNR indicates increased fidelity of the compression technique. Generally, when its value is 35dB or above, then the two images are almost indistinguishable. So if a compression technique offers higher value of PSNR and lower value of MSE that is considered to be the best. In case of a color image PSNR is given by Equation: (8).

$$PSNR = 10 \log_{10} \left(\frac{255^2}{MSE_{RGB}} \right) dB \tag{8}$$

and MSE_{RGB} is calculated by using Equation: (9).

$$MSE_{RGB} = \frac{MSE_{RED} + MSE_{GREEN} + MSE_{BLUE}}{3} \tag{9}$$

where MSE_{RED}, MSE_{GREEN}, MSE_{BLUE} are the MSE's calculated for the three color of the image respectively and the average of these three is used to find out the PSNR of the decompressed RGB image.

In addition to the PSNR and MSE, compression rate and C_R are also used to evaluate the performance of the image compression system. Compression rate is defined as the average number of bits used to represent a single pixel or a sample. Mathematically it is given by Equation: (10).

$$\text{Compression Rate} = \frac{\text{compressed image size in bits}}{\text{Number of pixels}} \quad \text{bpp} \quad (10)$$

Although, smaller value of compression rate and larger value of C_R indicates the better compression scheme but these alone doesn't justify the lossy compression scheme because the compression scheme which offers higher C_R may result in worst reconstructed image. So, there is always a tradeoff between the different image quality measurement parameters.

IMAGE COMPRESSION

Over the past few decades, the amount of information that is handled by digital computers has grown exponentially due to the advancement in Internet, teleconferencing, multimedia technologies etc. Hence, there is a dearth of storage space and the available transmission bandwidth of the digital image component of the multimedia. In order to present a huge image data with an acceptable quality, large storage space and transmission bandwidth is required, which the existing technology is incapable to handle technically as well as economically. One of the possible solutions to this problem is compression. It is a technique of minimizing the amount of data, required to represent assumed quantity of information. Data is a combination of redundancy and information. Redundancy (Gonzalez & Eugene, 2008) is defined as that portion of data which is not necessary to preserve permanently in its original form and therefore can be removed when it is not required. But this redundancy is removed in such a manner that it can be subsequently reinserted in order to reproduce the approximate form of data. While as information is necessary to preserve permanently. The technique used to lessen the redundancy of data is termed as Data Compression and the application of data compression on digital images is known as Image Compression. Image Compression has experienced extensive research growth through the realistic application of the hypothetical work that was initiated in the 1940s, when C.E. Shannon and others first devised the probabilistic view of information and its representation, transmission and compression. The key purpose of image compression is to store or transmit images in a proficient procedure. Image compression plays a vital role in numerous applications which include medical imaging, document, facsimile transmission (FAX), Tele-conferencing and video-conferencing, remotely piloted vehicles, and remote sensing.

Image Compression System

The general block diagram of an image compression system is shown in Figure 1. It consists of an Encoder and a Decoder. The Encoder and Decoder together are called 'Codec'.

Encoder

The Encoder consists of three components; Mapper, Quantizer and a Symbol Coder.

Mapper

Mapper basically performs the transformation of the input image signal from time domain to the frequency domain in order to reduce the inter-pixel redundancy. It maps the pixel values onto a set of coefficients by making use of a reversible, linear mathematical transform which ultimately proves to be more competent for performing the compression. The choice of transform used depends on the factors like coding gain and computational complexity (Martin, 1999). Currently, Discrete Cosine transform (DCT) (Rao & Hwang, 1996) and Discrete Wavelet transform (DWT) (Rioul & Vetterli, 1991) are the most frequently used transform coding techniques.

Figure 1. Image compression system

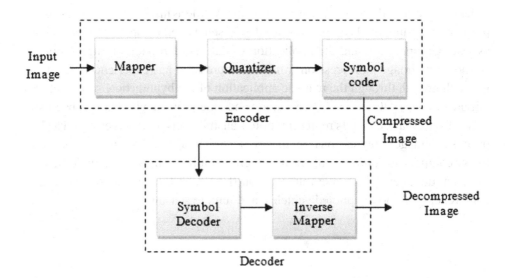

Quantizer

It helps to reduce the number of bits required to store the changed coefficients by reducing the accuracy of the coefficient values. Quantization is a many-to-one mapping and therefore irreversible. In fact, it is one of the simplest approaches to lossy compression (Wallace, 1991). The choice of the Quantizer depends on the transformation used.

Symbol Coder

The symbol coding or entropy encoding is performed in order to provide an additional compression of the quantized values. The basic idea of the Entropy encoder is to find a reversible mapping to the quantized coefficient values such that the average number of bits is reduced. Entropy encoding assigns shorter codes to the letters appearing frequently from Quantizer and longer codes to the letters appearing less frequently. The symbol coder provides the compressed image which can then be stored or transmitted using less space.

Decoder

The Decoder performs the inverse of the operations used in the Encoder. The entropy encoded output from the encoder is first decoded and afterwards an inverse mapping is applied to get the decompressed image. The inverse quantization of decoded coefficients is not possible because the information lost during the quantization step in the encoder cannot be recovered back completely. In the codec, if the transformation step for the removal of inter-pixel redundancy is reversible (Wang et al., 2004) and the quantization and inverse quantization steps are omitted, the decoder produces the same image as original.

Advantages of Image Compression

1. The most important benefit of image compression is that it requires less storage space because of the reduced file size. The reduced file size facilitates webmasters to design image-rich sites and hence works splendidly for the internet.
2. The reduced file size not only increases the speed of input-output operations in a computing device but also minimizes the probability of transmission errors.
3. By employing the process of compression, the audience can experience high quality signals for audio-visual representation.

4. The level of image security against illicit monitoring can be considerably improved by ciphering the decoding parameters and transmitting them independently from the compressed image database files.
5. Furthermore, the storage and transmission cost of huge image files is greatly reduced by storing or transmitting them in compressed form.

Disadvantages of Image Compression

1. The most serious drawback of image compression is the extra complexity and overhead expenses incorporated by the encoding and decoding process, which discard its use in some areas of application that require very low power VLSI implementation (Penebaker & Mitchell, 1993).
2. The compression of image files which are hundreds of megabytes in size, before storage or transmission require considerable amount of time depending upon the speed of the computing device.
3. It is very risky to transmit the extremely sensitive compressed images like medical and textual images through the noisy communication channel because the burst errors introduced by the channel can destroy the image information.
4. Compression schemes disrupt the original image data properties that are important in some applications. For example, in categorization and searching schemes.

CLASSIFICATION OF IMAGE COMPRESSION TECHNIQUES

The common goal of all the image compression techniques is to alter the representation of information contained within a given image, so that it can be represented efficiently by using lesser number of bits. The selection of a particular compression technique involves several antagonistic considerations which include extent of compression required, the speed of operation and the size of compressed file versus quality of decompressed image. Digital image compression techniques can be broadly classified into two types (1) Lossless image compression and (2) Lossy image compression as shown in Figure 2:

Figure 2. Classification of image compression techniques

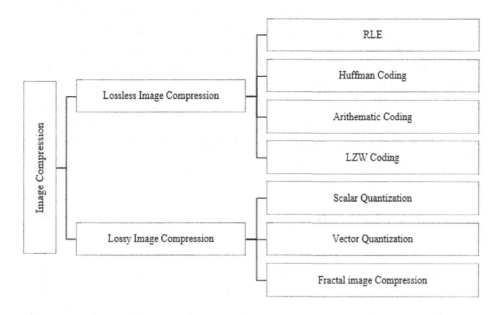

Lossless Image Compression

In Lossless image compression the original image is recovered after decompression. Lossless compression techniques normally involve two main operations: (1) a representation of the image data in which its inter-pixel redundancies are minimized. (2) Codification of the representation to abolish the coding redundancy. The techniques based on lossless compression are generally applied in those applications where difference between the uncompressed and the decompressed image cannot be tolerated. Lossless compression is generally used for computer generated data, medical images, text data. Lossless compression normally provides lesser C_R's of 2 to 10 and is equally applicable to both binary and grayscale images. One more reason for using lossless coding scheme in place of lossy schemes is their computational demand. There is always a well-known trade-off between coder complexity, C_R, and coder delay for all lossless compression techniques. Some of the lossless compression techniques are discussed below:

Run Length Coding (RLC)

RLC (Kim et al., 2005) also called as packed bits encoding was developed in 1950s. It is a simple and popular compression approach for maps, cartoon images etc. This lossless coding technique utilizes the fact that the neighboring pixels in an image are not independent, but highly correlated to each other. Also the consecutive pixels in the smooth regions of an image have identical values. Instead of coding the individual pixels, RLC codes the number of pixels in a run. The terms run and run-length are used to represent the value of the pixel and the number of repeated pixels respectively. The run-lengths can be coded by using code words of fixed length 'b' corresponding to a greatest run-length C_l-1, where $C_l=2b$. As the largest run-length decides the number of bits used to represent the length of each run, as a result of which, it may increase the memory requirement resulting in decreased transmission speed. Therefore, runs can be encoded more efficiently by Huffman encoding as variable length coding is more efficient as compared to the fixed length coding. For example, in binary images, there appears a long run of identical pixel values of 1's and 0's. Consider d = 00000 00001 11111 11110 00011 10000 00000 000000 a segment of binary image as shown in Figure 3, then it can be represented compactly by listing the lengths of alternate 0's and 1's simply as C(d)= (9,10, 4, 3, 15).

Figure 3. Run length encoding of binary segment

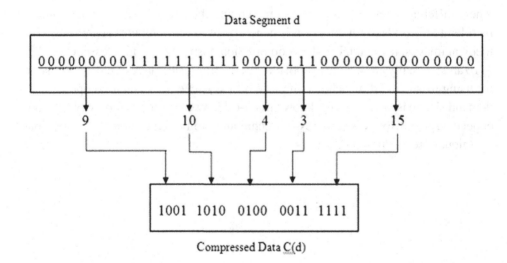

The original binary segment d requires 41 bits while as its compressed form C(d) requires only 20 bits, considering runs of length 4 bit each. Hence, instead of coding the individual 1's and 0's, it is more efficient to code their runs.

Huffman Coding

In 1952, David Albert Huffman, an American mathematician (Huffman, 1952) presented a new coding technique called Huffman Coding. It is one of the popular statistical coding techniques used for removing coding redundancy in the process of compression (O'Hanen & Wisen, 2005). Huffman coding generates the best minimal-length code when the associated probability of occurrence of the symbols is a negative power of 2. The codes produced using Huffman coding techniques are known as Huffman codes and the average length of these codes is close to the entropy of the source. It depends on the below stated comments concerning optimum prefix codes.

- The more probable symbols can be allocated with shorter code words than the less probable symbols (Sharma, 2010).
- The two least probable symbols will have code words of the same length, and they differ only in the least significant bit (LSB).

Let $\{S_1, S_2, S_3 \dots S_m\}$ represents the 'm' source symbols and $\{P_1, P_2, P_3 \dots P_M\}$ be the associated probability of occurrence. Then by using these values of probability, a set of Huffman codes of the source symbols can be generated and then mapped into a binary tree, popularly known as the Huffman Tree. The step by step procedure for generating the Huffman tree and hence Huffman code is given below:

1. Produce a set of 'm' nodes represented by $N= \{N_1, N_2, N_{3 \dots} N_m\}$ as leaves of a binary tree. Then, assign the node N_i by the source symbol S_i and label the node with the associated probability $P_i, i=1, 2, 3\dots M$.
2. In the second step, find the two nodes with the two least probability symbols from the current node set, and create a new node(called parent node) with probability equal to the sum of probabilities of the two least probable nodes(called child nodes).
3. Assign a value '1' to one of the branches of new parent node and a '0' to branch of the other child node. The assignment of 1 and 0 is arbitrary but it should be maintained throughout.

4. If the no. of nodes remaining in the new node set is greater than 1, then go on updating the node set by repeating the step 2 until left with a single node having probability 1. The remaining final node is called as root node of the Huffman tree.

5. The codes for the symbols S_i are obtained by going across the generated binary tree sequentially from the root node to each leaf node N_i, i=1, 2, 3, ..., m.

Consider a, b, c, d, e, f, g, h and 0.30, 0.10, 0.20, 0.06, 0.09, 0.07, 0.03, 0.15 be the eight source symbols and their probability of occurrence respectively. Figure 4 shows the Huffman Tree construction.

The average length of the generated Huffman code is below

$$L_{avg} = (0.30)(2) + (0.10)(3) + (0.20)(2) + (0.06)(5) + (0.09)(3) + (0.07)(4) + (0.03)(5) + (0.15)(3) \tag{11}$$

$$L_{avg} = 2.75 \frac{bits}{pixel} \tag{12}$$

Figure 4. Huffman tree construction

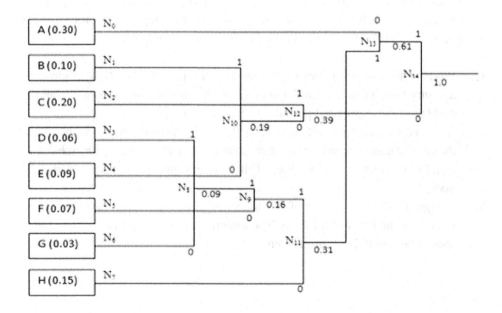

Despite many properties and applications of Huffman coding, there are certain limitations as well which are mentioned below:

1. When the exact probability allocation of the source symbol is known, only then the Huffman codes prove to be optimal.
2. Since the Huffman codes generated are of variable lengths therefore it turns out to be difficult for the decoder to know whether the given code has reached the last bit or not. Thus, if the Huffman coded data contains some additional error bits or missing bits then whatever the decoder decodes will be wrong and the resulting decompressed image displayed will be garbage.
3. The length of the codes of the least probable symbol could be very large to store into a single word or basic storage unit in a computing system.
4. It is very important to send the Huffman coding table to the de-compressor otherwise decoder will not be able to decode the codes. Hence, this adds to its cost.
5. Another important weak point of Huffman coding is that it is not competent to modify itself to the varying source statistics. A well-known example is when digitally halftoned images are compressed with the CCITT international digital facsimile data compression standard (Hunter & Robinson, 1980).

Arithmetic Coding

Although traditional Huffman coding is competent to generate the best codes for the individual data symbols but this is possible only when the probability of occurrence of the data symbols is a negative power of 2. Huffman coding allocates each coded symbol an integer number of bits but, Arithmetic coding deviates from this paradigm by assigning one Arithmetic code word to the entire sequence of source symbols (Rissanen & Langdon, 1979). Arithmetic encoding is a lossless variable-length coding technique that is gaining popularity in various image compression standards (Pasco, 1976; Rissanen, 1976). Its basic concept was given by Elias in the early 1960's and further improved by Pasco (Pasco, 1976), Rissanen (Rissanen, 1976) and Langdon (Langdon, 1984). The Arithmetic code word itself defines the unit interval of real numbers between 0 and 1. The size of the interval used to represent the source symbol becomes smaller as soon as the number of symbols from the source increases, and hence few bits are added in the encoded symbols. This coding technique actually involves the calculation of cumulative distribution function (CDF) of the probability of sequence of source symbols and afterwards represents the resulting value in a binary code. The obtained numerical value is labeled as Tag or Identifier. In Arithmetic coding there is no need for the encoder or decoder to store the code books. The decoder can decode the encoded sequence of symbols uniquely simply by using the Tag. But, in order to terminate the sequence, the decoder must know either the length of sequence or the code indicating the termination of deciphering. Arithmetic encoding is efficient for coding binary images and several multiplication-free arithematic coding techniques have been developed for their compression. Arithmetic coding is poor error resistant, complex and requires higher computation because of the number of multiplication required to calculate the intervals as compared to the Huffman coding. The arithmetic coding process is illustrated with the help of an example given below:

Consider an information source S= {a_1, a_2, a_3, a_4} with four letters a_1, a_2, a_3, a_4 and their corresponding probability of occurrence 0.5, 0.8, 0.9 and 1.0 respectively. Further consider $a_1a_3a_2a_4a_1$ be the sequence of symbols to be coded.

Firstly, divide the half open interval [0, 1] in proportion to the probabilities of the source symbols (Kavitha & Easwarakumar, 2008) starting with zero as shown in Figure 5 then calculate the cumulative probability of the symbols.

Since a_1 is the first symbol in the sequence to be transmitted. Hence, the new range is [0, 0.5]. At this point the tag lies in the new interval [0, 0.5]. Now find the

Figure 5. Arithematic coding procedure

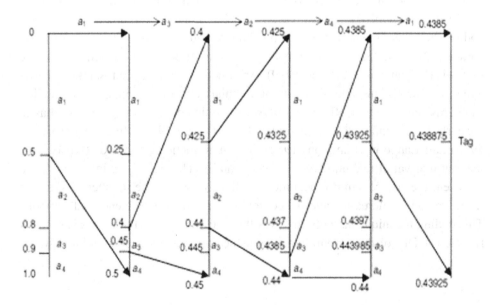

sub-range for all symbols in the new interval [0, 0.5]. The formula for computing the low and high sub-ranges is given as

$$Low = Low+(range \times Low\_range) \tag{13}$$

$$Hight=High+(range \times High\_range) \tag{14}$$

With the help of the given formula, the new boundary points for the symbols a_1, a_2, a_3, a_4 are 0.25, 0.4, 0.45, and 0.5 respectively. The next symbol of the sequence to be transmitted after a_1 is symbol a_3, which lies between 0.4 and 0.45. Divide the new interval [0.4, 0.45] in proportion to the probabilities of the symbols. Again at this point, the tag lies in the interval [0.4, 0.45]. By following the same procedure for the symbols a_2, a_4, a_1 the final tag interval is [0.4385, 0.43925]. If we choose the mid-point of the interval [0.4385, 0.43925] as the Tag, then the value of tag is 0.438875. The binary representation of the tag is 0.01110000010110... Now if this binary fraction is represented by using only 12 digits, then the value of the tag is given as 0.4387207 which lies in the tag interval [0.4385, 0.43925] and the Tag is unique. Hence, the arithematic code for the sequence $a_1a_3a_2a_4a_1$ is 0.01110000010. After the encoding, the Tag received by the decoder is 0.4387207 and the initial interval is assumed to be [0, 1]. The received Tag value is compared with the sub-ranges of the symbols. The tag value 0.4387207 lies in the interval [0, 0.5], then the first decoded symbol is a_1. Now [0, 0.5] becomes the new interval and the new tag value is computed using the formula given in Equation 15.

$$t^* = \frac{Tag - Low}{range} \tag{15}$$

Here Tag=0.4387207, Low= 0 and the range is 0.5-0=0.5. Therefore, new tag value is given in Equation 16.

$$t^* = \frac{0.4387207 - 0}{0.5} = 0.8774414 \tag{16}$$

The new tag t* lies in the interval [0.8, 0.9] and therefore the next decoded symbol is a_3. The new interval is now [0.8, 0.9]. By following the same procedure, the decoded sequence comes out to be $a_1a_3a_2a_4a_1$.

Lempel-Ziv-Welch (LZW) Coding

The method, what is called the LZ family of substitutional compressors was basically produced by Abraham Lempel and Jacob Ziv (Ziv & Lempel, 1977). Jacob Ziv and Abraham Lempel issued two research papers, one on "Dictionary" based compression and another on "Sliding Window" compression in 1978 and 1977 respectively. The former algorithm was named as LZ77 and later as LZ78. However, in 1984 (Welch, 1984), this method was published by Terry Welch while he was working for Unisys Corporation, as an improvement of the LZ78 compression algorithm and the outcome was LZW algorithm. LZW can compress any type of data such as executable codes, text file, and tremendously redundant data records to around half of its size because of its simplicity and adaptability. In this technique, variable length sequence of symbols is assigned with fixed-length code words.

In LZW coding the codebook is constructed at the beginning of the encoding process which contains the source symbols to be coded. For a grayscale image, the onset 256 words of the dictionary are allocated to the intensities varying from 0-255. Since the encoder inspects the image pixels successively and if the intensity strings are not found in the dictionary then they are placed in the next unused locations. For example, consider the first two white pixels of the image as "255-255", then this sequence may be assigned to location 256. If these two white pixels are encountered next time in the sequence then the address of the location containing "255-255" is used to represent these white pixels. Now if 9 bits are used, then the original (8+8) bits that were used to represent the two pixels are replaced by single 9-bit code word and 512-word dictionary is employed in the coding process. This clearly shows that the size of the dictionary is an important parameter in this coding technique. The working of LZW can be better understood with the help of an example given below.

Assume 4x4 vertical edge of an 8-bit image as:

```
39   39   126   126
39   39   126   126
39   39   126   126
39   39   126   126
```

Table 1 shows the steps involved in coding a 16-pixel image of the vertical edge.

Each pixel of the image is encoded starting from upper left corner in a left-to-right, top-to-bottom fashion. Each consecutive pixel representing the intensity value is linked with a variable called currently recognized sequence and is initially

Table 1. Steps involved in coding the 16 pixel image of the vertical edge

Currently Recognized Sequence	Pixel Being Processed	Encoded Output	Dictionary Location (Code word)	Dictionary Entry
Null	39	Null	Null	Null
39	39	39	256	39-39
39	126	39	257	39-126
126	126	126	258	126-126
126	39	126	259	126-39
39	39	Null	Null	Null
39-39	126	256	260	39-39-126
126	126	Null	Null	Null
126-126	39	258	261	126-126-39
39	39	Null	Null	Null
39-39	126	Null	Null	Null
39-39-126	126	260	262	39-39-126-126
126	39	Null	Null	Null
126-39	39	259	263	126-39-39
39	126	Null	Null	Null
39-126	126	257	264	39-126-126
126	Null	126	Null	Null

empty as shown in column one of the Table 1. For each linked sequence, the word list or dictionary is searched and if found, it is then, replaced by newly linked and located sequence. If it is not found, then neither the output codes are generated nor get the dictionary updated. However, the address of the currently recognized sequence is output as the next encoded value, the linked but unrecognized sequence is added to the dictionary and the currently recognized sequence is initialized to the current pixel value which can be seen in the second row of the table. Further, the intensity sequences that are added to the dictionary while scanning the entire 4x4 image is given by the details in the last two columns of the table. It is observed that the final dictionary contains 265 code words and the final encoded output is obtained by traversing third column from top to bottom. At the decoding end, the identical decompression dictionary is built in order to decode the encoded data stream simultaneously.

Lossy Image Compression

Lossy image compression completely discards the redundant information. For this reason, lossy compression is sometimes also called as the noisy or irreversible compression. Irreversible compression is suitable for compressing multimedia data such as still images etc., where the minor damage of fidelity is acceptable. Lossy compression techniques are capable of achieving higher C_R's of about 10:1 in case of photographic images as compared to the lossless compression techniques.

Scalar Quantization (SQ)

Since the lossy compression involves the mapping of high rate, digital pixel intensities into a relatively small no. of symbols therefore it results into loss of information. This mapping operation is called the Quantization and can be applied either to the individual pixels or groups of pixels in an image. Quantization is an irreversible process. In fact, the performance of the encoder depends on the design of Quantizer because it has a significant impact on the amount of compression obtained and the loss incurred in case of a lossy compression technique (Gersho & Gray, 1992). SQ is defined as the quantization in which the inputs and outputs of the Quantizer are scalars. Also in case of SQ, the individual input real numbers are repeatedly rounded to the nearest integers, called reproduction levels and the spacing between them is known as the Bin Width. The scalar Quantizer 'Qs' for N-points and the codebook 'C' for the set of 'N' output values are defined as

$$Q_S : R \rightarrow S \ \& \ C = \left\{ Y_n; \ n = 1, 2, \ldots N \right\} \sqsubset R \tag{17}$$

where R is set of real numbers. The Quantizer Q_S partitions the set of real numbers into non-overlapping intervals (x_i, x_i+1) according to the rule given below

$$
\begin{aligned}
&\text{if} \ \ X \in (x_i, x_i + 1) \\
&\text{then} \ \ Q_s(x) = y_i
\end{aligned}
\tag{18}
$$

SQ is effectively used in many image compression schemes such as (Cheng & Kingsbury, 1992) and is considered as the simplest form of Quantization.

Vector Quantization (VQ)

VQ is based on the principle of block coding (Nasrabadi, & King, 1988). It codes the sequence or blocks of input values by the indexes listed in the fixed table of quantization values. In VQ, the output from the source is grouped into vectors and then this vector output of the source is given as input to the Quantizer. Consequently, there is a set of vectors called the codebook both at the encoder and the decoder end of the vector Quantizer and the vectors in this codebook are called code vectors. Vector quantization can thus be described as follows:

Let $x=(x_1,x_2,....x_n)$ be an 'n' dimensional random vector belonging to R_n with probability function $P_x(x)=P_x(x_1,x_2,....x_n)$. A vector Quantizer Q_v, of size 'S' and 'n' dimensions, is defined as an application which associates one of the K reproduction vectors with a vector $x \in R_n$

$$Q_v:R^n \to C \tag{19}$$

where 'Q_v' is a function whose area is the set of all possible values of 'x' and whose range, a codebook, is a set of 'K' vectors

$$C = \{y_1,y_2,...,y_k\} \subset R^n \tag{20}$$

A vector quantization is therefore completely defined by the knowledge of the codebook and a partition $S= \{S_1,S_2,.....S_K\}$ of 'K' regions in R_n such that

$$\underset{i=1}{\overset{i=k}{U}} S_i = R^n \tag{21}$$

and $Si \cap Sj = 0$ for $i \neq j$, where $S_i = x \in R^n$ such that

$$Q_n(x) = Y_i, \text{ if } D_m(x,y_i) \leq D_m(x,y_j) \forall j \neq I \tag{22}$$

where Dm (…) is a quality criteria or distortion measure e.g., Mean Square Error.

Partition S for a given codebook is usually created using a classification algorithm and a training set. For instance, a vector x belonging to class Si is represented by the vector y_i belonging to the codebook. The distance between $x \in S_i$ and y_i can be computed using a distortion measure.

Figure 6 illustrates the principle of VQ in which a space of 2 dimensions is partitioned into K regions, called Voronoi Regions. The input signal is no longer a single data element but a block of elements, or n-dimensional vector. All the elements of the vector are jointly quantized. An interval along the line as in the

Figure 6. Partition of a space of dimension n = 2

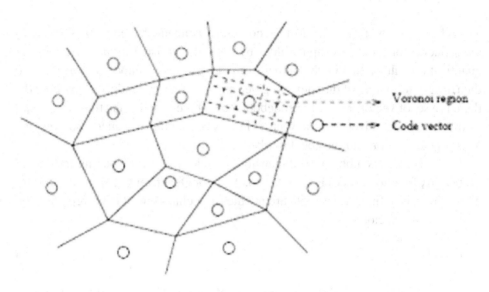

case of SQ is replaced by a region and the quantization level is replaced by specific point in the region.

The quantization consists of two steps: the codebook design, which involves an appropriate selection of the output vectors $y_1,...,y_K$, and the mapping of each input vector to one of the output vectors according to the rule $Q(x) = Y_i$ if $x \in S_i$. It can be seen that the vectors yi correspond to the quantization levels in a scalar quantizer and the collection of quantization levels is referred to as the codebook. A number of approaches to codebook design are presented in the literature such as in (Gersho & Gray, 1992).

Since the performance of an image coding technique using VQ depends on the performance of the vector quantizer, optimal VQ is expected to have small codebook which still provides the best approximation. In VQ, the input vector x, which consists of blocks of pixels is quantized by being encoded into a binary index 'i_n', which then serves as an index for the output reproduction vector or code-word. If the code has a fixed rate of 'm' then 'i_n' has length m. With a variable rate code, the indices 'i_n' have variable length and 'm' is their average length. The compressed image is represented by these indices 'i_n', and the compressed representation requires fewer bits than the original image.

The main goal in developing a vector quantizer is to find a codebook which minimizes the error according to a selected distortion criterion (Barlaud et al., 1993). Ideally, an optimal codebook is expected to yield a globally optimal quantization.

However, in practice this is rarely attained since codebook generation algorithms lead to a local optimal quantizer. For a given sequence of vectors to be encoded and a given codebook size, the task of constructing a codebook, which contains the best collection of reproduction vectors and efficiently represents a broad variety of source vectors to be encoded, is difficult. In addition, in SQ, it is trivial to test if a signal sample belongs to a given interval, however in VQ, an accurate and consistent quality criterion or a distortion measure, which is expected to parallel with human visual system, is used. The most commonly used distortion method in Quantization is still the MSE. The general optimality of VQ over SQ was discussed by Gersho and Gray in (Gersho & Gray, 1992). The application of VQ in several new image coders has also shown its advantage over SQ (Westerink, 1988; Senoo & Girod, 1992). The design of optimal VQ codebook with minimum search time has led to the development of different VQ techniques (Kim, 1988; Fisher et al., 1991).

Fractal Image Compression (FIC)

Benoit B. Mandelbrot (Gonzalez & Eugene, 2008), a French mathematician, first coined the word 'fractal' in 1975, while he introduced the principles of fractal geometry. However, in 1981, the mathematician John Hutchinson (Mandelbrot, 1993) used the Iterated Function theory(IFT) to model collection of contractive transformation in a metric space as a dynamical system. Later, Michael Barnsley (Hutchinson, 1981) a leading researcher generated the fractal model using the Iterated Function System (IFS) which was used to code images. However, Barnsley's IC algorithm (Hutchinson, 1981) based on fractal mathematics was insufficient due to the searching problem. In March 1988, one of Barnsley's Ph.D. students, Arnaud Jacquin (Barnsley & Hurd, 1992), arrived at a modified scheme for representing images (Jacquin, 1992) called the Partitioned Iterated Functions Systems (PIFS), which led to encoding of images to achieve significant compression.

Fractal may be defined as a geometrical figure, each part of which has the same statistical character as the whole. Fractals are usually classified into two main groups: linear and non-linear. The non-linear types of fractals are of the complex plane and are characterized by the popular Mandelbrot set and Julia sets. However, the group of fractals used in FIC is linear, and of the real plane. In fact, they are fractals from IFT. Therefore, the fractals used are not disordered. They are generated by an iterative process, starting from an initial tile. Heinz-Otto Peitgen introduced the idea of Iterated Function Systems (IFS) with the alluring metaphor of a special type of photocopying machine called as Multiple Reduction Copying Machine (MRCM)(Jacquin, 1989).

MRCM is imagined to be a normal photocopying machine that reduces the size of the image to be copied by half and reproduces it three times on the output copy. If the output image is fed back to the copying machine as input and the process is repeated several times, then the initial image will be reduced to a point. In fact, the final shape of the image depends on the position and orientation of the copies. Such a procedure for different input images is shown in Figure 8, for several iterations. All of these copies appear to converge to the same output image shown in Figure 7(C). The final image achieved is known as the attractor for the output image (Fisher, 1992).

From this example, it is quite clear that fractals possess 'Self Similarity' and there is no characteristic size associated with it. In FIC, exact self-similarity means that the fractal object is created by scaled down copies of itself that are translated, stretched, and rotated based on a transformation which is popularly known as Affine Transformation (Mitra et al., 1998). The affine transformation is actually used to express relations between different parts of an image and is given in matrix form in Equation: (23):

$$w_i \begin{bmatrix} x \\ y \end{bmatrix} = \begin{bmatrix} a_i & b_i \\ c_i & d_i \end{bmatrix} \begin{bmatrix} x \\ y \end{bmatrix} \begin{bmatrix} e_i \\ f_i \end{bmatrix} \tag{23}$$

where 'w_i' is called the set of an affine transformation and (x, y) is the initial coordinate vector. The constants a_i, b_i, c_i, d_i denotes the rotation, scaling and stretching operations. The values of e_i and f_i control the translation. 'w_i' used must

Figure 7. Image for first three iterations of the MRCM (Jacquin, 1989)

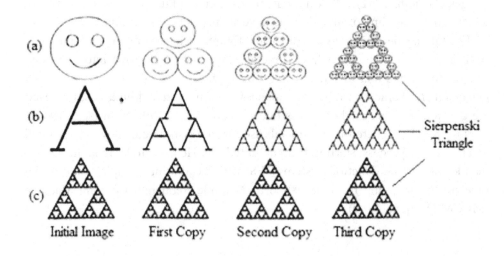

Figure 8. 1-D Cosine basis function for N=8 (Penebaker & Mitchell, 1993)

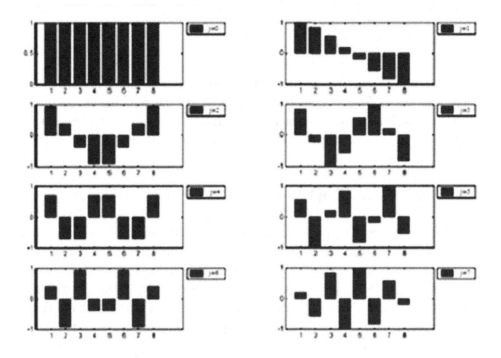

be contractive in nature i.e. it must bring any two points in the input image closer to each other in the copy. If the transformation is not contractive then the two points in the copy will spread out the final image which results in an infinite size of output image. The general procedure of FIC is summarized as:

1. The first step involved in the fractal encoding is the partitioning of the input image into non-overlapping sub-images or range blocks or parent blocks. The partitioning of the input image can be done in a number of ways. The partitioning process continues until a covering tolerance is satisfied.
2. For each parent block, the compression technique searches for a part of the image or domain block which is similar to the range in a statistical sense. The range must be smaller in size than the domain to ensure that the mapping from the domain to the range is contractive in the spatial dimensions.
3. Once the best match is found, calculate the transformation, which is basically a combination of a luminance transformation and an affine transformation. Such a transform is expressed in matrix form as:

$$w_i \begin{bmatrix} x \\ y \\ z \end{bmatrix} = \begin{bmatrix} a_i & b_i & 0 \\ c_i & d_i & 0 \\ 0 & 0 & p \end{bmatrix} \begin{bmatrix} x \\ y \\ z \end{bmatrix} \begin{bmatrix} e_i \\ f_i \\ q_i \end{bmatrix} \tag{24}$$

where z, p, q denotes the pixel intensity, contrast and brightness respectively.

The efficiency of the FI compressor depends very much on the choice of the partitioning used in the very first step of encoding. It is used in image processing applications such as feature extraction, ECG, and image retrieval etc.

TRANSFORM CODING(TC)

Transform coding relies on the premise that, there always exists a correlation between the neighboring pixels of an image. Consequently, these correlations can be exploited to predict the value of a pixel from its respective adjacent neighbors. In TC, an image is basically transformed or mapped from spatial domain to a different form of representation by employing some well-known transform. The set of transformed coefficients, which is relatively small is quantized and then coded in order to achieve greater compression.

The transformation can be broadly classified into two types: orthogonal and non-orthogonal (Moulin, 1995) transform. Orthogonal transforms are preferred because they can preserve the energy in the transform domain. As a result, the image can be recovered or reconstructed by the inverse transform. There are a number of transforms available which can be used in image coding e.g., Karhunen-Loeve Transform (KLT), Walsh Hadamard Transform (WHT), Discrete Fourier Transform (DFT), Discrete Cosine transform (DCT) and the Discrete Wavelet Transform (DWT) etc. However, the most efficient transform is the discrete cosine transform and will be discussed in detail in this chapter.

One-Dimensional DCT (1-D DCT)

The mathematical expression for calculating the DCT of 1-D sequence of length N is given by Equation (25):

$$Y[j] = C[j] \sum_{n=0}^{N-1} X[n] \mathrm{Cos}\left[\frac{(2n+1)j\pi}{2N}\right] \tag{25}$$

where j=0,1,2,….N-1.

Similarly, the inverse discrete cosine transform (IDCT) of 1-D sequence is given by Equation (26).

$$X[n] = \sum_{j=0}^{N-1} C[j] Y[j] \text{Cos}\left[\frac{(2n+1)j\pi}{2N}\right] \tag{26}$$

where n=0,1,2,….N-1. For Equations (25) and (26) C[j] is defined as

$$C[j] = \begin{cases} \sqrt{\frac{1}{N}} & \text{for } j = 0 \\ \sqrt{\frac{2}{N}} & \text{for } j = 1,2,...,N-1 \end{cases} \tag{27}$$

On putting j=0 in Equation (25)

$$Y[j=0] = \sqrt{\frac{1}{N}} \sum_{n=0}^{N-1} X[n] \tag{28}$$

Therefore, the first DCT coefficient is the average value of the sample sequence and is referred as the DC coefficient. The other transform coefficients are referred as the AC coefficients. The 1-D DCT is useful for analyzing speech waveforms (Watson, 1994). On the other hand, for analyzing 2-D signals such as images, a 2-D version of DCT is needed. Figure 8 shows the 1-D cosine basis functions obtained by Plotting $\sum_{n=0}^{N-1} \text{Cos}\left[\frac{(2n+1)j\pi}{2N}\right]$, for N=8 and varying values of 'j'.

On observing these basis functions or waveforms, it is found that the top-left waveform (j=0) provide a constant DC value whereas the other waveforms (j=1, 2, 3, …, 7) represent progressively increasing frequencies. These waveforms are known as the cosine basis functions and all of these functions are orthogonal in nature.

Two-Dimensional DCT (2-D DCT)

The 2-D DCT is simply calculated by applying the 1-D DCT first on each of the individual rows and then on each of the individual columns of the 2-D image. The mathematical equation for 2-D DCT of an NxN image is given by Equation (29).

$$Y[j,k] = C[j]C[k]\sum_{m=0}^{N-1}\sum_{n=0}^{N-1} X[m,n]\mathrm{Cos}\left[\frac{(2m+1)j\pi}{2N}\right]\mathrm{Cos}\left[\frac{(2n+1)k\pi}{2N}\right] \quad (29)$$

where j, k = 0, 1, 2,..., N-1 and C[j], C[k] are defined by Equation (27). The reconstructed image is calculated by using the 2-D IDCT which is given in Equation (30).

$$X[m,n] = \sum_{j=0}^{N-1}\sum_{k=0}^{N-1} C[j]C[k]Y[j,k]\mathrm{Cos}\left[\frac{(2m+1)j\pi}{2N}\right]\mathrm{Cos}\left[\frac{(2n+1)k\pi}{2N}\right] \quad (30)$$

where m, n =0,1,2,.......,N-1.

Similarly, the plot of 2-D cosine basis functions; for N=8 and varying values of both j and k in Equation (29) is represented in Figure 9.

The neutral gray, white and black color in Figure 9 represents the zero amplitude, positive amplitude and negative amplitude respectively. From Figure 9, it is also

Figure 9. 2-D Cosine basis functions for N=8 (Penebaker & Mitchell, 1993)

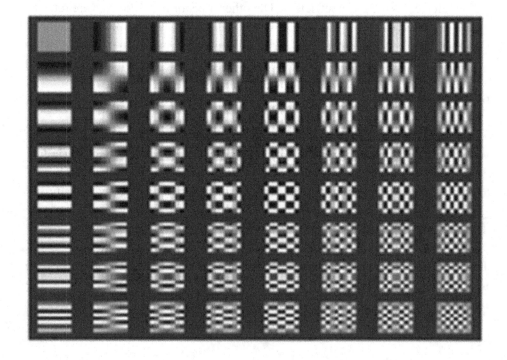

observed that 2-D cosine basis functions shows a progressive increase in frequency both in the horizontal and vertical direction.

PROPERTIES OF DCT

There are a number of properties of DCT, but some of them which are of particular importance to image processing applications are explained below.

De-Correlation

The most important advantage of image transformation from spatial domain to the frequency domain is the removal of inter-pixel redundancy between its adjacent pixels. This removal of redundancy permits the encoding of the transformed coefficients independently and therefore helps to achieve a greater compression. The DCT represents the image pixels by using only a few transformed coefficients and is therefore found to exhibit an outstanding de-correlation property.

Energy Compaction

The efficiency of a transformation based compression method can be measured by the ability of the transform to pack input image data into as few coefficients as possible. This allows discarding of the small magnitude coefficients during the quantization step without introducing visual loss of quality in the reconstructed image. DCT is having better energy packing ability for highly correlated images and therefore offers higher C_R's.

Separability

This property has the principle advantage that Y [j,k] given in Equation (29) can be calculated in two steps; first by computing the successive 1-D DCT on rows and then on columns of the image. The idea of separability can be identically applied to the IDCT computation.

Symmetry

Again from Equation (29), it is clear that the row and column transformations are functionally same. Therefore, such a transformation is known as symmetric transformation. The mathematical expression for a separable and symmetric transform is presented in Equation (31).

$T=AfA$ (31)

where f is an NxN image matrix and A is symmetric transformation matrix of order NxN with entries a(x,y), given by

$$a\left(x,y\right) = \alpha\left(y\right)\sum_{y=0}^{N-1}\text{Cos}\left[\frac{\left(2y+1\right)x\pi}{2N}\right]$$ (32)

The symmetry property is extremely useful because it involves pre-computing of the transformation matrix offline and then applying it to the image thus providing order of magnitude improvement in computation efficiency.

Orthogonality

The inverse transformation of Equation (31) can be written as

$f=A^{-1}TA^{-1}$ (33)

Since DCT basis functions are orthogonal in nature therefore, the inverse transformation matrix A^{-1} of A is equal to its transpose i.e. $A^{-1}=A^{T}$. So, in addition to its De-correlation characteristics, the orthogonal property provides reduction in the pre-computation complexity).

IMAGE COMPRESSION USING DCT

The DCT algorithm is commonly used for image and video compression as JPEG and MPEG (Gonzalez & Eugene, 2008). However, only JPEG compression standard will be discussed in this chapter. The acronym "JPEG" stands for "Joint Photographic Experts Group", which is a standard committee that has its origin within the International Standard Organization. The DCT based image compression method is proficient of compressing Continuous-tone images with pixel depth ranging from 6 to 24 bits with reasonable efficacy and speed. It is a lossy compression method having extension .jpeg, .jpg, .jpe which was specifically designed to discard the information content that the human eye is not able to see. Since the human eye can notice the slight variations in intensity well as compared to the changes in color; therefore, JPEG's lossy encoding tends to be more careful with the gray-scale part of an image and more playful with the color. Figure 10 describes the JPEG compression model clearly.

Figure 10. JPEG Compression Model (Das & Sethy, 2013)

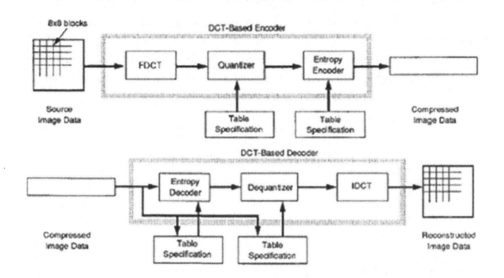

In JPEG compression process, the source input image is first and foremost partitioned into non-overlapping NxN pixel sub-images known as blocks (where N is usually multiple of 2, say 8). The block size used is an important factor since they determine the effectiveness of the transform over the source input image. If the block size is too large then the local features of the image are not exploited but if it is too small then the image is not effectively de-correlated. Followed by partitioning, the Forward DCT is applied to each NxN pixel blocks of the image working in a left to right, top to bottom method. To enhance the exactness of DCT the image is 'zero shifted', before the DCT is applied. This changes a $0 \rightarrow 255$ image intensity range to a $-128 \rightarrow 127$ range, which works more competently with the DCT. The total number of transformed coefficients for an 8x8 block is 64. Out of these 64 coefficients, the first transformed coefficient is referred to as the DC coefficient and the other 63 as AC coefficients.

After the computation of DCT coefficients, the elements of each block are compressed through quantization which involves dividing by some specific NxN matrix called Q_{matrix} and rounding to the nearest integer value by using the relation shown in Equation (34).

$$D_{quant}(x,y) = round\left(\frac{D_{DCT}(x,y)}{Q(x,y)}\right) \qquad (34)$$

151

The Q_{matrix} is a user-defined matrix and it gives the quality levels ranging from 1 to 100. The quality value of 100 gives the best reconstructed image and lowest C_R while as the quality value of 1 gives the poor reconstructed image and highest C_R. Although there are many quantization matrices available that are employed in JPEG compression but the standard matrix is given by Q_{matrix}. The Q_{matrix} is having a quality equal of 50 that offers both high C_R and outstanding output reconstructed image.

$$
Q_{matrix} = \begin{bmatrix}
16 & 11 & 10 & 16 & 24 & 40 & 51 & 61 \\
12 & 12 & 14 & 19 & 26 & 58 & 60 & 55 \\
14 & 13 & 16 & 24 & 40 & 57 & 69 & 56 \\
14 & 17 & 22 & 29 & 51 & 87 & 80 & 62 \\
18 & 22 & 37 & 56 & 68 & 109 & 103 & 77
\end{bmatrix}
$$

After the quantization step, most of the high frequency coefficients found in the bottom-right part of the matrix are zeros and therefore, can be truncated because the human eye is more sensitive to the lower frequencies as compared to the higher frequencies. The resulting sparse matrix after quantization can be reordered or zigzag scanned into a 64x1 vector that contains all of the non-zero entries of the matrix in the first few entries of the new vector and zero entries following the last non-zero entry. The removal of the zero entries results in the compression.

For further compression, the lossless coding such as Huffman coding etc. is applied after the scanning of the quantized coefficients. The encoded one dimensional array is then transmitted to the receiver. For decompression process, the receiver decodes the quantized coefficients and calculates the inverse 2-D DCT of each block, then places the blocks back together into a single image.

Despite many advantages such as less complexity, reasonable coding efficiency, availability of special purpose hardware for implementation, high C_R and high speed etc., DCT based image compression techniques suffer from a number of distortions which appear in the form of artifacts. These artifacts are not noticed by the human eye at lower compression ratios. Some of the common artifacts that results from an aggressive DCT based image compression technique are discussed below:

- **Blocking Artifact**: It is a distortion that seems as an even pattern of noticeable block boundaries in the compressed image. This type of artifact results from the uneven quantization of the DCT coefficients and the independent processing of the 8x8 pixel blocks which does not take into account the inter-block correlations. It is a primary distortion found in all DCT based image compression techniques.

- **Ringing Artifact**: Ringing artifact is a distortion that becomes apparent near the sharp edges of an image as spurious signals called rings. It is caused due to the loss or truncation of high frequency information in an image during the compression process. This causes ripples or oscillations around sharp edges or contours in an image in the spatial domain. This is popularly known as the Gibbs phenomena (Yang et al., 2001) and is found in different classes of images like compressed images, over-sharpened images, Magnetic Resonance Images (MRI) and images transmitted over analog channels etc.

- **Blurring Artifact**: Blurring is another artifact which means loss of fine details and smearing of edges of the image in comparison to the original image. This artifact also appears around the sharp edges in an image and hence sometimes it is very difficult to differentiate between the two.

- **Color Distortion**: Since HVS is not sensitive to the changes in the color of an image as to its brightness; consequently, a large amount of color information is disposed during compression while brightness is preserved. This process is known as "chroma subsampling". As a consequence, the compressed image seems to be slightly washed-out with less brilliant color.

CONCLUSION

The study presented in this chapter is primarily concerned with the study of image compression, its classification into different lossless and lossy compression techniques and the quality measurements used to evaluate the performance of the image compression system. The motivation for this study emanated, because image compression techniques are finding a great deal of applications in medical imaging, document, facsimile transmission (FAX), Tele-conferencing and Video-conferencing etc. by offering a number of advantages such as efficient utilization of the storage space, transmission time and bandwidth etc. However, the amount of compression achieved by a particular image compression system depends on various factors which include system hardware, type of the image and the compression method employed. Further, the quality of the compressed image can be evaluated by using parameters like MSE, PSNR and C_R. The higher value of PSNR and lower value of MSE gives the better image quality. So, if an image compression technique provides higher PSNR and lower MSE that is considered to be the best. Hence, it can be concluded that there is always a trade-off between the different image quality parameters.

REFERENCES

Barlaud, M., Sole, P., Gaidon, T., Antonini, M., & Mathieu, P. (1993). Elliptical codebook for lattice vector quantization. *Proceedings of IEEE International Conference on Acoustics, Speech and Signal Processing*, 590-593. 10.1109/ICASSP.1993.319880

Barnsley, M. (1989). *Fractals Everywhere*. San Diego, CA: Academic Press.

Barnsley, M. F., & Hurd, L. P. (1992). *Fractal Image Compression*. Wellesley, MA: AK Peters Ltd.

Cheng, N. T., & Kingsbury, N. G. (1992). The erpc: An efficient error resilient technique for encoding positional information or sparse data. *IEEE Transactions on Communications*, *40*(1), 140–148. doi:10.1109/26.126715

Cosman, P. C., Gray, R. M., & Vetterli, M. (1996). Vector quantization of image sub-bands: A review. *IEEE Transactions on Image Processing*, *5*(2), 202–225. doi:10.1109/83.480760 PMID:18285108

Fisher, T. R., Marcellin, M. W., & Wang, M. (1991). Trellis-coded vector quantization. *IEEE Transactions on Information Theory*, *37*(6), 1551–1566. doi:10.1109/18.104316

Fisher, Y. (1992). A Discussion of Fractal Image Compression. In chaos and fractals. New York: Springer-Verlag.

Fisher, Y. (1992). *Fractal Image Compression*. Siggraph 92 course notes.

Gersho, R., & Gray, R. M. (1992). *Vector quantization and signal compression*. Boston: Kluwer Academic Publishers. doi:10.1007/978-1-4615-3626-0

Gonzalez, R. & Eugene, R. (2008). *Digital Image Processing*. Academic Press.

Huffman, D. A. (1952). A Method for the Construction of Minimum-Redundancy Codes. *Proceedings of the IRE*, *40*(9), 1098–1101. doi:10.1109/JRPROC.1952.273898

Hunter, R., & Robinson, A. H. (1980). International Digital facsimile Standards. *Proceedings of the IEEE*, *68*(7), 854–867. doi:10.1109/PROC.1980.11751

Hutchinson, J. E. (1981). Fractals and Self Similarity. *Indiana University Mathematics Journal*, *35*(5), 713. doi:10.1512/iumj.1981.30.30055

Jacquin, A. (1989). *Fractal Theory of Iterated Markov Operators with applications to Digital Image Coding* (Doctoral Thesis). Georgia Institute of Technology.

Jacquin, E. (1992). Image Coding Based on a Fractal Theory of Iterated Contractive Image Transformation. *IEEE Transactions on Image Processing*, *1*(1), 18–30. doi:10.1109/83.128028 PMID:18296137

Kavitha, V., & Easwarakumar, K. S. (2008). Enhancing Privacy in Arithmetic Coding. *ICGST-AIML Journal, 8*(1).

Kim, T. (1988). New finite-state vector quantizer for images. *IEEE International Conference on Acoustics, Speech and Signal Processing*, 1180-1183.

Kim, W. J., Kim, S. D., & Kim, K. (2005). Fast Algorithms for Binary Dilation and Erosion Using Run-Length Encoding. *ETRI Journal*, *27*(6), 814–817. doi:10.4218/etrij.05.0205.0013

Langdon, G. G. (1984). An introduction to arithmetic coding. *IBM Journal of Research and Development*, *28*(2), 135–149. doi:10.1147/rd.282.0135

Lewis, A. S., & Knowles, G. (1992). Image compressions using the 2-D wavelet transform. *IEEE Transactions on Image Processing*, *1*(2), 244–250. doi:10.1109/83.136601 PMID:18296159

Mandelbrot, B. B. (1993). *The Fractal Geometry of Nature.* W.H. Freeman and Company.

Martin, M. B. (1999). *Applications of Multi-wavelets to Image Compression.* M.S. Thesis.

Mitra, S. K., Murthy, C. A., & Kundu, M. K. (1998). Technique for Fractal Image compression Using Genetic Algorithm. *IEEE Transactions on Image Processing*, *7*(4), 586–593. doi:10.1109/83.663505 PMID:18276275

Moulin, P. (1995). A multi-scale relaxation algorithm for SNR maximization in non-orthogonal sub-band coding. *IEEE Transactions on Image Processing*, *4*(9), 1269–1281. doi:10.1109/83.413171 PMID:18292023

Nasrabadi, N. M., & King, R. A. (1988). Image coding using vector quantization: A review. *IEEE Transactions on Communications*, *36*(8), 957–971. doi:10.1109/26.3776

O'Hanen, B., & Wisan M. (2005). *JPEG Compression.* Academic Press.

Pasco, R. (1976). *Source Coding Algorithms for Fast Data Compression* (Ph.D. thesis). Stanford University.

Penebaker, W., & Mitchell, J. (1993). *JPEG Still Image Data Compression Standard.* Van Nostrand.

Rao, K., & Hwang, J. (1996). *Techniques and Standards for Image, Video and Audio Coding*. Prentice-Hall.

Rioul, O., & Vetterli, M. (1991). Wavelets and Signal Processing. *IEEE Transactions on Signal Processing, 8*(4), 14–38. doi:10.1109/79.91217

Rissanen, J. J. (1976). Generalized Kraft inequality and Arithematic coding. *IBM Journal of Research and Development, 20*(3), 198–203. doi:10.1147/rd.203.0198

Rissanen, J. J., & Langdon, G. G. (1979). Arithmetic Coding. *IBM Journal of Research and Development, 23*(2), 146–162. doi:10.1147/rd.232.0149

Saha, S. (2001). *Image Compression from DCT to Wavelet: A Review*. Retrieved from http://www.acm.org/crossroads/xrds6-3/sahaimgcoding.html

Senoo, T., & Girod, B. (1992). Vector quantization for entropy coding of image sub-bands. *IEEE Transactions on Image Processing, 1*(4), 526–533. doi:10.1109/83.199923 PMID:18296186

Sharma, M. (2010). Compression Using Huffman Coding. *International Journal of Computer Science and Network Security, 10*(5).

Shi, Y. Q., & Sun, H. (2000). *Image and Video Compression for Multimedia Engineering: Fundamentals, Algorithms, and Standards* (1st ed.). Boca Raton, FL: CRC Press LLC.

Singh, P., & Duhan, M., & Priyanka. (2006). Enhancing LZW Algorithm to Increase Overall Performance. *Annual IEEE Indian Conference*, 1-4. 10.1109/INDCON.2006.302770

Timo, K., Pasi, F., & Olli, N. (1996). Empirical study on subjective quality evaluation of compressed images. *Proceedings of the Society for Photo-Instrumentation Engineers*, 78–87.

Wallace, G. K. (1991). The JPEG Still Picture Compression Standard. *Conference of the ACM, 34*, 30–44.

Wallace, G. K. (1992). The JPEG Still Picture Compression Standard. *IEEE Transactions on Consumer Electronics, 38*(1), 18–34. doi:10.1109/30.125072

Wang, Z., Bovik, A. C., Sheikh, H. R., & Simonelli, E. P. (2004). Image Quality Assessment: From Error Visibility to Structural Similarity. *IEEE Transactions on Image Processing, 13*(4), 600–612. doi:10.1109/TIP.2003.819861 PMID:15376593

Welch, T. A. (1984). A technique for high-performance data compression. *IEEE Computer, 17*(6), 8–19. doi:10.1109/MC.1984.1659158

Westerink, P., Biemond, J., Boekee, D., & Woods, J. W. (1988). Subband coding of images using vector quantization. *IEEE Transactions on Communications*, *36*(6), 713–719. doi:10.1109/26.2791

Yang, S., Hu, Y. H., Nguyen, T. Q., & Tull, D. L. (2001). Maximum-Likelihood Parameter Estimation for Image Ringing Artifact Removal. *IEEE Transactions on Circuits and Systems for Video Technology*, *11*(8).

Ziv, J., & Lempel, A. (1977). A Universal Algorithm for Sequential Data Compression. *IEEE Transactions on Information Theory*, *23*(3), 337–342. doi:10.1109/TIT.1977.1055714

KEY TERMS AND DEFINITIONS

HVS: Human Visual System
RD: Data Redundancy
CR: Compression Ratio
PSNR: Peak Signal to Noise Ratio
MSE: Mean Square Error
DCT: Discrete Cosine Transform
DWT: Discrete Wavelet Transform
RLC: Run Length Coding
LZW: Lempel-Ziv-Welch
SQ: Scalar Quantization
VQ: Vector Quantization
FIC: Fractal Image Compression
IFT: Iterated Function Theory
MRCM: Multiple Reduction Copying Machine
KLT: Karhunen-Loeve Transform
WHT: Walsh Hadamard Transform
DFT: Discrete Fourier Transform
JPEG: Joint Photographic Experts Group
MPEG: Motion Picture Experts Group
MRI: Magnetic Resonance Images

Chapter 7
Bio–Medical Image Processing:
Medical Image Analysis for Malaria With Deep Learning

Rasmita Lenka
KIIT University (Deemed), India

Koustav Dutta
KIIT University (Deemed), India

Ashimananda Khandual
(iD) https://orcid.org/0000-0002-9357-9749
College of Engineering and Technology, India

Soumya Ranjan Nayak
(iD) https://orcid.org/0000-0002-4155-884X
Chitkara University, India

ABSTRACT

The chapter focuses on application of digital image processing and deep learning for analyzing the occurrence of malaria from the medical reports. This approach is helpful in quick identification of the disease from the preliminary tests which are carried out in a person affected by malaria. The combination of deep learning has made the process much advanced as the convolutional neural network is able to gain deeper insights from the medical images of the person. Since traditional methods are not able to detect malaria properly and quickly, by means of convolutional neural networks, the early detection of malaria has been possible, and thus, this process will open a new door in the world of medical science.

DOI: 10.4018/978-1-7998-0066-8.ch007

INTRODUCTION

Application of Digital Image Processing and Deep Learning for analyzing the occurrence of Malaria from the Medical Reports is an important poverty. This approach is helpful in quick identification of the disease from the preliminary tests which are carried out in a person affected by Malaria. The combination of Deep Learning has made the process much advanced as the Convolution Neural Network is able to gain deeper insights from the medical images of the person. Since, traditional methods are not able to detect malaria properly and quickly, so by means of Convolution Neural Networks, the early detection of malaria has been possible and thus, this process will open a new door in the world of medical science. Automatic In this chapter, the main problems regarding the disease malaria is being discussed as well as the problems faced due in the quick diagnosis of malaria due to absence of advanced medical techniques is being brought into light. Most importantly, the solution to handle such a big problem using Deep Learning algorithms (Antony et al., 2016) is being provided in this chapter. The techniques to handle the problem and possible benefits by the use of Deep Learning (Kumar et al., 2013) technique is also being discussed.

BACKGROUND OF RELATED WORK

There are many components that make an area susceptible to an infectious disease outbreak. We'll the primary constituents below

- **Poverty Level**: When assessing the risk of infectious disease outbreak, we typically examine how many people in the population or at or below poverty levels. The higher the poverty level, the higher the risk of infectious disease, although some researchers will say the opposite — that malaria causes poverty. Whichever the cause we all can agree there is a correlation between the two.
- **Access to Proper Healthcare**: Regions of the world that are below poverty levels most likely do not have access to proper healthcare. Without good healthcare, proper treatment, and if necessary, quarantine, infectious diseases can spread quickly.
- **War and Government**: An area of the world that either has a corrupt government or is experiencing civil war will also have *higher* poverty levels and *lower* access to proper healthcare. Furthermore, if may be impossible for a corrupt government to provide emergency medical treatment or issue proper quarantines during a massive outbreak.

- **Disease Transmission Vectors**: A disease vector is an agent that carries the disease and spreads it to other organisms. Mosquitoes are notorious for carrying malaria.

Once infected, a human can also be a vector and can spread malaria through blood transfusions, organ transplants, sharing needles/syringes, etc.

Furthermore, warmer climates of the world allow mosquitoes to flourish, further spreading disease. Without proper healthcare, these infectious diseases can lead to endemic proportions.

MAIN FOCUS OF THE CHAPTER

Here, in this section, the existing methods of the tests being conducted for detection of Malaria (Fabio, Gonzalez & Romero, 2009) and the problems faced due the existing methods are being discussed.

Tests for Malaria

T There are a handful of methods to test for Malaria (Hartl, 2004), but the two I most frequently have read about include:

1. Blood smears
2. Antigen testing (i.e., rapid tests)
    a. First, a blood sample is taken from a patient and then placed on a slide.
    b. The sample is stained with a contrasting agent to help highlight malaria parasites in red blood cells
3. clinician then examines the slide under a microscope and *manually counts* the number of red blood cells that are Infected.

According to the official WHO malaria parasite counting protocol, a clinician may have to manually count up to 5,000 cells, an extremely tedious and time-consuming process.

In order to help make malaria testing a faster process (Mitiku, Mengistu & Gelaw, 2000) in the field, scientists and researchers have developed antigen tests for Rapid Diagnosis Testing (RDT).

For RDTs, a small device that allows both a blood sample and a buffer to be added. Internally, the device performs the test and provides the results While RDTs are significantly faster than cell counting they are also much less accurate.

An ideal solution would, therefore, need to combine the *speed* of RDTs with the *accuracy* of microscopy.

SOLUTIONS AND RECOMMENDATIONS

Thus, Using Deep Learning we will be tackling the same problem and thus bring out a solution which will monitor all the requirements as well as help in using the application in any moment of time. The malaria dataset we will be using in deep learning and medical image analysis tutorial is the exact same dataset that Rajaraman (at NIH -United States National Institutes of Health). used in their 2018 publication as shown in Figure 1.

The Convolution Neural Network Architecture used by us is Res-Net Architecture. The main problem with the approach taken by Rajaraman et al. is that it took 24 hrs to train the model. The Convolution Neural Network Architecture (Mitiku, Mengistu & Gelaw, 2000) makes use of Input Layers, Convolution Layers, Zero Padding Layers, Drop out Layers, Batch Normalization Process, Flatten Layers, Dense Layers and Output Layers with appropriate Activation Functions applied in between the layers while passing the Inputs. The complete Convolution Neural Network Architecture of the Res-Net Model is given below in Figure 2.

The dataset consists of 27,588 images belonging to two separate classes:

Figure 1. Data set image

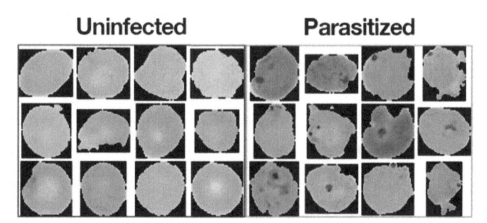

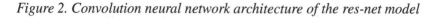

Figure 2. Convolution neural network architecture of the res-net model

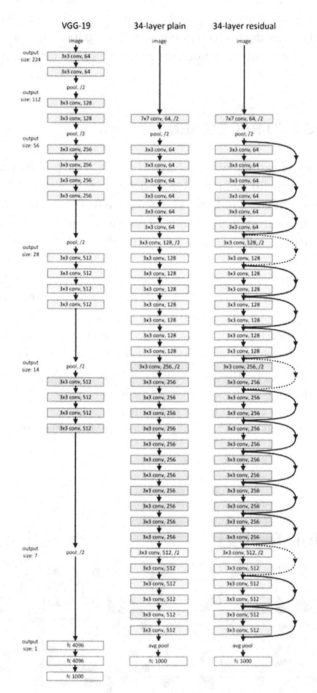

- **Parasitized:** Implying that the region contains malaria.
- **Uninfected:** Meaning there is no evidence of malaria in the region.

The number of images per class is equally distributed with 13,794 images per each respective class.

The code is given in below

```
# set the matplotlib backend so figures can be saved in the background
importmatplotlib
matplotlib.use("Agg")
# import the necessary packages
fromkeras.preprocessing.image importImageDataGenerator
fromkeras.callbacks importLearningRateScheduler
fromkeras.optimizers importSGD
frompyimagesearch.resnet importResNet
frompyimagesearch importconfig
fromsklearn.metrics importclassification_report
fromimutils importpaths
importmatplotlib.pyplot asplt
importnumpy asnp
importargparse
# construct the argument parser and parse the arguments
ap = argparse.ArgumentParser()
ap.add_argument("-p","--plot",type=str,default="plot.png",
help="path to output loss/accuracy plot")
args = vars(ap.parse_args())
# define the total number of epochs to train for along with the
# initial learning rate and batch size
NUM_EPOCHS = 50
INIT_LR = 1e-1
BS = 32
defpoly_decay(epoch):
# initialize the maximum number of epochs, base learning rate,
# and power of the polynomial
maxEpochs = NUM_EPOCHS
baseLR = INIT_LR
power = 1.0
# compute the new learning rate based on polynomial decay
alpha = baseLR * (1 - (epoch / float(maxEpochs))) ** power
# return the new learning rate
```

```
returnalpha
# determine the total number of image paths in training, validation,
# and testing directories
totalTrain = len(list(paths.list_images(config.TRAIN_PATH)))
totalVal = len(list(paths.list_images(config.VAL_PATH)))
totalTest = len(list(paths.list_images(config.TEST_PATH)))
# initialize the training training data augmentation object
trainAug = ImageDataGenerator(
rescale=1 / 255.0,
rotation_range=20,
zoom_range=0.05,
width_shift_range=0.05,
height_shift_range=0.05,
shear_range=0.05,
horizontal_flip=True,
fill_mode="nearest")
# initialize the validation (and testing) data augmentation object
valAug = ImageDataGenerator(rescale=1 / 255.0)
# initialize the training generator
trainGen = trainAug.flow_from_directory(
config.TRAIN_PATH,
class_mode="categorical",
target_size=(64,64),
color_mode="rgb",
shuffle=True,
batch_size=BS)
# initialize the validation generator
valGen = valAug.flow_from_directory(
config.VAL_PATH,
class_mode="categorical",
target_size=(64,64),
color_mode="rgb",
shuffle=False,
batch_size=BS)
# initialize the testing generator
testGen = valAug.flow_from_directory(
config.TEST_PATH,
class_mode="categorical",
target_size=(64,64),
color_mode="rgb",
```

```
shuffle=False,
batch_size=BS)
# initialize our ResNet model and compile it
model = ResNet.build(64,64,3,2,(3,4,6),
(64,128,256,512),reg=0.0005)
opt = SGD(lr=INIT_LR,momentum=0.9)
model.compile(loss="binary_crossentropy",optimizer=opt,
metrics=["accuracy"])
# define our set of callbacks and fit the model
callbacks = [LearningRateScheduler(poly_decay)]
H = model.fit_generator(
trainGen,
steps_per_epoch=totalTrain // BS,
validation_data=valGen,
validation_steps=totalVal // BS,
epochs=NUM_EPOCHS,
callbacks=callbacks)
# reset the testing generator and then use our trained model to
# make predictions on the data
print("[INFO] evaluating network...")
testGen.reset()
predIdxs = model.predict_generator(testGen,
steps=(totalTest // BS) + 1)
# for each image in the testing set we need to find the index of the
# label with corresponding largest predicted probability
predIdxs = np.argmax(predIdxs,axis=1)
# show a nicely formatted classification report
print(classification_report(testGen.classes,predIdxs,
target_names=testGen.class_indices.keys()))
# plot the training loss and accuracy
N = NUM_EPOCHS
plt.style.use("ggplot")
plt.figure()
plt.plot(np.arange(0,N),H.history["loss"],label="train_loss")
plt.plot(np.arange(0,N),H.history["val_loss"],label="val_loss")
plt.plot(np.arange(0,N),H.history["acc"],label="train_acc")
plt.plot(np.arange(0,N),H.history["val_acc"],label="val_acc")
plt.title("Training Loss and Accuracy on Dataset")
plt.xlabel("Epoch #")
plt.ylabel("Loss/Accuracy")
```

plt.legend(loc="lower left")
plt.savefig(args["plot"])

RESULTS AND DISCUSSION

Overall, the entire training process took *only 54 minutes* (*significantly* faster than the 24-hour training process of NIH's method). At the end of the 50th epoch we are obtaining:

- **96.50% accuracy** on the *training* data
- **96.78% accuracy** on the *validation* data
- **97% accuracy** on the *testing* data

There are a number of benefits to using the ResNet-based model we are training for medical image analysis.

Thus, our model is a complete end-to-end malaria classification system.

Unlike NIH's approach which leverages a multiple step process of (1) feature extraction from multiple models and (2) classification, we instead can utilize only a *single, compact model* and obtain comparable results.

Speaking of compactness, our serialized model file is only 17.7MB. Quantizing the weights in the model themselves would allow us to obtain a model < 10MB (or even smaller, depending on the quantization method) with only slight, if any, decreases in accuracy.

Our approach is also faster in two manners.

First, it takes less time to train our model than NIH's approach Our model took only 54 minutes to train while NIH's model took ~24 hours.

>Secondly, our model is faster in terms of both (1) forward-pass inference time and (2) significantly fewer parameters and memory/hardware requirements.

Considering the fact that NIH's method requires pre-trained networks for feature extraction. Each of these models accepts input images that have input image spatial dimensions in the range of 224×244, 227×227, and 299×299 pixels.

Our model requires only 64×64 input images and obtains near identical accuracy.

Based on our results we can see that we have created an automatic malaria classifier that is not only *more* accurate but significantly smaller, requiring less processing power as well. Given below is the Visualized final result:

Figure 3. Graph between accuracy and epoch

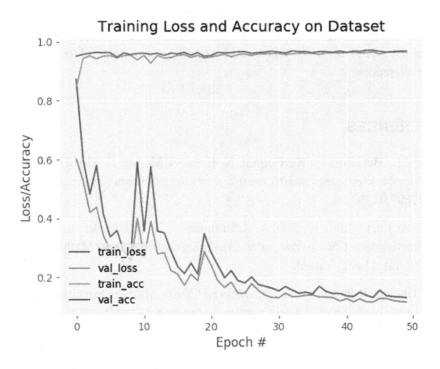

FUTURE RESEARCH DIRECTIONS

This Research work of combining Deep Learning based Model in the case of Medical Imaging will be more modified by us and we will further focus on handling more complex diseases like Liver Cirosis, for MRI Segmentation and in Lungs Imaging which will thus open a new door in the field of Medical Science in handling different diseases.

CONCLUSION

Thus, our technique of using Residual Network based Deep Learning in case of Malaria Analysis has proved to be much better both taking into consideration the training time required during the process and also with respect to the accuracy level attained. Thus, our model and technique is robust and thus, much useful in analysis of Malaria .

ACKNOWLEDGMENT

The authors are sincerely thankful to the Department of Computer Science and Engineering, KL University Vijayawada. And we are also thankful to all the authors of the references.

REFERENCES

Antony, J., McGuinness, K., Connor, N. E. O., & Moran, K. (2016). *Quantifying radiographic knee osteoarthritis severity using deep convolutional neural networks.* arxiv:1609.02469

Barbu, A., Lu, L., Roth, H., Seff, A., & Summers, R. M. (2016). *An analysis of robust cost functions for CNN in computer-aided diagnosis Comput.* Methods Biomech. Biomed. Eng. Imag. Visual.

Dasa, Ghosha, Palb, Maitib, & Chakraborty. (2013). Machine learning approach for automated screening of malaria parasite using light microscopic images. *Micron (Oxford, England), 45*(February), 97–106. PMID:23218914

Fabio, G. D., González, A., & Romero, E. (2009, April). A semi-automatic method for quantification and classification of erythrocytes infected with malaria parasites in microscopic images. *Journal of Biomedical InformaticsVolume, 42*(2), 296–307. doi:10.1016/j.jbi.2008.11.005 PMID:19166974

Hartl, D. (2004). The origin of malaria: Mixed messages from genetic diversity. *Nature Reviews. Microbiology, 2*(1), 15–22. doi:10.1038/nrmicro795 PMID:15035005

Mitiku, K., Mengistu, G., & Gelaw, B. (2000). The reliability of blood film examination for malaria at the peripheral health unit. *Tropical Medicine & International Health, 5*, 3–8. PMID:10672199

Ruberto, C. D., Dempster, A., Khan, S., & Jarra, B. (2002). Analysis of infected blood cell images using morphological operators. *Image and Vision Computing, 20*(2), 133–146. doi:10.1016/S0262-8856(01)00092-0

KEY TERMS AND DEFINITIONS

Antigen: A toxin or other foreign substance which induces an immune response in the body, especially the production of antibodies.

Convolution: A function derived from two given functions by integration which expresses how the shape of one is modified by the other.

Malaria: An intermittent and remittent fever caused by a protozoan parasite which invades the red blood cells and is transmitted by mosquitoes in many tropical and subtropical regions.

Neural Network: A computer system modeled on the human brain and nervous system.

Normalize: Multiply (a series, function, or item of data) by a factor that makes the norm or some associated quantity such as an integral equal to a desired value (usually 1).

Chapter 8
Fatigue Monitoring for Drivers in Advanced Driver–Assistance System

Lakshmi Sarvani Videla
Koneru Lakshmaiah Education Foundation, India

M. Ashok Kumar P
Koneru Lakshmaiah Education Foundation, India

ABSTRACT

The detection of person fatigue is one of the important tasks to detect drowsiness in the domain of image processing. Though lots of work has been carried out in this regard, there is a void of work shows the exact correctness. In this chapter, the main objective is to present an efficient approach that is a combination of both eye state detection and yawn in unconstrained environments. In the first proposed method, the face region and then eyes and mouth are detected. Histograms of Oriented Gradients (HOG) features are extracted from detected eyes. These features are fed to Support Vector Machine (SVM) classifier that classifies the eye state as closed or not closed. Distance between intensity changes in the mouth map is used to detect yawn. In second proposed method, off-the-shelf face detectors and facial landmark detectors are used to detect the features, and a novel eye and mouth metric is proposed. The eye results obtained are checked for consistency with yawn detection results in both the proposed methods. If any one of the results is indicating fatigue, the result is considered as fatigue. Second proposed method outperforms first method on two standard data sets.

DOI: 10.4018/978-1-7998-0066-8.ch008

INTRODUCTION

The symptoms of fatigue are the driver feels difficulty to be awake. He will be constantly yawning or closing his eyes. The person's fatigue impacts the alertness and response of a driver which results in increasing rate of accident. There may be several factors that would result in accidents. One of the major factors in crashes is due to drowsiness. The rates of accidents are due to the fact that the sleepy person fails to make correct decisions when necessary. The National Transport Commission conveys that at least 45 percent of heavy vehicle persons were impaired by fatigue. The survey also revealed fifty percent of all long-distance truck people had nodded off while driving more than once.

Different techniques are used in detecting the person-fatigue. These techniques are divided into three categories. The first category includes intrusive techniques, which are mostly based on monitoring biomedical signals, and therefore require physical contact with the person. The second category includes non-intrusive techniques based on visual assessment of person's bio-behavior from face images such as head movement and eye state positions. The third category includes methods based on person's performance, which monitor vehicle behaviors such as moving course, steering angle, speed, brake.

There are different ways to reduce the person fatigue and behavior at the driving time by alerting them. Different measure involves Face detection, eye state measurement, lip detection, yawn detection, head tilt detection are the major visual symptoms considered.

BACKGROUND

The steps involved in fatigue detection are face detection, feature detection and then classifying whether the person is fatigue or not. In literature, the features mostly considered are eye state and yawn. Some researchers considered head tilt detection for determination of fatigue. Xie Y. et al (2018) built a model using deep neural network for yawn detection. The network learns from yawning video clips and also images using transfer and sequential learning. They are able to distinguish between yawning, talking and laughing. Also, yawn is detected even when the face is turned 70 degrees away from camera. Huang R et al. (2018) has built fatigue detection convolutional network (FDCN) based on common convolutional neural network (CNN). projection cores were incorporated into FDCN to make the features learnt invariant to scale. Achieving an accuracy of 94.9% to detect fatigue using eye state.

F. Zhang et al (2017) used AdaBoost and Local Binary Features to detect features and CNN for classifying and achieved an accuracy of 95%. B. N. Manu et al. (2016) used binary support vector machines to detect closed eye detection and yawn. They used linear kernel and achieved an accuracy of 95%.

Automatic fatigue detection of drivers through yawning analysis is done by Azim, Tayyaba, et al. (2009). After locating face in a video frame, the mouth region is extracted, where lips are searched using spatial fuzzy c-means (s-FCM) clustering. If the yawning state of the driver is detected for several consequent frames, the driver is said to be drowsy. Fuzzy C-means uses spectral and optimal information to segment lips region. Danisman et al. (2010) proposed variations in eyes location based on the symmetry feature along horizontal direction of the eyes. If the symmetry doesn't occur, it corresponds to a closed eye state. Omidyeganeh et al. (2011) detected drowsiness by analyzing eye and mouth states. The person's face is captured from a camera and then converted to color spaces of YCbCr and HSV. To extract eyes, Structural Similarity Measure (SSIM) was used which uses properties which are statistical such as mean and variance. The SSIM values vary between -1 and 1. The maximum value is gained when two images are the same. It is used along with a template to find out the best match for the eyes.

Different techniques used to detect face and facial features are presented in Table 1. Of all the face detection techniques Modified Viola –Jones technique proposed by Videla, L.S. et al. (2018) and Histogram of Oriented Gradients coined by Navneet Dalal et. al. (2006). HOG+ Support Vector Machine (SVM) based face detector gave state of the art results. A brief description of Viola Jones and Histogram of Oriented Gradients is presented in this paper.

Viola Jones Face Detection Algorithm

The Viola-Jones algorithm is proposed by Viola, P. et al. (2004) is used for object detection. It specifies whether an image contains a human face or not. For detecting face objects from frames, we use Haar classifiers. Haar Features impulse a real-time performance with high detection and low false positive rates. At first, the integral image is calculated and Haar classifiers are applied on each frame of the input image to find the location of objects. The integral image makes feature extraction faster. The different Haar cascades used to find the features are:

Haar classifier has two rectangle features which are computed using the difference between the sums of pixels within two rectangular regions. A three-rectangle feature calculates the sum of two outside rectangles subtracted from the sum in a center rectangle. The feature is a four-rectangle feature is determined by finding the difference between diagonal pairs of rectangles.

Table 1. Different techniques to detect features

	Technique used	Advantages	Disadvantages
Face Detection	Viola-Jones is used by Azim, Tayyaba, et al. (2009) and by Danisman, Taner, et al (2010).	Matches face exactly using similarity measures like sum of absolute differences (SAD), the sum of squared difference (SSD), and the normalized cross correlation (NCC).	Yields better result when combined with Linear Discriminant Analysis (LDA).
	Principal Component Analysis (PCA) approach is used by Karim, Tahia Fahrin, et al.(2010).		
	Detected using skin color technique by Omidyeganeh et. al.		
	Karhunen–Loève transform (KLT) used by Qian et. al. (2011).	Face recognition is done by using the Euclidean distance measure along with different tilt angles.	Percentage of face recognition decreases when database has many samples.
	Combination of Color image segmentation, Belief Propagation and PCA used by Kamencay et. al.	Belief propagation used to find marginal probabilities.	Gives better result using LDA and 2D PCA.
	SIFT - PCA and Graph Based Segmentation is used by Kamencay et. al. (2012).	(Scale-invariant feature transform) SIFT is insensitive to illumination.	
	Segmentation using thresholding is used by Rezaee, Khosro, et al (2013).	Gives better result in different varying light conditions.	It is not robust to extreme expression variation.
	Tiesheng, Pengfei, et al. (2005) detects using YCbCr, HSV color spaces along with RGB color space. Then it matches with the database by using template matching. It then uses Daubechies function.	Detects face exactly.	Lengthy process to detect the face.
Mouth and Yawn	Spatial fuzzy c-means (s-FCM) by Azim, Tayyaba, et al. (2009).	Better performance than k-means cluster.	Number of clusters should be known in advance.
	Haar Features and Linear Support Vector Machine is used by Kumar, K., et al (2012).	It finds the minimum distance between the classes.	Selection of structural elements plays very crucial.
	K-means clustering is used by Rezaee, Khosro, et al (2013).		Numbers of clusters should be known in advance.
Eye	Neural Network is used by Danisman, Taner, et al (2010).	Various conditions of eye blinks are measured by using symmetry property.	Presence of glass affects eye detection.
	Structural Similarity Measure was used by Omidyeganeh et. al.	Obtains similarity by using some statistical measures such as mean and variance.	Doesn't yield better result when the template doesn't match with eye.
	Morphological top hat and bottom hat operations are done by Kumar, K., et al (2012).	The exact eyes are identified using eye localization process.	It varies based on the structuring element taken.
	Edge detection using Sobel is used by Rezaee, Khosro, et al (2013).	Using convolution process of mask on image gives exact result of edges.	Not much performance observed when compared to canny edge detection.
Head	Eye Localization process and mouth contour are used to detect head angle by Kumar, K., et al (2012)	Triggers alarm as soon as the (Hierarchical Dirichlet Process) HDP values crosses the threshold value.	Detect angle when angle of deviation is much higher.
	Detection of head lowering using HDP is used by Rezaee, Khosro, et al (2013).		Varies based on the color values of Red.

Figure 1. Haar classifiers used in Viola Jones

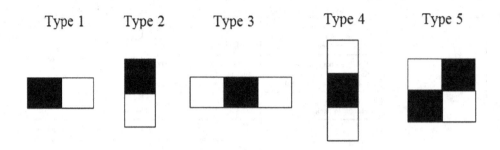

Here the feature detection of input image is done by means of sub-window capable of detecting features. Then the sliding window is made traversed over the image for each scale increment. Here a cascade of classifiers is used to detect the presence of face regions. In each stage, it rapidly rejects regions which do not contain the face part. If the desired face location is not found at any stage in the cascade, the detector rejects the region and the process is terminated.

For each scale increment, the sliding window traverses over the image by producing multiple detections around the face. These multiple detections are merged into a single bounding box of the target object. The size of the final output box is the average of the sizes of the bounding box for individual detections.

The Viola-Jones algorithm steps are as below:

1. Integral Image Calculation
2. Feature Computation
3. Adaboost Feature Selection
4. Classifier Cascade

All the Haar features in different scales are used to produce approximately 1,80,000 features. Viola Jones uses 24x24 windows as the base window size to evaluate the Haar features.

Integral Image Calculation

Integral Image of Figure 2 is calculated as follows:

For each pixel, we draw a line as follows. All the pixel intensities above the line must be added to get the integral image.

5	2
3	6

The value of first pixel remains the same.

Figure 2. 4x4 pixel image with pixel intensities

5	2	5	2
3	6	3	6
5	2	5	2
3	6	3	6

$\begin{array}{cc} 5 & 2 \\ \hline 3 & 6 \end{array}$ The value of first row second column value changes from 2 to 7

$\begin{array}{c|c} 5 & 2 \\ 3 & 6 \end{array}$ So, in place of 6 we get 6+5+2+3 = 16

We calculate like this for all the pixels in the image and when a Haar classifier is run on the image. We sum all the pixels under black region and subtract from sum of all pixels under white region. This computation will be easy, if we calculate the integral image.

Feature Computation

The feature computation is done by overlapping the Haar Classifier over the integral image and is shown in Figure 3.

Sum of pixels under black region = 5+32-(7+16) =14 (same as 6+2+6 =14 in given image)

Sum of pixels under white region = 7+48-(12+32) =11 (same as 3+5+3 in given image)

Figure 3. Feature computation to detect objects

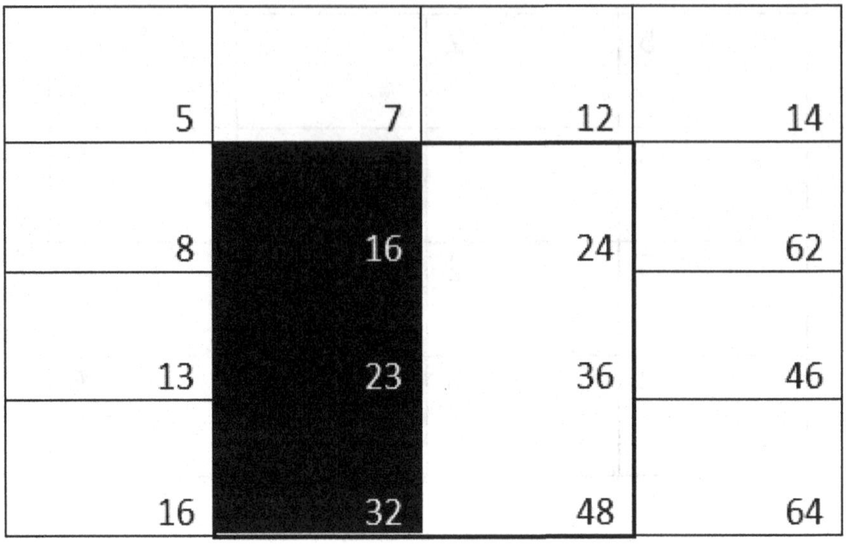

5	7	12	14
8	16	24	62
13	23	36	46
16	32	48	64

AdaBoost Classifier

Adaboost is used to train Strong Classifier which is linear combination of weak classifier. It also decides whether a feature is relevant or not. The steps in Adaboost are:

1. Training set of positive and negative examples (Ex: faces and non-faces images).
2. Initially all the positive training images are given weights equal to 1/(2*number of positive examples) and negative training images are given weights equal to 1/(2*number of negative examples).
3. All the 1,80,000 Haar features or weak classifiers are run on the training images
4. A good threshold (for ex: decision tree) such that any image above threshold is face and below threshold is non-face is determined.
5. Now, Error rate is calculated as sum of weights of images misclassified by each weak classifier. Of the 1,80,000 error rates choose the weak classifier with lowest error rate.

The chosen weak classifier is added to the strong classifier. Now, increase the weights of misclassified images and decrease the weights of correctly classified by normalizing the weights. Repeat the steps 3 to 5 for 1,80,000 times and all the Haar features are run on the images with updated weights and each round selects one weak classifier, which is added as linear combination to obtain final Strong Classifier. The output of weak classifier is 1 or 0 for classifying the image as face or non-face.

Cascading of Stages

After all the rounds of Adaboost, we build a strong classifier which is a linear combination of selected weak classifiers (let's say, 2,000). Instead of running all the 2,000 weak classifiers on the 24x24 window of test image, we build a cascade of classifiers.

To train a cascade, we must choose

- Number of stages or Strong classifiers in cascade
- Number of weak classifiers in strong Classifier (which is done by Adaboost)

A heuristic algorithm, Manual Tweaking is used to train the cascade as follows

1. Select Maximum Acceptable False Positive rate.
2. Select Minimum Acceptable True Positive rate.
3. Threshold for each Strong Classifier (which decided by Adaboost)


```
Let the User select the Target Overall False Positive for all
the stages
Until Target Overall False Positive is met
    Add new Stage
    Until Maximum Acceptable False Positive rate and Minimum
Acceptable
    True Positive rate are met
    Keep adding weak classifiers and train Strong Classifier
using Adaboost
```

Histogram of Oriented Gradients

In Histogram of Oriented Gradients proposed by Navneet Dalal et. al. (2006), first Gaussian Smoothing Mask is applied on the image. The given image is divided into 16x16 blocks each of 2x2 cell and each cell is 8x8. If the image is of size 64x128, we get 105 blocks. Each block is as shown in Figure 4

Figure 4. Blocks in histogram of oriented gradients

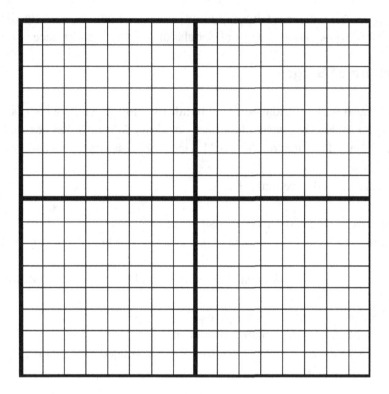

Gradient magnitude and gradient direction is computed for each block. By looking at Gradient direction, gradient orientation is quantized into any of 9 bins (0- 180 degrees) as shown in Figure 5.

If direction is not in one of the bins, interpolation is used. All descriptors i.e., 105 blocks each of 9 dimensions as we have 9 bins are concatenated. Hence a total of

Figure 5. Quantization of gradient orientation into bins

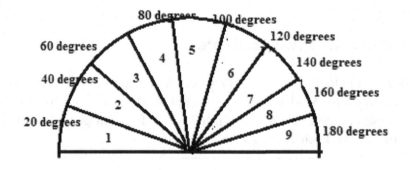

3780 descriptors are used to plot a histogram. X-axis of histogram is the bin values say (20 degrees, 40 degrees...as shown in the above figure 4). Y-axis is the count. One counts how strong the gradient direction is using gradient magnitude(vote)

Proposed Method

In proposed method1, the eyes and mouth are detected in test image using Viola –Jones Eye and mouth detection algorithm. Then HOG features are computed for both eyes. These features are fed to SVM classifier that classifies the test image as eye state closed or not. Mouth map area is computed for the detected mouth by separating the chromium parts of blue and red. The distance between upper lip and lower lip is calculated for normal mouth using mouth map. If the distance between upper lip and lower lip of mouth is greater than the distance of normal mouth, then yawning is detected. If either the eye state and mouth determines fatigue, it is considered as fatigue. But this method is not fully automatic and requires calculating of normal mouth distance.

Modified Feature Extraction proposed by Videla, L.S. et al. (2018) is used for Eye Detection. HOG features are extracted from the detected eye bounding box as follows

1.   Convert the image into gray scale
2.   Divide the cells and group of cells are called blocks
3. Calculate the gradients in x and y direction

$$|G| = \sqrt{G_x^{\,2} + G_y^{\,2}}$$

where

D_x=[-1 0 1] and D_y=[-1 0 1]^T

$G_x = I*D_x$

$G_y = I*D_y$

where * denotes convolution operator.

4.   4. Orientation is computed by

$$\theta = \tan^{-1}\left(\frac{G_y}{G_x}\right)$$

5. The angle transformed into degrees is which gives values in range $\alpha=\theta*180/\Pi$ which gives values in range of (-180, 180] in degrees

6. 6. For signed gradient, we need to change the range of gradient (-180, 180] to [0,360) degrees. It is done using the formula

$$a_{signed} = \begin{cases} a & a \geq 0 \\ a + 360 & a < 0 \end{cases}$$

7. Group the cells into large spatially connected blocks. Normalize over overlapping spatial blocks. Hog is then vector of components of normalized cell histograms.

Let v be the non-normalized vector which has all histograms in a given block and $\| v_k \|$ be k-norm. Then the normalization factor used by Song, Fengyi, et. al. (2014) is

L1-norm is $\dfrac{v}{\|v\|_1 + e}$

L2-norm is $\dfrac{v}{\sqrt{\|v\|_2^2 + e^2}}$

8. This vector is fed to the SVM classifier to detect the closed eye state.
9. End

Initial distance is calculated dynamically by considering the distance between intensity changes in the mouth map of normal mouth. If the calculated distance is greater than the initial distance, then it is considered as yawning.

The Figure 6 shows the mouth map area detected during yawn by separating the chromium parts of blue and red

Proposed method 2

In this method Dlib's HOG+SVM based face detector proposed by D. E. King et. al (2009) which is based on HOG is used. HOG descriptors are calculated for the given image and SVM classifier is used to detect the faces. Facial landmarks are detected for each face detected. Dlib facial landmark detector is used to detect the

Figure 6. Mouth map area for yawning

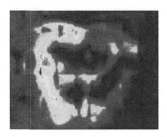

landmarks by Christos Sagonas et. al. (2013) and Vahid Kazemi et. al.(2014) . An ensemble of regression trees is used in Dlib facial landmark detector. Gradient boosting is used to detect the pixel intensities. These intensities are used to detect the landmarks. The landmarks determined by Dlib for eyebrow, eye and mouth are same as proposed by Ralph Gross et. al (2010) and are as shown in Figure 6 and 8. Eye aspect ratio is used by Cech, J. et. al (2016) to detect the eye state. In this paper eye state is determined as Eye distances are depicted in Figure 7.

EyeDistance1=E1~E2 where
E1 = Euclidean distance between landmark 19 and 38;
E2 = Euclidean distance between landmark 19 and 42
EyeDistance2=E3~E4 where
E3 = Euclidean distance between landmark 20 and 38;
E4 = Euclidean distance between landmark 20 and 42
EyeDistance3=E5 ~ E6 where
E5 = Euclidean distance between landmark 21 and 38;
E6 = Euclidean distance between landmark 21 and 41

If eye distance is less than or equal to 3 then the eye is closed else eye is open. The eye distances are calculated for both the eyes. The Eye distances for 1001 images provided by Song, Fengyi, et al (2014) are as shown in Figure 8 and the threshold considered is 3.

Figure 7. Eye distances

Figure 8. Eye distances plotted for 1001 images taken from dataset by Song, Fengyi, et al (2014)

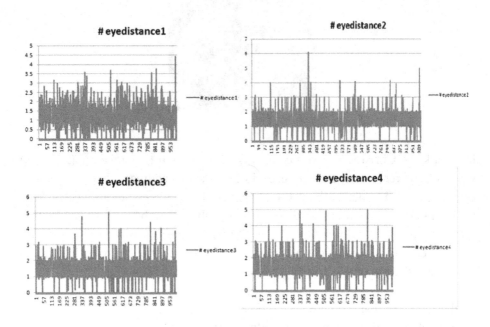

New method has been proposed to detect yawning. For simultaneous yawning detection, the mouth distance is calculated from Figure 9 as follows

Mouth Distance1= Euclidean distance between landmark 49 and 52
Mouth Distance2= Euclidean distance between landmark 55 and 52
Mouth Distance3= Euclidean distance between landmark 49 and 51
Mouth Distance4= Euclidean distance between landmark 55 and 51
Mouth Distance5= Euclidean distance between landmark 49 and 50
Mouth Distance6= Euclidean distance between landmark 55 and 50

Figure 9. Euclidean distances considered for yawn detection

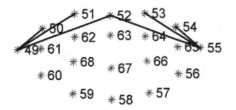

After analysis it is found that if the mouth distance1 or mouth distance2 >16 then a yawn is detected. Also, if mouth distance 3 or mouth distance4 > 13 then a yawn is detected and mouth distance5 or mouth distance6 >7 then a yawn is detected. When the eyes are occluded by glasses, the mouth distance helps to evaluate the drowsiness of the person. If either or both closed eye state and yawn are detected, the person is determined to be fatigue

Yawn images are extracted from the videos in YawnDD dataset provided by Abtahi, S. et. al. (2014). The images on which face is detected are only considered. These images are used as test images to analyze the accuracy of the performance of proposed methods. All the images are resized to 60x60 pixels. Results of proposed method2 are shown in Figure 10 and the performance of proposed methods for detecting yawn are shown in Table 2.

Closed Eyes in the Wild dataset provided by Song, Fengyi, et. al. (2014) consists of 2423 subjects, among which 1192 subjects with both eyes open are downloaded

Figure 10. Results of proposed method 2 on YawnDD dataset provided by Abtahi, S. et. al. (2014)

Table 2. Performance of proposed methods for detecting yawn

Camera inserted	Number of images considered	Proposed Method1 Yawn detection Accuracy	Proposed Method2 Yawn detection accuracy
In the front mirror of car	80	55%	96.55%
On Dash of Car	29	79.31%	96.55%

from internet and 1231 subjects with open eyes are provided by G. B. Huang et. al. (2007). Results of proposed method2 are shown in Figure 11.

Performance of proposed methods for detecting closed eye state in CEW dataset are shown in Table 3.

CONCLUSION

A novel metric has been proposed to detect the closed eye state and yawn detection. The state of the art face detection and landmark detection are used to measure the accuracy of the proposed method. The proposed method gives high accuracy on two standard datasets. The work can be can be extended to real time videos.

Figure 11. Results of proposed method 2 on CEW dataset

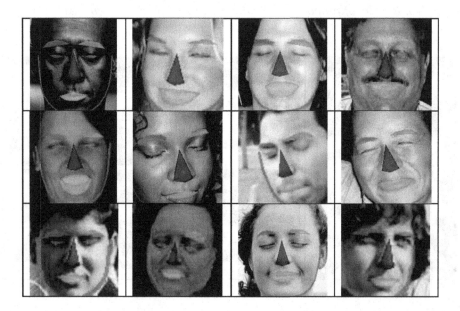

Table 3. Performance of proposed methods on CEW dataset

Number of images considered	Proposed Method1 Eye State detection Accuracy	Proposed Method2 Eye State detection accuracy
2000	85%	96%

NOTE

In this chapter, we presented two algorithms for detecting human fatigue. Algorithm that uses off the shelf facial landmark detectors performed better. A novel mouth and eye metric is proposed to detect yawning and eye closure.

REFERENCES

Abtahi, S., Omidyeganeh, M., Shirmohammadi, S., & Hariri, B. (2014). YawDD: A Yawning Detection Dataset. *Proc. ACM Multimedia Systems.* 10.1145/2557642.2563678

Azim, T. (2009). *Automatic fatigue detection of drivers through Yawning analysis.* Signal Processing, Image Processing and Pattern Recognition. Springer Berlin Heidelberg. doi:10.1007/978-3-642-10546-3_16

Cech, J., & Soukupova, T. (2016). *Real-Time Eye Blink Detection using Facial Landmarks. 21st Comput.* Vis. Winter Work.

Dalal, N., Triggs, B., & Schmid, C. (2006). Human detection using oriented histograms of flow and appearance. In *European conference on computer vision*, (pp. 428–441). Springer. 10.1007/11744047_33

Danisman, T. (2010). Drowsy driver detection system using eye blink patterns. In *Machine and Web Intelligence (ICMWI), 2010 International Conference on.* IEEE. 10.1109/ICMWI.2010.5648121

Gross, R., Matthews, I., Cohn, J., Kanade, T., & Baker, S. (2010). Multi-pie. *Image and Vision Computing*, *28*(5), 807–813. doi:10.1016/j.imavis.2009.08.002 PMID:20490373

Huang, R. Berg, & Learned-Miller. (2007). *Labeled faces in the wild: A database for studying face recognition in unconstrained environments* (Tech. Rep. 07-49). University of Massachusetts, Amherst.

Huang, R., Wang, Y., & Guo, L. (2018, October). P-FDCN Based Eye State Analysis for Fatigue Detection. In *2018 IEEE 18th International Conference on Communication Technology (ICCT)* (pp. 1174-1178). IEEE. 10.1109/ICCT.2018.8599947

Kamencay, Jelsovka, & Zachariasova. (2011). The impact of segmentation on face recognition using the principal component analysis (PCA). *Signal Processing Algorithms, Architectures, Arrangements, and Applications Conference Proceedings (SPA).* IEEE.

Kamencay, P. (2012). Improved face recognition method based on segmentation algorithm using SIFT-PCA. *Telecommunications and Signal Processing (TSP), 2012 35th International Conference on*. IEEE. 10.1109/TSP.2012.6256399

Karim, T. F. (2010). Face recognition using PCA-based method. In *Advanced Management Science (ICAMS), 2010 IEEE International Conference on., 3*. IEEE.

Kazemi & Josephine. (2014). One millisecond face alignment with an ensemble of regression trees. In *27th IEEE Conference on Computer Vision and Pattern Recognition, CVPR 2014* (pp. 1867–1874). IEEE Computer Society.

King, D. E. (2009). Dlib-ml: A Machine Learning Toolkit. *Journal of Machine Learning Research, 10*, 1755–1758. doi:10.1145/1577069.1755843

Kumar, K. (2012). Morphology based facial feature extraction and facial expression recognition for driver vigilance. *International Journal of Computers and Applications, 51*(2), 17–24. doi:10.5120/8578-2317

Manu, B. N. (2017). Facial features monitoring for real time drowsiness detection. *Proc. 2016 12th Int. Conf. Innov. Inf. Technol. IIT 2016*, 78–81.

Omidyeganeh, M., Javadtalab, A., & Shirmohammadi, S. (2011). Intelligent driver drowsiness detection through fusion of yawning and eye closure. In *Virtual Environments Human-Computer Interfaces and Measurement Systems (VECIMS), 2011 IEEE International Conference on*. IEEE. 10.1109/VECIMS.2011.6053857

Qian, J. (2011). Face detection and recognition method based on skin color and depth information. In *Consumer Electronics, Communications and Networks (CECNet), 2011 International Conference on*. IEEE. 10.1109/CECNET.2011.5768500

Rezaee, K. (2013). Real-time intelligent alarm system of driver fatigue based on video sequences. In *Robotics and Mechatronics (ICRoM), 2013 First RSI/ISM International Conference on*. IEEE. 10.1109/ICRoM.2013.6510137

Sagonas, C., Tzimiropoulos, G., Zafeiriou, S., & Pantic, M. (2013). 300 faces in-the-wild challenge: The first facial landmark localization challenge. In *Computer Vision Workshops (ICCVW), 2013 IEEE International Conference on*, (pp. 397–403). IEEE.

Song. (2014). Eyes closeness detection from still images with multi-scale histograms of principal oriented gradients. *Pattern Recognition, 47*(9).

Tiesheng, P. (2005). Yawning detection for determining driver drowsiness. *VLSI Design and Video Technology, 2005. Proceedings of 2005 IEEE International Workshop*, 373 – 376.

Videla, L.S., & Ashok Kumar, M. (2018, March). Modified Feature Extraction Using Viola Jones Algorithm. *Journal of Advanced Research in Dynamical & Control Systems, 10*(3), 528-538.

Viola, P., & Jones, M. J. (2004). Robust real-time face detection. *International Journal of Computer Vision, 57*(2), 137–154. doi:10.1023/B:VISI.0000013087.49260.fb

Xie, Y., Chen, K., & Murphey, Y. L. (2018, November). Real-time and Robust Driver Yawning Detection with Deep Neural Networks. In *2018 IEEE Symposium Series on Computational Intelligence (SSCI)* (pp. 532-538). IEEE.

Zhang, F., Su, J., Geng, L., & Xiao, Z. (2017). Driver fatigue detection based on eye state recognition. *Proc. - 2017 Int. Conf. Mach. Vis. Inf. Technol. C. 2017*, 105–110. 10.1109/CMVIT.2017.25

KEY TERMS AND DEFINITIONS

Gradient Boosting: Gradient boosting is a machine learning technique for regression and classification problems, which produces a strong classifier in the form of an ensemble of weak classifiers. Gradient boosting combines weak classifiers in iteratively. Gradient boosting generalizes by minimizing loss function and loss function must be differentiable. Gradient boosting involves weak classifiers, a loss function that has to be minimized and an additive model to add weak classifiers to minimize loss function.

Mouth Map: Color map is matrix of values. Color map can be of any length and depends on the number of colors that make the color space. Each row in the matrix defines one color. For example, in RGB image, each pixel is combination of intensities of red, green and blue colors. Each row of color map matrix contains 3 columns for storing the intensities of red, green and blue colors. Image with only red component can be used for image processing. Red component dominates around mouth area than blue component in humans. Mouth can be prominently identified by considering only chromium component in YCbCr color space. Mouth Map is generally image of the detected mouth with only one component used.

Support Vector Machines: A support vector machine (SVM) is a classifier that separates classifiers by outputting a hyperplane. In supervised learning where labeled training data is given, SVM generates a hyperplane such that data belonging to same class will be on one side of hyperplane.

Chapter 9

Automatic Article Detection in a Jumbled Scene Using Point Feature Matching

Cmak Zeelan Basha
Koneru Lakshmaiah Education Foundation, India

Azmira Krishna
Koneru Lakshmaiah Education Foundation, India

S. Siva Kumar
Koneru Lakshmaiah Education Foundation, India

ABSTRACT

Recognition of items in jumbled scenes is a basic test that has as of late been generally embraced by computer vision frameworks. This chapter proposes a novel technique how to distinguish a specific item in jumbled scenes. Given a reference picture of the article, a method for recognizing a particular article dependent on finding point correspondences between the reference and the objective picture is presented. It can distinguish objects in spite of a scale change or in-plane revolution. It is additionally strong to little measure of out-of-plane rotation and occlusion. This technique for article location works for things that show non-reiterating surface precedents, which offer rising to exceptional part coordinates. This method furthermore works honorably for reliably shaded articles or for things containing repeating structures. Note that this calculation is intended for recognizing a particular article.

DOI: 10.4018/978-1-7998-0066-8.ch009

INTRODUCTION

According to many standard surveys tracking of an object in jumbled scene stands very difficult. Many reports says that human verification of an object in a jumbled image stands almost impossible. It has been very difficult to say manually that same object is available in all image modes. Here this paper proposes an Automatic Article Detection in a jumbled Scene Using Point Feature Matching People perform object capturing easily and quickly by Bradski (1998). A frontal face classifier constructed from 200 features yields a detection rate of 95% with a false positive rate of 1 in 10284 presented by Viola (2001). In this section we discuss about various steps in catching an item in jumbled scene. We look at the impulsiveness of these errands and present techniques which helps in various ways of the catching assignment. The item catching problem can be categorized as a marking subject dependent on models of known articles. Giving an item as input and extracting the strongest feature points from the input image. The strongest feature points from a cluttered scene also taken into consideration for this analysis. The item capturing issue is firmly attached to the division issue: without something like a fractional catching of articles, division is impossible, and without division, object catching is beyond the realm of imagination presented by Jugessur (2000). In this paper we converse about essential parts of item catching. In our venture, the item can be caught by utilizing point include coordinating method. It is one of the procedures of the neighbourhood features by Lowe (2004).

POINT FEATURE MATCHING TECHNIQUE

Highlight is portrayed as an "entrancing" some segment of a picture and features are used as a starting stage for some PC vision figuring. The appealing property for a part locator is repeatability, paying little heed to whether a comparable component will be distinguished in something like two extraordinary photos of a comparable scene. Feature recognizable proof is computationally exorbitant and there are time-impediments, a progressively raised sum figuring may be used to deal with the part acknowledgment sort out, with the objective that simply certain bits of the image are searched for features. Point incorporate recognizable proof is an effective technique to recognize a foreordained concentration in a muddled scene. This procedure is to separate one express thing as opposed to that kind of articles. For instance, by using this procedure, we can recollect one unequivocal individual in a scrambled scene and we will in all likelihood be unfit to see diverse individuals in a cluttered scene.

The count of this system is, essentially, established on differentiating and separating point correspondences between the reference target picture and the confused scene picture. If any bit of the cluttered scene shares correspondences more unmistakable than the farthest point, that bit of disordered scene picture will be centred around and could be considered to have the reference object there.

Feature Detection and Extraction

A component is a fascinating piece of a picture, for example, a corner, mass, edge, or line. Highlight extraction Brown and Lowe (2002) empowers you to determine a lot of highlight vectors, likewise called descriptors, from a lot of identified highlights. PC vision structure toolbox offers capacities for feature area and extraction that include: Corner acknowledgment, including Shi and Tomasi, Harris, and FAST methodologies

- BRISK, MSER, and SURF recognizable proof for masses and regions
- Extraction of BRISK, FREAK, SURF, and clear pixel neighbourhood descriptors
- Histogram of Oriented Gradients (HOG) feature extraction.

Feature planning is the examination of two courses of action of feature descriptors gained from different pictures to give point correspondences between pictures. Our philosophy In this paper, we propose a SURF estimation for evacuating, portrayal and planning the photos.

SURF FEATURE ALGORITHM

The SURF Algorithm is made by Ester (1996). Likewise, it speaks to Speeded up the Robust Features. SURF count is truly established on the SIFT computation. It uses basic pictures and approximations for achieving higher speed than SIFT. These fundamental pictures are used for convolution. Like SIFT, SURF works in three rule stages: extraction, depiction, and planning. The qualification among SIFT and SURF is that SURF isolates the features from an image using imperative pictures and box channels. The extraction of the key concentrations from an image is a methodology that requires picture isolating. SURF executes these channels using box channels. An entrancing pre-taking care of step is the difference in the primary picture into an implied vital picture. Essential pictures are all around adequately enrolled by including the right pixel regards. In a crucial picture every pixel is the aggregate of all pixels arranged in a rectangular window melded by that pixel and the origin, with the reason being the most upper left pixel. Box channels are used as a gauge of the exact channel cover. By using vital pictures together with box channels an imperative quicken is made sense of it. Another refinement in the extraction of key centres is that SIFT rescales the image, while SURF changes the channel cloak. The term box-space is used to remember it from the run of the mill scale-space. While the scale space is gotten by convolution of the fundamental pictures with Gaussians, the discrete box-space is procured by convolving the main picture with box channels at a couple of particular discrete sizes. In the acknowledgment step, the adjacent maxima of a Hessian-like chairman, the Box Hessian manager, associated with the container space are figured to pick interest point contenders. These hopefuls are then endorsed if the response is over a given edge. Both box size and territory of these contenders are then refined using an iterated approach fitting locally a quadratic limit. Routinely, two or three a few interest centres are distinguished in a propelled picture of one pixel. In this manner, SURF fabricates a descriptor that is invariant by both (Felzenszwalb, 2010; Fouhey, 2014) to see point changes of the nearby neighbourhood of the focal point. Like in SIFT, the area of this point in the case space gives invariance to scale and gives scale and interpretation invariance. To accomplish revolution invariance, a predominant introduction is characterized by considering the nearby slope introduction conveyance, evaluated with Haar wavelets. Making utilization of a spatial restriction grid by Carreira (2012) and Ester (1996), a 64-dimensional descriptor is then constructed, relating to a neighbourhood histogram of the Haar wavelet responses by Geiger et al. (2011). In this methodology an input image is given along with the cluttered scene. The objective is to catch the input image object in cluttered scene. Point features are extracted for both input image and the cluttered scene. Then based on the putative matching points an object can be detected in a jumbled scene. The below figure description (Figure 1-7) represents our experimental analysis. From this we have clearly observed that the proposed techniques out-performs well with given own capture dataset. All figure represented in this chapter are own capture images.

This paper shows the obtained result with 7 output images. Figure 1 is input image which is to be detected in a cluttered scene. Figure 2 is input image of a cluttered scene. Figure 3 represents strongest feature points from an image. Figure4 represents strongest feature points of cluttered image. Figure 5 results a putative matched points along with outliers. Figure 6 results putative matched points of only in liners Figure 7 is output of detected image in a cluttered scene.

Figure 1. Image of a box

Figure 2. Image of a cluttered scence

CONCLUSION

The method of object capturing work best for objects that exhibit non-repeating texture patterns, which give rise to unique feature matches. This technique is not likely to work well for uniformly-coloured objects, or for objects containing repeating patterns. Note that this algorithm is designed for detecting a specific object, for example, the elephant in the reference image, rather than any elephant. For detecting objects of a particular category, such as people or faces, see vision. Cascade Object Detector.

Figure 3. 100 stongest feature points from box image

Figure 4. 300 stongest feature points from box image

Figure 5. Putatively matched points (including outliers)

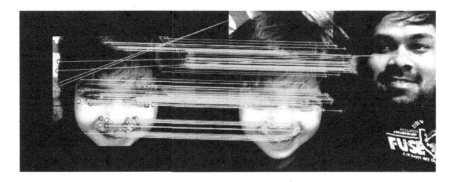

Figure 6. Matched points (inliers only)

Figure 7. Detected Box

REFERENCES

Bradski, G. R. (1998). Real Time Face and Object Tracking as a Component of a Perceptual User Interface. In *Fourth IEEE Workshop on Applications of Computer Vision WACV '98* (pp. 214-219). IEEE. 10.1109/ACV.1998.732882

Brown, M., & Lowe, D. (2002). Invariant features from interest point groups. BMVC02. doi:10.5244/C.16.23

Carreira, J., & Sminchisescu, C. (2012). Cpmc: Automatic object segmentation using constrained parametric min-cuts. *IEEE Transactions on Pattern Analysis and Machine Intelligence*, *34*(7), 1312–1328. doi:10.1109/TPAMI.2011.231 PMID:22144523

Ester, M., Kriegel, H. P., Sander, J., & Xu, X. (1996). A density-based algorithm for discovering clusters in large spatial databases with noise. In *KDD'96 Proceedings of the Second International Conference on Knowledge Discovery and Data Mining* (pp. 226-231). ACM.

Felzenszwalb, P. F., Girshick, R. B., McAllester, D., & Ramanan, D. (2010). Object detection with discriminatively trained part-based models. *IEEE Transactions on Pattern Analysis and Machine Intelligence, 32*(9), 1627–1645. doi:10.1109/TPAMI.2009.167 PMID:20634557

Fouhey, D. F., Gupta, A., & Hebert, M. (2014). Unfolding an indoor origami world. In *ECCV: European Conference on Computer Vision* (Vol. 8694, pp. 687–702). Springer. 10.1007/978-3-319-10599-4_44

Geiger, A., Wojek, C., & Urtasun, R. (2011). Joint 3d estimation of objects and scene layout. *Neural Information Processing Systems 24 (NIPS 2011).*

Jugessur, D., & Dudek, D. (2000). Local appearance for robust object recognition. In Computer Vision and Pattern Recognition (ICCVPR 2000) (pp. 834-840). IEEE. doi:10.1109/CVPR.2000.855907

Lowe, D. G. (2004). Distinctive image features from scale-invariant key points. *International Journal of Computer Vision, 60*(2), 91–110. doi:10.1023/B:VISI.0000029664.99615.94

Viola & Jones. (2001). Rapid Object Detection using a Boosted Cascade of Simple Features. *Proceedings of the 2001 IEEE Computer Society Conference on Computer Vision and Pattern Recognition (CVPR 2001).*

Chapter 10

R-HOG Feature-Based Off-Line Odia Handwritten Character Recognition

Abhisek Sethy
Koneru Lakshmaiah Education Foundation, India

Prashanta Kumar Patra
College of Engineering and Technology Bhubaneswar, India

ABSTRACT

Offline handwritten recognition system for Odia characters has received attention in the last few years. Although the recent research showed that there has been lots of work reported in different language, there is limited research carried out in Odia character recognition. Most of Odia characters are round in nature, similar in orientation and size also, which increases the ambiguity among characters. This chapter has harnessed the rectangle histogram-oriented gradient (R-HOG) for feature extraction method along with the principal component analysis. This gradient-based approach has been able to produce relevant features of individual ones into the proposed model and helps to achieve high recognition rate. After certain simulations, the respective analysis of classifier shows that SVM performed better than quadratic. Among them, SVM produces with 98.8% and QC produces 96.8%, respectively, as recognition rate. In addition to it, the authors have also performed the 10-fold cross-validation to make the system more robust.

DOI: 10.4018/978-1-7998-0066-8.ch010

INTRODUCTION

Automatic Character Recognition has considered as to be one of the emerging fields of Pattern Recognition. Henceforth it was quite impressive for researchers to do more qualitative work to solve the real-world problems. An automated recognition model has been developed not only for printed, handwritten characters along with degrade characters are also reported by Govindan et al. (1990). Each recognition system has certain intermediate stages such as acquisition, preprocessing, feature extraction and last the classification are accepted in well- defined manner so to report high recognition rate (Mantas, 1986). As on context of recognition of handwritten one is quite challenging as compared with printed one, it is so because handwritten more complex in nature and various individual's various way of writing skills in terms of shape orientation of writing (Plamondon et al., 2000). In this paper we have try to build a recognition system for Odia Handwritten characters. Handwritten Character of Odia is one of the oldest scripts and the official language of Odisha state, India. In this regard several recognition techniques have been evolved for variance kind of languages but writing pattern of Odia character is just like as curve appearance. Hence, it adds more complex analysis to the recognition model for handwritten ones (Pal et al., 2004).

In context to automatic recognition handwritten Odia Characters is most challenging task among the individual's characters and its due that most the characters are mostly alike to each other that is in terms of shapes size and orientation. These reported variations make researchers to work more to provide robust techniques towards this problem domain. To have a successive recognition accuracy for any OCR system one should put more emphasis on feature extraction technique. There was certain well-defined feature extraction technique has been listed up which was used in recent year is described by to have a proper solution to above mentioned (Pal et al., 2012; Sethi et al., 1977). Here in this paper we have shown how cell-based approach is quite efficient to achieve high recognition rate for the hand-written characters. For implementing a cell based we have harnessed the Rectangle Histogram Oriented Gradient (R-HOG) over the data image in the feature extraction segment. In addition to it we have shown the reduction in feature dimension through implementing Principal Component Analysis (PCA) (Sethy et al., 2018). At last the reduced feature vector are forwarded to SVM and Quadratic Classifier and report the respective recognition rate. In order to make the recognition system effective we have segmented the model into certain section. Where section 2 represents the related work done by various researchers, section 3 depicts the overall proposed model where all the significant stages are explained precisely, and Section 4 and Section 5 represents the result analysis and conclusion along with future scope of the proposed model.

BACKGROUND OF RELATED WORK

To the context literature survey, we have noticed that many researchers has done both printed and offline Odia characters and numerals. Basically, from Brahmi script Odia script is generated and in the part Devanagari script, which is considered as the most ancient languages among Indian regional language. Odia is usually most spoken eastern part of India basically in state Odisha, West-Bengal, Gujarat etc. Initially all the researcher was done to Devanagari scripts in early 1970s which was extended to various regional scripts among them Odia is one of them. Sethi et al. (1977) and Sinha et al. (1979) has started the on-Devanagari scripts. Initially some work was related printed scripts was reported by Pal et al. (2001). In which he has shown the importance of feature analysis and reported in terms of stroke analysis of the individuals of printed characters. Once again by Pal et al. (2007) evaluates a new robust method which says about curvature analysis of individual characters for which he had reported the curvature feature in feature extraction step. As on simulation analysis he has reported 94.6% as a recognition accuracy. Chen and Kundu (1998) has solve a real tine analysis over postal words, where they had conducted over 100 postal words. In addition to it they had also reported curvature analysis over the character and on simulation analysis achieved 88.2% recognition accuracy with the help of HMM. Similar problem domain was reported in Jindal et al. (2007). In that they had listed eight different major Printed scripts for the recognition system and achieved all the recognition accuracy varying from 96.45 to 99%. Patra et al. (2002) had introduced the variant and invariant feature of the Odia characters. These invariant features were listed from by applying certain transformation such as Zernike and Mellin over invariant images. Upon certain analysis he reported 99% as overall recognition rate and chosen Neural Network as the classifier in the recognition model. Bhowmik et al. (2006) had reported the stroke analysis where they listed both vertical and horizontal stroke and perform the simulation part into training and testing of the system. In addition to it they had achieved recognition rate achieved as 95.89% for training and 90.50% recognition rate for testing data. Once again Kale et al. (2013) also put emphasis on Zernike moments in the feature extraction section. In addition to it they had also performed normalize the individual images and segmented into various zones and calculated the feature of each zone.

Pallin et al. (2006) has proposed a histogram based approached for the successful implementation upon to the printed scripts. They had taken a vertical histogram of the line which is generally represents the distance between two consecutive words of a line is bigger than the distance between two consecutive characters in a word.

In Senapati et al. (2012) had performed the segmentation of both word and line. Vertically, horizontally projection was drawn and reported the different zones. As a result, they had achieved well defined recognition rate up to 99%. Later, some additional analysis of stroke was adopted by Pujari et al. (2013). In which the authors had reported 10 various algorithms and perform the comparison among them. Rather on stroke analysis some work has also reported for evaluating the feature along one directional. Dash et al. (2013) had performed over the handwritten numerals and reported the statistical feature vector, in addition zone optimization had been done over the zone wise and validate the proposed system with an accuracy of 99.1%. Once Again Dash et al. (2015) had suggested the histogram orientation of the handwritten characters and performed the recognition with the help of evolutionary approach. They had drawn symmetric projection over the unconstrained hand-written characters and suggested a two-way approach for classification, subsequently reported the analysis over three classifier such as Random forest, SVM, K-NN and listed up 89.92%, 93.77% and 95.01% recognition rate respectively.

ADOPTED RECOGNITION MODEL FOR HANDWRITTEN CHARACTER RECOGNITION

To have a well define recognition system it must focused with every stage of the recognition model Here in this we have listed all the essential steps like Image Acquisition, Image processing, Feature extraction and classification provides a unique way of approach for recognize of Odia Character and the complete model is shown in graphically in Figure 1. The details discussion can be made in several sub-chapters in subsequent section. Apart from this some reduction algorithm has included as dimension reduction of feature vector in the proposed model.

MATERIALS USED

To suggest any recognition model is the good one that depends upon recognition rate achieved. For achieving high accuracy all we need a good database. To implement the above said system we have harnessed over benchmark handwritten Odia characters that the captured image characters should be in good quality. In the experimental set up of the proposed model we have considered the handwritten character dataset received from NIT, Rourkela by Mishra et al. (2014) and one of the samples is shown in Figure 2. In the respective dataset it contains the scanned images of handwritten characters of various aged group from 10 to 50 years people.

Figure 1. Suggested model for handwritten character recognition

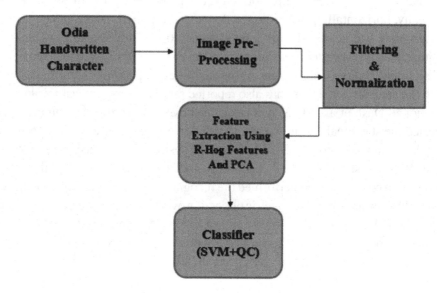

Figure 2. A sample of handwritten Odia character database of NIT, RKL

ODIA HANDWRITTEN CHARACTER PRE-PROCESSING

This is the next phase of the model is the Pre-processing step, where we have performed removal of noise from the original image. In order to have the character image noise free we have deployed median filter to the respective images. After that we have harnessed some morphological operation like dilation to detect the exact boundary of the character images efficiently. In addition to it to we have performed the normalization the image matrix after reading the handwritten images from the benchmark database which leads to make all the character in uniform size.

R-HOG BASED FEATURE EXTRACTION

As we all know each feature extraction is the most crucial part of any recognition model. Basically, it is way of conversion of input handwritten image to certain set of feature values which is termed as Feature Extraction. Here in this handwritten Odia characters most of the characters are identical to each other in terms of orientation, shape so it is added challenges in the recognition of handwritten characters. By retrieving the minimum feature which is used to predict the correct pattern class. Rectangle Histogram Oriented Gradient (R-HOG) is most useful to report the features of the data image suggested by Mishra et al. (2014). So, we have harnessed the R-Hog over each handwritten image and the gradient value used to report the direction along with the magnitude. In context to this magnitude it must be maximum variation of intensity which is present in small zone of each pixel gradient and that has been calculated by Sobel filter. These Sobel filters is quite helpful to report the horizontal (H_h) and vertical (H_v) that are shown in Figure 3.

$$G_x\left(x,y\right) = H * F\left(x,y\right) \, and \, G_y\left(x,y\right) = H^T * F\left(x,y\right) \tag{1}$$

$$G\left(x,y\right) = \sqrt{G_x^2\left(x,y\right) + G_y^2\left(x,y\right)} \tag{2}$$

Usually all the images are in 2D format, so handwritten Odia character $F(x,y)$ and its respective gradient is represented as $G(x,y)$ which is calculated in Equation 2. And their respective Sobel mask component H and H^T. In addition to it also we had reported the gradient magnitude (θ) is computed as below

Figure 3. (a) Horizontal gradient; (b) Vertical gradient value

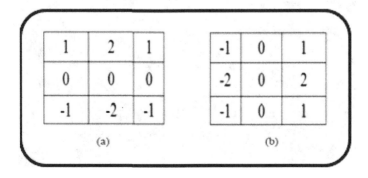

$$\theta\left(x,y\right) = tan^{-1} \frac{G_x\left(x,y\right)}{G_y\left(x,y\right)} \tag{3}$$

By obtaining the gradient magnitude all the histogram is in block size and depicted in blink, in this way we can calculate the respective HOG feature values as below and repective HOG Feature (λ) one sample is given Figure 4.

$$\lambda = \begin{cases} G\left(x,y\right), & if\ \theta\left(x,y\right) \in bin_k \\ 0, & Otherwise \end{cases} \tag{4}$$

PRINCIPAL COMPONENT ANALYSIS (PCA) OVER FEATURE VECTOR

To make less complex and more performance oriented we have employed PCA (Sethy et al., 2018) over high dimension feature vectors. Already we known that less the number of features it will take less computation time, and this can achieve

*Figure 4. Respective HOG feature of one sample in 4*4 block*

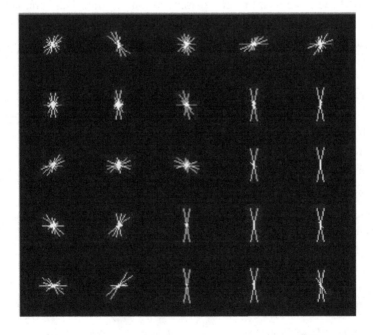

by mapping the higher dimensional value to the lesser dimensional one. PCA by Nasrabadi (2007), Already we known that less the number of features it will take less computation time, and this can achieve by mapping the higher dimensional value to the lesser dimensional one. It usually evaluates depending upon the orthogonal parameters by Mishra et al. (2014) of transform from which variance and Eigen values are reported. Subsequently a covariance matrix is formed, and the highest Eigen values are treated as the principal component and shown in Algorithm I. The After application of PCA to the feature vector of size $P \times Q$ a new reduced feature matrix $P \times R$ is yielded, where $R << Q$ and the procedure is given in Algorithm I.

Algorithm I: Feature Reduction

Input: FV [1: M, 1: N]: Feature value matrix, P: total numbers of image and R: number of features.

Output: RFV [1: M, 1: N]: Reduction in dimension to get reduced feature vector.

PCA (RFV, N) – calculates the principal co-efficient values

1. Input the vale value of R (reduce in dimension).
2. Report RFV [1:P,1: R]
3. $RFV[1:P, 1:R] \leftarrow pca(FV,R)$
4. Obtain the RFV

CLASSIFIER USED

After harnessing the PCA over the larger feature set and as an outcome we have get ready with the least feature set termed as primary features. We have collected 40,50 significant features and process to next step that is classification. Here we have suggested a two-way approach of classification. Initially all the primary features were processed to SVM (Sharma et al., 2006) classifier and followed up by Quadratic Classifier Kimura et el. (2006). SVM is one of the most powerful machine learning algorithms due its supervised in nature and here we have considered a Multi-Class SVM (Chang, 2011) one with having linear kernel function. We have first evaluated the SVM Classifiers and secondly quadratic classifier is executed. In this work which is statistical classifier one and works linearly depending on the measurement of the surface among various classes. All the performance was listed depending upon the value of the mean square error. And tells about which classifier is the best one.

IMPLEMENTATION

Here in this section we have proposed a well-defined step and make it all in an algorithm and listed in Algorithm II. For successful implementation of recognition handwritten Odia Character, we have focused in various aspect in terms of pre-processing, feature technique used and at last classifier used. Again, we had classified into two stage one is offline and online procedure and mentioned below.

Algorithm II: Implementation Offline Procedure

1. Read the Handwritten Odia Character Image One by One and make it into 4* 4 block.
2. Perform the pre-processing stage along with normalisation of the pixel values.
3. Apply R-HOG to each individual handwritten character.
4. Extract the primary features through feature descriptors.
5. Perform the dimension reduction using PCA and retain the principal components (PCs)
6. Apply the SVM and Quadratic Classifier for Classification.
7. Evaluate the model based on testing data

On-Line Procedure

1. Load the input query image of the User.
2. Forwarded the query image to preprocessing section.
3. Report the features through harnessing R- Hog to handwritten images.
4. Retained PCs by harnessing the PCA over the primary features.
5. Apply the trained classifiers separately and predict the class label.

RESULTS AND DISCUSSION

All the experiments were performed on a system having specification as windows 8, 64-bit operating system, and Intel (R) i7 – 4770 CPU @ 3.40 GHz. Simulations were conducted through Matlab2014a on a standard database named as NIT Rourkela Odia Database. Here in the dataset it consists of various aged group handwritten Odia characters. These characters are leveled up to 47 categories Handwritten

Odia characters and in total 350 number of each 47 are inputted into the proposed model. Hence all image putted over 4*4 block to make the calculation process easier. Henceforth we had performed certain preprocessing with the image along with normalization to get better accuracy over the dataset. For to extract the desired feature vector we have reported R-HOG in it. This rectangle gradient based feature is quite impressive to report the minimum feature of each one. Though the feature set very large in number to increase the complexity of the model. To avoid such situation PCA has introduced and successfully 50 number PC Score are extracted as primary features. Here we have shown how the least feature leads to have high recognition rate. A 10-fold cross validation scheme has been deployed which avoids overfitting and leads a more stable model. Cross-validation is used in the present study in order to overcome the overfitting issues of the recognition system. Then the reduced features are fed to both the classifiers SVM and Quadratic Classifier and their respective recognition rate has been reported in below Table 1 and Table 2. In the tables, N_{CC} represents the number of correctly classified samples, N_{MC} indicates the number of misclassified samples and RR indicates the recognition accuracy.

CONCLUSION AND FUTURE SCOPE

In this paper we have adopted a new direction of recognition of Handwritten scripts based upon its gradient's values. To achieve such, we had considered the recant angle- HOG for which we have shown how effectively we have shown direction wise along with their gradient components much helpful in recognition of handwritten characters. In addition to make the system performance oriented we have reduced the dimension of the feature vector by implementing PCA over the feature set and obtain the primary feature. In the classification section we have processed the input vector of 50*350*47 of total size to the two classifiers one by one. Initially Multi-class SVM is executed followed up by Quadratic Classifier. After performing proper training and testing of data the classifier we have optimize the mean square of classifiers, as an outcome SVM achieved 98.8% overall recognition rate and Quadratic classifier achieved 96.8% as the overall all recognition rate. We have achieved very good recognition rate over benchmark handwritten data set. Apart from its various invented machine learning approaches such as direction based, extreme learning based can be applied to such problem domain. Further, other techniques are to be explored for better recognition accuracy.

Table 1. Recognition rate obtained by SVM classifier

SL. No	N_{CC}	N_{MC}	Accuracy (RR in %)	SL. No	N_{CC}	N_{MC}	Accuracy (RR in%)
1	346	4	98.8	25	346	4	98.8
2	346	4	98.8	26	343	7	98
3	346	4	98.8	27	343	7	98
4	346	4	98.8	28	343	7	98
5	346	4	98.8	29	343	7	98
6	346	4	98.8	30	343	7	98
7	346	4	98.8	31	341	9	97.4
8	346	4	98.8	32	341	9	97.4
9	346	4	98.8	33	341	9	97.4
10	346	4	98.8	34	341	9	97.4
11	343	7	98	35	341	9	97.4
12	343	7	98	36	341	9	97.4
13	341	9	97.4	37	341	9	97.4
14	341	9	97.4	38	341	9	97.4
15	343	7	98	39	341	9	97.4
16	343	7	98	40	341	9	97.4
17	346	4	98.8	41	346	4	98.8
18	346	4	98.8	42	346	4	98.8
19	343	7	98	43	346	4	98.8
20	343	7	98	44	346	4	98.8
21	346	4	98.8	45	341	9	97.4
22	346	4	98.8	46	341	9	97.4
23	346	4	98.8	47	346	4	98.8
24	341	9	97.4	**Average Recognition Rate = 98.8%**			

ACKNOWLEDGMENT

The authors are sincerely thankful to the Department of Computer Science and Engineering, KL University Vijayawada. And we are also thankful to all the authors of the references.

Table 2. Recognition rate obtained by confusion matrix of quadratic classifier

SL. No	N_{CC}	N_{MC}	Accuracy (%)	SL. No	N_{CC}	N_{MC}	Accuracy (%)
1	339	11	96.8	25	339	11	96.8
2	339	11	96.8	26	339	11	96.8
3	339	11	96.8	27	339	11	96.8
4	339	11	96.8	28	339	11	96.8
5	346	4	98.8	29	339	11	96.8
6	339	11	96.8	30	339	11	96.8
7	339	11	96.8	31	339	11	96.8
8	346	4	98.8	32	339	11	96.8
9	339	11	96.8	33	339	11	96.8
10	339	11	96.8	34	339	11	96.8
11	343	7	98	35	341	9	97.4
12	343	7	98	36	341	9	97.4
13	341	9	97.4	37	341	9	97.4
14	341	9	97.4	38	341	9	97.4
15	343	7	98	39	341	9	97.4
16	343	7	98	40	341	9	97.4
17	346	4	98.8	41	339	11	96.8
18	339	11	96.8	42	339	11	96.8
19	339	11	96.8	43	339	11	96.8
20	339	11	96.8	44	346	4	98.8
21	339	11	96.8	45	341	9	97.4
22	339	11	96.8	46	339	11	96.8
23	339	11	96.8	47	339	11	96.8
24	341	9	97.4	Average Recognition Rate = 96.8%			

REFERENCES

Bhowmik, T. K., Parui, S. K., Bhattacharya, U., & Shaw, B. (2006, December). An HMM based recognition scheme for handwritten Oriya numerals. In *9th International Conference on Information Technology (ICIT'06)* (pp. 105-110). IEEE.

Chang, C. C. (2011). LIBSVM: a library for support vector machines. *ACM Transactions on Intelligent Systems and Technology, 2*. Retrieved from http://www. csie. ntu. edu.tw/~cjlin/libsvm

Chaudhuri, B. B., Pal, U., & Mitra, M. (2002). Automatic recognition of printed Oriya script. *Sadhana, 27*(1), 23–34. doi:10.1007/BF02703310

Dalal, N., & Triggs, B. (2005, June). Histograms of oriented gradients for human detection. In *International Conference on computer vision & Pattern Recognition (CVPR'05)* (Vol. 1, pp. 886-893). IEEE Computer Society. 10.1109/CVPR.2005.177

Dash, K. S., Puhan, N. B., & Panda, G. (2015). Handwritten numeral recognition using non-redundant Stockwell transform and bio-inspired optimal zoning. *IET Image Processing, 9*(10), 874–882. doi:10.1049/iet-ipr.2015.0146

Dash, K. S., Puhan, N. B., & Panda, G. (2016). BESAC: Binary External Symmetry Axis Constellation for unconstrained handwritten character recognition. *Pattern Recognition Letters, 83*, 413–422. doi:10.1016/j.patrec.2016.05.031

Govindan, V. K., & Shivaprasad, A. P. (1990). Character recognition—A review. *Pattern Recognition, 23*(7), 671–683. doi:10.1016/0031-3203(90)90091-X

Jindal, M. K., Sharma, R. K., & Lehal, G. S. (2007). Segmentation of horizontally overlapping lines in printed Indian scripts. *International Journal of Computational Intelligence Research, 3*(4), 277–286. doi:10.5019/j.ijcir.2007.109

Kale, K. V., Deshmukh, P. D., Chavan, S. V., Kazi, M. M., & Rode, Y. S. (2013, October). Zernike moment feature extraction for handwritten Devanagari compound character recognition. In *2013 Science and Information Conference* (pp. 459-466). IEEE.

Kimura, F., Wakabayashi, T., Tsuruoka, S., & Miyake, Y. (1997). Improvement of handwritten Japanese character recognition using weighted direction code histogram. *Pattern Recognition, 30*(8), 1329–1337. doi:10.1016/S0031-3203(96)00153-7

Kundu, A., He, Y., & Chen, M. Y. (1998). Alternatives to variable duration HMM in handwriting recognition. *IEEE Transactions on Pattern Analysis and Machine Intelligence, 20*(11), 1275–1280. doi:10.1109/34.730561

Mantas, J. (1986). An overview of character recognition methodologies. *Pattern Recognition, 19*(6), 425–430. doi:10.1016/0031-3203(86)90040-3

Mishra, T. K., Majhi, B., Sa, P. K., & Panda, S. (2014). Model based odia numeral recognition using fuzzy aggregated features. *Frontiers of Computer Science, 8*(6), 916–922. doi:10.100711704-014-3354-9

Mitra, C., & Pujari, A. K. (2013). Directional decomposition for odia character recognition. In *Mining Intelligence and Knowledge Exploration* (pp. 270–278). Cham: Springer. doi:10.1007/978-3-319-03844-5_28

Mitra, C., & Pujari, A. K. (2013). Directional decomposition for odia character recognition. In *Mining Intelligence and Knowledge Exploration* (pp. 270–278). Cham: Springer. doi:10.1007/978-3-319-03844-5_28

Nasrabadi, N. M. (2007). Pattern recognition and machine learning. *Journal of Electronic Imaging, 16*(4), 049901. doi:10.1117/1.2819119

Pal, U., & Chaudhuri, B. B. (2001). Machine-printed and hand-written text lines identification. *Pattern Recognition Letters, 22*(3-4), 431–441. doi:10.1016/S0167-8655(00)00126-4

Pal, U., & Chaudhuri, B. B. (2004). Indian script character recognition: a survey. *Pattern Recognition, 37*(9), 1887-1899.

Pal, U., Jayadevan, R., & Sharma, N. (2012). Handwriting recognition in indian regional scripts: A survey of offline techniques. *ACM Transactions on Asian Language Information Processing, 11*(1), 1–35. doi:10.1145/2090176.2090177

Pal, U., Wakabayashi, T., & Kimura, F. (2007, December). A system for off-line Oriya handwritten character recognition using curvature feature. In *10th international conference on information technology (ICIT 2007)* (pp. 227-229). IEEE. 10.1109/ICIT.2007.63

Patra, P. K., Nayak, M., Nayak, S. K., & Gobbak, N. K. (2002). Probabilistic neural network for pattern classification. In *Proceedings of the 2002 International Joint Conference on Neural Networks. IJCNN'02 (Cat. No. 02CH37290)* (Vol. 2, pp. 1200-1205). IEEE.

Plamondon, R., & Srihari, S. N. (2000). Online and off-line handwriting recognition: A comprehensive survey. *IEEE Transactions on Pattern Analysis and Machine Intelligence, 22*(1), 63–84. doi:10.1109/34.824821

Senapati, D., Rout, S., & Nayak, M. (2012, July). A novel approach to text line and word segmentation on odia printed documents. In *2012 Third International Conference on Computing, Communication and Networking Technologies (ICCCNT'12)* (pp. 1-6). IEEE. 10.1109/ICCCNT.2012.6396063

Sethi, I. K., & Chatterjee, B. (1977). Machine recognition of constrained hand printed Devanagari. *Pattern Recognition*, 9(2), 69–75. doi:10.1016/0031-3203(77)90017-6

Sethy, A., Patra, P. K., & Nayak, D. R. (2018). Off-Line Handwritten Odia Character Recognition Using DWT and PCA. In Progress in Advanced Computing and Intelligent Engineering (pp. 187-195). Springer. doi:10.1007/978-981-10-6872-0_18

Sharma, N., Pal, U., Kimura, F., & Pal, S. (2006). Recognition of off-line handwritten devnagari characters using quadratic classifier. In *Computer Vision, Graphics and Image Processing* (pp. 805–816). Berlin: Springer. doi:10.1007/11949619_72

Sinha, R. M. K., & Mahabala, H. N. (1979). Machine recognition of Devanagari script. *IEEE Transactions on Systems, Man, and Cybernetics*, 9(8), 435–441. doi:10.1109/TSMC.1979.4310256

Tripathy, N., & Pal, U. (2006). Handwriting segmentation of unconstrained Oriya text. *Sadhana*, 31(6), 755–769. doi:10.1007/BF02716894

Chapter 11
Image Enhancement:
Application of Dehazing and Color Correction for Enhancement of Nighttime Low Illumination Image

Rasmita Lenka
KIIT University (Deemed), India

Koustav Dutta
KIIT University (Deemed), India

Asimananda Khandual
(iD) https://orcid.org/0000-0002-9357-9749
College of Engineering and Technology, India

Soumya Ranjan Nayak
(iD) https://orcid.org/0000-0002-4155-884X
Chitkara University, India

ABSTRACT

This chapter describes a novel method to enhance degraded nighttime images by dehazing and color correction method. In the first part of this chapter, the authors focus on filtering process for low illumination images. Secondly, they propose an efficient dehazing model for removing haziness Thirdly, a color correction method proposed for color consistency approach. Removing nighttime haze technique is an important and necessary procedure to avoid ill-condition visibility of human eyes. Scattering and color distortion are two major problems of distortion in case of hazy image. To increase the visibility of the scene, the authors compute the preprocessing using WLS filter. Then the airlight component for the non-uniform illumination presents in nighttime scenes is improved by using a modified well-known dark-channel prior algorithm for removing nighttime haze, and then it uses α-automatic color equalization as post-processing for color correction over the entire image for getting a better enhanced output image free from haze with improved color constancy.

DOI: 10.4018/978-1-7998-0066-8.ch011

INTRODUCTION

Main degradation of outdoor images occurs due to bad atmospheric phenomena such as hazy or foggy weather effect. Scattering of atmospheric particles reduces the visibility in terms of color variation contrast and makes difficult to recognize the object's prominent features to be identified by human and computer vision systems. So haze process yield pour visibility in day as well as night time or on low dim light effect. In the past few years images taken from worst weather situations and restoring them has made greater impact and progress. These image restorations are vital in various outdoor applications like surveillance, intelligent vehicles, object recognition, and remote sensing. Due to the ambiguity between the unknown depth of haze and the object underlying scene haze removal is very difficult. Another major issue related to haze images is perceivability degradation due to lag of missing information in terms of color effect due to effect of low illumination.

Considering into account of the illumination characteristics of night-time imaging, a modified algorithm for image enhancement is proposed in this chapter. In the first phase of proposed method Weighted Least-Squares (WLS) is used for filtering application to visualize the fine detail within an image respectively by Perona et. al (1900). WLS is an edge preserving filter which computes detail layers and recombines them with approximate pixel intensity value. The dehazing method based on Prior method is adopted as the key parameters of dehazing method using the local patch process Tarel et. al (2009) to obtain the better conditions of nighttime imaging. The illumination level of nighttime hazy image can be artificially enhanced through flexibly selecting the color correction method. In contrast to the classical model of color transfer with the strategy of overall to overall transfer, the modified model focuses on the different characteristics of various regions in the original image, and it works well even though the nighttime image is interfered by various artificial light sources. Various preprocessing methods are providing in terms of histogram, bilateral histogram, spatial filtering, Homo-morphic filtering. But in this chapter, the application of edge preserving application is done for better result. Similarly, for dehazing Presented by Perona et. al (1900) in order to use for haze removal methods are based on a) Image Enhancement b) Image Fusion c) Image restoration. The main object of haze removal algorithms is to enhance and restore the exact information of the scene from hazy image. In a haze removal model, primarily a haze density distribution map of hazy image is created. It enables to segment the hazy image into scenes according to generated density distribution function improving the scene with proper brightness, contrast and information contest of image. Here in, we focus to find methods to enhance and restore the dehazed images. Visibility restoration plays an important role in image processing applications.

Based on restoration methods for dehazing many methods are open to new avenues for the image degradation and scrutinize the imaging procedure, then recover the scene by an inverse transformation. Due to the use of better assumptions and priors single image dehazing has made progress efficiently. With the progression of innovation, numerous single image Haze removal strategies have been proposed based on Additional information, multiple images methods, and prior knowledge. Various models as described further are taken as reference in our method. Fattal (2014) strategy was based on Independent Component Analysis. Tarel et. al (2009) presented visibility restoration strategy depending on linear operations computed by numerous parameters for alteration. Kaiming et. al (2011) proposed an image dehazing method using cloudiness combined with Dark and re-estimated by soft matting. Tripathi et. al (2012) presented a novel effective mist expulsion algorithm with a pre-processing step as histogram equalization individually. Multi-scale fusion approach is deployed for dehazing Ancuti et. al (2013) and Wang et. al (2014) in terms of white adjustment, and a differentiate upgrading utilizing two original hazed pictures. Farbman et. al (2008) once more proposed a modern haze removal method for a picture employing a neighborhood color-line demonstrate that exhibit a one-dimensional conveyance of pixels of little picture patches. He employed a 'Gamma variable' adjustment to re-establish the color images with tall high precision at lower commotion levels as it were, but the picture limits the execution of color-line dehazing algorithm like other strategies in sky region. Color distortion corresponds to the varying degrees of attenuation encountered by light traveling in different medium. This means that the colour correction is not a linear transformation Economopoulos et. al (2010). Many underwater image enhancement techniques are embedded with colour correction algorithms. But some authors are only confined to colour correction techniques, which are discussed here. Hou et. al (2007) enhanced the colour of the underwater image using Markov Random Field (MRF). The algorithm used training image patches to colour correct the images. It has training image patches which are both bluish and original colored image patches. For each input image patch closest patches are selected. The color value of center of each estimated maximum probability patch is assigned to the corresponding pixel in output image. Farbman et. al (2008) presented algorithm which is based on the modeling of the color modification by the water. Backscattered component is not considered in this algorithm. All the discussed method is time consuming, so it is improved by new approach for image colorization very fast, named αACE presented by Imatiyaz et. al (2017) are also taken care in this chapter.

BACKGROUND OF RELATED WORK

Various preprocessing methods provide in terms of histogram, bilateral histogram, spatial filtering, Homo-morphic filtering. But in this chapter application of edge preserving application is done for better result. Similarly, for dehazing by Perona et. al (1900) that are used for haze removal methods are based on a) Image Enhancement b) Image Fusion c) Image restoration. The main object of haze removal algorithms is to enhance and restore the exact information of the scene from hazy image. In a haze removal model, primarily a haze density distribution map of hazy image is created. It enables to segment the hazy image into scenes according to generated density distribution function improving the scene with proper brightness, contrast and information contest of image. Here in, we focus to find methods to enhance and restore the dehazed images. Visibility restoration plays an important role in image processing applications.

Based on restoration methods for dehazing many methods are open to new avenues for the image degradation and scrutinize the imaging procedure, then recover the scene by an inverse transformation. Due to the use of better assumptions and priors single image dehazing has made progress efficiently. With the progression of innovation, numerous single image Haze removal strategies have been proposed based on Additional information, multiple images methods, and prior knowledge. Various models as described further are taken as reference in our method. Fattal (2014) strategy was based on Independent Component Analysis. Tarel et. al (2009) presented visibility restoration strategy depending on linear operations computed by numerous parameters for alteration. Kaiming et. al (2011) proposed an image dehazing method using cloudiness combined with Dark and re-estimated by soft matting. Tripathi et. al (2012) presented a novel effective mist expulsion algorithm with a pre-processing step as histogram equalization individually. Multi-scale fusion approach is deployed for dehazing Ancuti et. al (2013) and Wang et. al (2014) in terms of white adjustment, and a differentiate upgrading utilizing two original hazed pictures. Farbman et. al (2008) once more proposed a modern haze removal method for a picture employing a neighborhood color-line demonstrate that exhibit a one-dimensional conveyance of pixels of little picture patches. He employed a 'Gamma variable' adjustment to re-establish the color images with tall high precision at lower commotion levels as it were, but the picture limits the execution of color-line dehazing algorithm like other strategies in sky region. Color distortion corresponds to the varying degrees of attenuation encountered by light traveling in different medium. This means that the colour correction is not a linear transformation Economopoulos et. al (2010). Many underwater image enhancement techniques are embedded with colour correction algorithms. But some authors are only confined to colour correction techniques, which are discussed here. Hou et. al (2007) enhanced the colour of the underwater image using Markov Random Field (MRF). The algorithm used training image patches to colour correct the images. It has training image patches which are both bluish and original colored image patches .For each input image patch closest patches are selected. The color value of center of each estimated maximum probability patch is assigned to the corresponding pixel in output image. Farbman et. al (2008) presented algorithm which is based on the modeling of the color modification by the water. Backscattered component is not considered in this algorithm.

HAZE REMOVAL MODEL FOR IMAGE RESTORATION

In this chapter a fusion process of filter application, haze removal algorithm and improvement of color restoration is applied to obtain an image free from haze and restoration of color components is achieved by αACE represented in Figure 1. The details discussion can be made in several sub-chapters in subsequent section. Apart from this the algorithm has used as color correction in the proposed model.

Figure 1. Model for image dehazing

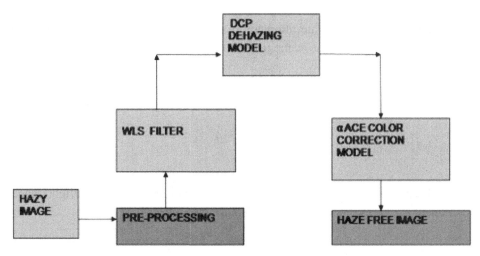

PROPOSED METHOD

The primary focus of this chapter is the development of a fast and robust exposure fusion approach based on local texture features computed from edge-preserving filter. WLS filter is used as a preprocessing technique that produces a composite image without blurring or loss of detail.

In WLS pre-processing is done. Edge preserving filters have received considerable attention in computational photography over the last decade. From the literature we have observed that the both techniques presented by both Ancuti et. al (2012) and Hou et. al (2007) are the most popular edge-preserving operators. Standard BLT uses distances of neighboring pixels in space and range. The space varying weighting function is computed at a space of higher dimensionality than the signal being filtered. As a result, such filters have high computational speed by Liu et. al (2017). The motivation behind weight map computation by Wang et. al (2017) is to yield nonlinear adaptive function for controlling the contribution of pixels from base layers and detail layers computed across all input exposures. Then the filtered image is dehazed by DCP (Dark channel prior) model and processed according to the steps given below

THEORETICAL CONCEPT OF DCP

According to his law, the impact of haze or fog is presented as:

$$I(i,j) = I_{an}(i,j) + A_{airlight}(i,j) \ (1).$$

On, the right-hand side value, attenuation, and air-light are the function of distance from capturing devices of the scene in form of:

$$I_{an}\left(I, j\right) = I_o\left(I, j\right) e^{-\beta l(I,j)} \ (2).$$

$$A_{airlight}\left(i, j\right) = I_{pS}\left(1 - e^{-\beta l(i,j)}\right) \tag{3}$$

Combining all the parameters of Attenuated image component and Airlight image component the Haze model can be entitled as:

Algorithm 1: Implementation procedure for dehazing model

- ◦ Read a low light mist or fog picture taken from output of WLS filter
- ◦ The shade of the air light - An is near the shade of the sky so simply pick the initial couple of pixels that are nearest to in Dark and take the normal pick top 0.01% brightest pixels oblivious channel
- ◦ Accommodate a vector of pixels in Dark of picture
- ◦ Sort the vector and need the last couple of pixels on the grounds that those are nearest to 1 named as A
- ◦ Re Estimate RT – reclassified Transmission utilizing A
- ◦ Get Radiance utilizing picture, 'T' transmission and Atmospheric light 'An' acquiring dehazed yield picture
- ◦ Get Radiance utilizing picture, 'RT' transmission and Atmospheric light 'A' acquiring Redefined dehazed yield picture
- ◦ Enhance the dehazed yield picture with boosting the picture pixels of shading data RGB
- ◦ utilizing local inclination methods
- ◦ Apply the dehazed output for color correction

Finally color correction is consider for color distortion corresponds to the varying degrees of attenuation encountered by light traveling in different medium with different wavelengths, rendering ambient environments dominated by a bluish tone. The algorithm has been implemented in following the ways. The first stage accounts for chromatic spatial adjustment and models two important mechanisms: bilateral inhibition and global/local adaptation by Imtiyaz et. al (2017). These two mechanisms form the basis of the appearance computation of each area in the image, taking into account their neighboring and dimensional relationship. Then, the second stage maximizes the image dynamic, normalizing the white at a global level and performing a global gray world behavior. The proposed αACE-improved the degraded images by color correction method with different color vision well than the state-of-the-art methods, also with little computation time. The proposed methods are suitable for real-time computing in night time also. This method also contains some problems such as the influence of the possible presence of an artificial lighting source is not considered.

RESULTS AND DISCUSSION

Subjective Analysis of Enhancement Results Considering Data Base Image and Real Time Image

It is observed from the table that quality index varies because of low illumination effect and devices standard parameter while capturing images. It is good for images taken from high quality devices. The images are taken from Samsung and Asus phone but at different illumination effect so there SSIM, MSSIM, FSIM, FSIMc varies a lot. The software simulation tool used is MATLAB R2014. Two reference images one low contrast, one high illumination image along with two other real images are taken from Samsung and Asus phone but at different illumination effect. Two methods are used for comparison of image clarity and visibility such DCP and combining DCP with color correction factor .Since these images have low intensity value they appear lighter as shown in Figure (2) and the corresponding quality assessment is shown in Table 1. The images 3 and 4 which are taken at night time from different mobiles the output carrying information and clarity is different in for both the algorithm as presented in Table 1. The proposed algorithms enhance the contrast of the input image of low as well as images taken from mobiles at same instant as in Figure 2(b), 2(c). The simulation results clearly show that the improved output images have more clarity than the output images processed with only DCP. The Image quality assessment (IQA) measure the image quality consistently with subjective evaluations The parameters such as PSNR SNR SSIM(structural-similarity index), MSSIM(multi-scale SSIM index) FSIM(feature-similarity index), FSIMc (feature-similarity index with chromatic) are calculated as an objective quality assessment .So both subjective analysis as shown in Figure (2) and objective analysis as shown in Table 1.

PROBLEMS

The model proposed in this chapter presents a good result for images taken at proper illumination condition. It is better than previous method where enhancement is done by applying Dehazing model as shown in Figure 2a with respect to Figure 2b for real time images also. In the proposed algorithm involves three step which consumes more time than the previous method. In this paper images are captured from different capturing devices which indicates for correction of illumination is also considerable factor. But the overall result analysis is good from subjective point of view

Figure 2. Result analysis of proposed scheme

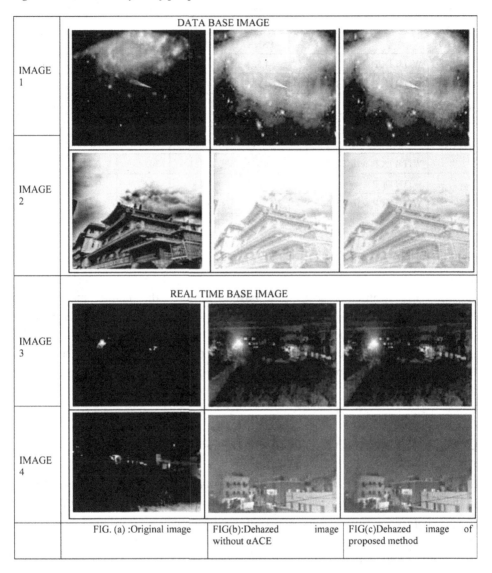

| | FIG. (a) :Original image | FIG(b):Dehazed image without αACE | FIG(c)Dehazed image of proposed method |

SOLUTIONS AND RECOMMENDATIONS

As hazy image is considered here so better illumination condition is difficult to provide as it depends on natural resources in some cases. So developing a more improved algorithm is necessary where filtering process that can be made adaptive in nature, the dehazing model can be performed by clearly getting depth and the improvement of contrast after haze removal process.

Table 1. Quality index assessment comparison between DCP Image and Dehazed image with αAce

SL N0		PSNR	SSIM	MSSIM	FSIM	FSIMc
IMAGE 1	WITH DCP	64.535	0.678	0.766	0.711	0.704
	WITH DCP & αACE	66.535	0.786	0.811	0.716	0.737
IMAGE 2	WITH DCP	62.534	0.567	0.678	0.714	0.697
	WITH DCP & αACE	65.533	0.768	0.798	0.756	0.735
IMAGE 3	WITH DCP	65.411	0.611	0.490	0.647	0.646
	WITH DCP & αACE	66.961	0.721	0.664	0.741	0.739
IMAGE 4	WITH DCP	61.011	0.430	0.572	0.865	0.841
	WITH DCP & αACE	66.313	0.623	0.752	0.863	0.842

FUTURE RESEARCH DIRECTIONS

As discussed in previous section we have considered the natural images which have some references data base and result is good .If this proposed method can be implemented in case where there is no reference image as shown in Figure 2a, 2b, and 2c and out can be further increased .Hence there should be more improved in the process to get more better quality image in output when it is consider as a non-reference image.

CONCLUSION AND FUTURE SCOPE

In this chapter we have adopted a new direction of restoration of hazy image based on both preprocessing and post processing in terms of WLS filter and color correction. In this chapter the proposal method is applied for images at different haze depth. But it can be extend to medical image processing confined to collect for information from color component and nuclear medical detection process. Developed in image acquisition process is also required as one of the major problem. Apart from its various invented machine learning approaches such as regression model can be applied to such problem domain. Further, other techniques are to be explored for betterdehazing process with proper image clarity.

ACKNOWLEDGMENT

The authors are sincerely thankful to the School of Electronics Engineering, KIIT, Deemed University Bhubeneswar. And we are also thankful to all the authors of the references.

NOTE: *In this chapter we presented an algorithm for color correction in dehazing process. The weighted least squares (WLS) filter is a well-known edge preserving smoothing technique, but its weights highly depend on the image gradients. It helps to calculate the smoothing weights for pixels based on both their isotropy and gradients.*

REFERENCES

Ancuti, C., & Ancuti, C. (2013). Single image dehazing by multi-scale fusion. *IEEE Transactions on Image Processing, 22*(8), 3271–3282. doi:10.1109/TIP.2013.2262284 PMID:23674449

Ancuti, C., Ancuti, C. O., Haber, T., & Bekaert, P. (2012). EnhancingUnderwater Images and Videos by Fusion. In *Conference on Computer Vision and Pattern Recognition (ICCVPR 2012)* (pp. 81-88). IEEE. 10.1109/CVPR.2012.6247661

Economopoulos, T. L., Asvestas, P. A., & Matsopoulos, G. K. (2010). Contrast enhancement of images using partitioned iterated function systems. *Image and Vision Computing, 28*(1), 45–54. doi:10.1016/j.imavis.2009.04.011

Farbman, Z., Fattal, R., Lischinski, D., & Szeliski, R. (2008). Edge-preserving decompositions for multi-scale tone and detail manipulation. *ACM Transaction on Graphics, 27*(3), 67:1-67:10.

Fattal, R. (2014). Dehazing using color-lines. *ACM Transactions on Graphics, 34*(1), 1–4. doi:10.1145/2651362

Hou, W., Gray, D. J., Weidemann, A. D., Fournier, G. R., & Forand, J. L. (2007) Automated Underwater Image Restoration and Retrieval of Related Optical Properties. In *International Symposium of Geoscience and Remote Sensing (ISGRS 2007)* (pp. 1889-1892). IEEE. 10.1109/IGARSS.2007.4423193

Imtiyaz, A., & Arun, K. (2017). Vision enhancement through single image fog removal. *Engineering Science and Technology, 20*, 1075-1083.

Kaiming, H., Jian, S., & Xiaoou, T. (2011). Single image haze removal using dark channel prior. *IEEE Transactions on Pattern Analysis and Machine Intelligence, 33*(12), 2341–2353. doi:10.1109/TPAMI.2010.168 PMID:20820075

Lagendijk, R., Biemond, J., & Boekee, D. E. (1988). Regularized iterative image restoration with ringing reduction. *IEEE Transactions on Acoustics, Speech, and Signal Processing, 36*(12), 1874–1888. doi:10.1109/29.9032

Levin, A., Lischinski, D., & Weiss, Y. (2008). A closed-form solution to natural image matting. *IEEE Transactions on Pattern Analysis and Machine Intelligence, 30*(2), 228–242. doi:10.1109/TPAMI.2007.1177 PMID:18084055

Liu, Y., Li, H., & Wang, M. (2017). Single image dehazing via large sky region segmentation and multiscale opening dark channel model. *IEEE Access: Practical Innovations, Open Solutions, 5*, 8890–8903. doi:10.1109/ACCESS.2017.2710305

Perona, P., & Malik, J. (1990). Scale-space and edge detection using anisotropic diffusion. *IEEE Transactions on Pattern Analysis and Machine Intelligence, 12*(7), 629–639. doi:10.1109/34.56205

Tarel, J., & Hautiere, N. (2008). Fast visibility restoration from a single coloror gray level image. In *Conference on Computer Vision and Pattern Recognition (ICCVPR 2008)* (pp. 2201-2208). IEEE.

Tarel, J. P., & Hautiere, N. (2009). Fast visibility restoration from a single color or gray level image. In *12th International Conference on Computer Vision (ICCV 2009)* (pp. 2201-2208). IEEE. 10.1109/ICCV.2009.5459251

Tripathi, A. K., & Mukhopadhyay, S. (2012). Single image fog removal using anisotropic diffusion. *IET Image Processing, 6*(7), 966–975. doi:10.1049/iet-ipr.2011.0472

Wang, W., Yuan, X., Wu, X., & Liu, Y. (2017). Fast image dehazing method based on linear transformation. *IEEE Transactions on Multimedia*.

Wang, Y., & Fan, C. (2014). Single image defogging by multi-scale depth fusion. *IEEE Transactions on Image Processing, 23*(11), 4826–4837. doi:10.1109/TIP.2014.2358076 PMID:25248180

KEY TERMS AND DEFINITIONS

Color Correction: Color distortion corresponds to the varying degrees of attenuation encountered by light traveling in medium with different wavelengths, rendering ambient hazy, low light environments dominated by a bluish tone. Color correction model used to compensate the attenuation discrepancy along the propagation path in various medium, automatic color enhancement algorithm enhanced images by reducing noised level, better exposedness of the dark regions, improved global contrast while the finest details and edges are enhanced significantly.

Dehazing Model: Images obtained under adverse weather conditions, such as haze or fog, typically exhibit low contrast and faded colors, which may severely limit the visibility within the scene. Restoring the image structure under the haze layer and recovering vivid colors out of a single image is known as dehazing process. Various models such as DCP and CAP are used as prior based dehazed model.

WLS Filter: The weighted least squares (WLS) filter is a well-known edge preserving smoothing technique, but its weights highly depend on the image gradients. It helps to calculate the smoothing weights for pixels based on both their isotropy and gradients.

Chapter 12
Analysis of Biomedical Image for Alzheimer's Disease Detection

Rashmi Kumari
Birla Institute of Technology, India

Shashank Pushkar
Birla Institute of Technology, India

ABSTRACT

Image analysis is giving a huge breakthrough in every field of science and technology. The image is just a collection of pixels and light intensity. The image capturing was done in two ways: (1) by using infrared sensors and (2) by using radiography. The normal images are captured by using the infrared sensors. Radiography uses the various forms of a light family, such as x-ray, gamma rays, etc., to capture the image. The study of neuroimaging is one of the challenging research topics in the field of biomedical image processing. So, from this note, the motivation for this work is to analyze 3D images to detect Alzheimer's disease and compare the statistical results of the whole brain image data with standard doctor's results. The authors also provide a very short implementation for brain slicing and feature extraction using Freesurfer and OpenNeuro dataset.

DOI: 10.4018/978-1-7998-0066-8.ch012

INTRODUCTION

The most common neurodegenerative disease is Alzheimer's (AD). It also goes a major health care issue of the future. During the next four decades, it has been estimated that the occurrence of AD will quadrivial the population of affected people from 27 million to 106 million vide Brookmeyer et al. (2007). According to Koenders et al. (2016), the count of Alzheimer patient has increased to 1 in 85 persons across the world. Any delay in detection and taking preventing step on Alzheimer disease lead to serious damage to brain cells. Intervention at an early stage of Alzheimer disease help in slowing down the process of mental disorder. In the initial stage, mild cognitive impairment (MCI) is found in the patient. It is a heterogeneous syndrome but it is not necessary that all MCI subjects develop into Alzheimer patients.

GENETIC FACTOR BEHIND ALZHEIMER'S DISEASE

Alzheimer's disease (AD) is a common form of neurodegenerative disease. Individuals who are impacted by this disease are aware of causes of dementia. The clinical characterization of Alzheimer's involves progressive loss of memory deficits in thinking, problem-solving and it has an impact on language abilities. Neuropathlogically AD can be characterized as progressive cortical atrophy due to neural loss and characteristic intracellular and extracellular deposits as insoluble tau and amyloid beta proteins vide Cauwenberghe et al. (2015), this is typically the process in which the disease manifests itself. Study of this disease based on genetically classification provides some important insights. Patients can be divided into two groups one is early onset and the other is late onset. For early onset, studies represent that there is a small set of genes that can be responsible for early onset of the disease but early-onset cases are fraction around five to 10 percent of total observed cases of these patients of early onset 2 to 10 percentage first display symptoms their 20s or their 30s. But the late onset of Alzheimer's tends to manifest itself after the age of 65. Late onset is pretty complex and is multifactorial, which means multiple genes could be involved and contributing to the disease and it has been found there is a pretty strong genetic predisposition. We have seen that about 30 to 48 percent of patients with Alzheimer's tend to have a first degree relatives that are also affected. So in trying to pinpoint which genetic risk are contributing to the disease, a number of Genome-wide association studies (GWAS) have been conducted GWAS helped in identifying as a community of 20 plus genetic risk loci, but these loci have small odds ratio. Hence none of them are really clear contenders to contribute to the disease. These loci include both common functional variants, and also rare and structural variants in that makeup. These are shown in Figure 1.

Genetics is a very important and interesting factor. Every individual is born with a particular set of genes and the assortment of genes that we have determined the number of things that might happen to us during life. Alzheimer's disease is no exception and there are different types of genetic effects on people's risk of developing Alzheimer's disease. Some of these can be very extreme or strongly predictive. These are associated with rather rare families who are at risk for developing early onset of Alzheimer's disease in a familial fashion. In this case, multiple people within a family will be affected. The age of onset is usually under the age of 50 and very often in the 30s as well as 40s. So, in these families, the fact is that a mutation in a gene really causes Alzheimer's disease. There are three genes that were identified in the 1990s that are responsible for early-onset familial Alzheimer's disease Cauwenberghe et al. (2015) and Brookmeyer et al. (2007).

Figure 1. Complex genetic makeup of AD

<u>MANIFOLD GENETIC FOUNDATION OF ALZHEIMER'S DISEASE</u>

I. Genetically split into two various groups: early-onset as well as late-onset.

II. Related exposure for first degree relatives is 3.5 – 7.5

III. 30-48% of AD patients have a damaged first-degree relative.

Early-onset AD:	Late-onset AD:

• For 2-10% of patients first significant occur in their 20s or 30s.
 • Four genes details for 5-10% of early onset AD:
     o APP
     o PSEN1
     o PSEN2
     o APOE
	• Declare later 65 years
	 • Multifactorial with stable genetic predisposition.
	 • GWAS have classify 20+ genetic risk loci along short odds ratios (1.1-2.0 per risk allele) together with two trivial functional variants as well as rare and structural variants

BIOLOGICAL BEHAVIOUR OF ALZHEIMER'S DISEASE

A centurial, German doctor, Alois Alzheimer's spotted anomalies in brain sections from patients with dementia. Since then people have been studying the strange plaques and tangles in the hope that we could one day understand and cure Alzheimer's disease. Inside Alzheimer's disease plaques is insoluble deposit the peptide of the tangles called amyloid beta or Abeta. They are formed when a protein called amyloid precursor protein is sequentially separated by two enzymes beta as well as gamma-secretase. Other molecules are generated by this cleavage and may show an act in the disease but Abeta is the main culprit. Abeta tends to misfold and become sticky eventually clumping together to form soluble oligomers. Some of these aggregates into large fibrils that deposited in the brain as plaques vide Tobin (1987). The oligomers come in several forms or species. We do not know which species are toxic, but research shows that they weaken communication and plasticity at synapses. This could stop the brain from forming or retrieving memories. Neurons are not only cells affected in Alzheimer's disease, astrocytes and microglia also play a role. Microglia are immune cells that clear our waste and prune synapses during development. Microglia take up Abeta but they also get activated by it triggering the release of inflammatory cytokines that can damage neurons. The microglia also start to remove synapses by phagocytosis. As synapses start to misfunction and neuron die, an abnormal pattern of activity emerge and eventually the brain cannot process and store information properly. Another key feature of Alzheimer's disease is neurodegeneration. In this neuron death is triggered by Abeta, but some time Abeta's effects seem to be mediated by another protein like Tau component. A healthy neuron, molecules are carried along the axon on a series of tracks made by microtubules and established by Tau. But in Alzheimer's disease, Tau is modified, causing it to dissociate from the microtubules, adopt an abnormal shape and move from the axon to the cell body. Like Abeta, Tau comes in a variety of forms and we do not know which one contribute to what type of disease. According to a neurologist, Tau will remain soluble, or stick together and make a tangled structure in the brain. Eventually, these processes kill the neuron. Another problem seen in animal models is that misfolded Tau protein can spread, across synapses into healthy neurons. There they make healthy Tau proteins which start to misfold as well, spreading the pathology across the brain. The pattern of spreading through the different brain regions matching the changing symptoms from early to late stage of Alzheimer's disease. This pattern also reflects how certain neurons are more vulnerable than other dying neurons. Despite these advances in our understanding of Alzheimer's disease, no cure of AD exists. While drugs are being developed to target Amyloid Beta or Tau, it is unclear whether they will eventually be successful in treating the disease. There is only one certainty: continued support for basic and clinical research will enable us one day to diagnose and treat this devastating condition.

EVOLUTION OF ALZHEIMER'S DISEASE

Curing of Alzheimer's disease (AD) is one of the most challenging tasks. Researchers are trying to understand the main mechanism of the brain. The brain plasticity is a very important mechanism in the brain hippocampus. This mechanism is really elaborate on learning as well as memory functions. The question arises: what are the mechanisms that initiate experience the gradual transition of physiology to pathology? Most of them are unknown. Alzheimer's disease (AD) is the biggest frequent and common form of Dementia. In the last 10 years, unfortunately, all the clinical trials fail. Doctors are trying to understand why it happens, and if you are looking through the research during the last 50 years, it is clear that Alzheimer's disease (AD) is uncommon of the serious problems for every individual vide Ng et al. (2007). So, Pharmacist tried to design drugs which help to reduce the plaques in the brain. But it didn't work out and if you reckon current research it clearly shows the dysfunction of synapses. According to Ming et al. (2005), the neurons in the brain are really the primary cause of the disease. The reduction of synapse inside the brain will be caused by the cognitive decline in remembering things. Hence the question is arises: What will initiate the synaptic loss? Loss of synaptic integrity is combined with the pathogenesis of Alzheimer's disease (AD). However, it also correlates with cognitive decline in amyotrophic lateral sclerosis (ALS). Synaptic loss is the strongest pathological cognitive decline in the frontal cortex and it can predict whether or not someone would have a cognitive problem as well as the motor problem in ALS. According to the neurologist, it is found that people who had cognitive problems, as well as their motor symptoms, did have significantly lower synapse density in BA9 which is frontal cortex than people who only had the motor symptoms. This support the hypothesis of synapse and generation of multiple neurodegenerative diseases. The brain consists of amyloid beta peptide that can be produced by different lenses short like 42 amino acids. During the last 20 years, many patients are suffering from Alzheimer's disease due to mutations which are given by the ancestor. The increase in production of toxic amyloid beta 42 has a high tendency of Alzheimer. So, the amyloid beta peptide can be the monomeric form which can be reduced by eating the legume in the daily diet. The novel studies view that higher levels of soluble oligomers can cause the end of the synaptic depression to vide Ng et al. (2007). So, reduction in synaptic activity and brain activity will end the memory decline. The huge progress has been done during the last 20 years in biochemistry related to Alzheimer's disease. Causes of Synaptic dysfunction are still not known. In fact, there are several key questions to be answered. In upcoming years we have to gather more information about ancestor based Alzheimer's disease (AD). The ratio of Alzheimer's disease patients is increasing every day. We have to find how the synaptic depression was caused and how the molecular mechanism is working for the synaptic change. The overall study of Alzheimer diseases (AD) is described in Figure 2.

COMPUTER SCIENCE SUPPORT IN ALZHEIMER'S DISEASE DIAGNOSIS

Biomedical image processing is used for the interpretation of Alzheimer's disease (AD). The ability of an earlier diagnosis of any disease is achieved by using different techniques of computer science. Various breakthroughs and researches have been done to increase the ability for diagnosis of Alzheimer's disease. Whereas doctors are used in doing brain slicing to examine the different blocks of the brain at the microscopic level. But using the Advance imaging tools will also provide the visualization of brain parts in 2D and 3D forms. We can see the amyloid image which is responsible for Alzheimer. There are various tools present to analyze the spinal fluid. Traditional techniques like lupuncture used a small needle to obtain

Figure 2. Method of study

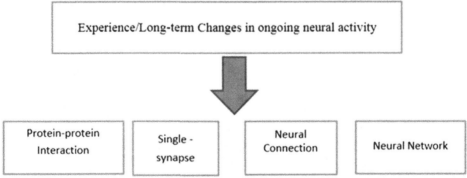

the spinal fluid sample. A critical way to measure in spinal fluid defines whether the patient is anguish from Alzheimer's disease (AD) or not.

According to Reisberg et al. (1982), scale vide the Global Deterioration Scale for assessment of primary degenerative dementia Alzheimer is divided into seven stages which are shown in Figure 3.

Stage 1: No Impairment: In this stage, memory and cognitive abilities are normal. If there are any impairments, they might only be slightly apparent to the patient themselves.

Stage 2: Very mild cognitive decline: In this stage, we can see some trouble in remembering the recent events or information, but it could be a more subtle thing like forgetting a word or misplacing things. Friend, family and medical workers cannot detect these lapses and change in thoughts. The reasons is that half of peoples over the age of 65 experience the loss of concentration and difficulty in recalling names or words.

Figure 3. Stages of Alzheimer Diseases

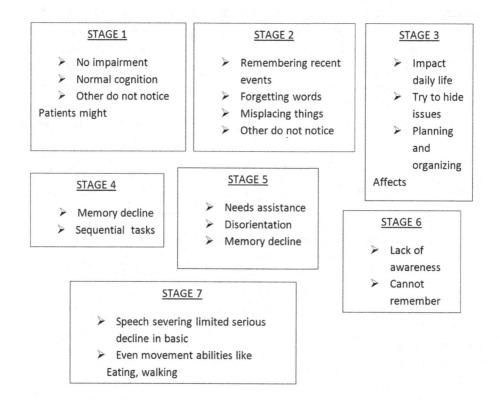

Stage 3: Mild Cognitive Impairment: According to Gauthier et al. (2006), it is a point where subtle difficulties can start to impact their daily life. The patients might consciously or even subconsciously try to hide these issues. They might remember what was just said or read and planning and organizing, which can all start to affect life at home or at work. It could be still difficult though, to diagnose Alzheimer's at this very early stage.

Stage 4: Mild Alzheimer's disease: This stage lasts about two years, and during these two years things like financials and math start to become very challenging. And the ability to remember recent events and what was just learned become increasingly difficult. The patient might have trouble carrying out tasks especially if there are specific sequences, like cooking and driving. But the patients are still usually able to recognize their family and friends although a diagnosis at this stage is usually accurate.

Stage 5: Moderate Alzheimer's disease: More drastic and the patients require some assistance. They will probably have trouble remembering things like an address or phone number and can be disoriented very easily regarding the time or place. This stage can last an average of about 1.5 years.

Stage 6: Moderately Severe Alzheimer's Disease: In this stage, there is a significant lack of awareness of current measures as well as the inability to remember the past and carry on the conversation; they will likely need help with essential regular functions like getting dressed, eating, as well as going to the bathroom. The patients will likely be unable to recall the names of family members yet will likely notice they are familiar. This stage lasts about 2.5 years

Stage 7: Severe Alzheimer's disease: Speech becomes severely limited, and there is a serious decline in basic abilities. Even movement abilities like eating, walking, sitting or standing up all start to fade as the disease starts to spread to more areas of the brain. Patients need extensive assistance in eating and drinking as they can lose the ability to discern when they are thirsty or hungry. Therefore they need total assistance and care around the clock for all functions of daily life. Due to these inabilities, they become much more susceptible to secondary complications such as diseases and infections especially pneumonia and falls. This final stage can last from one to two and a half years. But again it is very important to stress the flexibility in the timeline in these stages. Not all patients with Alzheimer's will experience this exact progression, some may deviate significantly from the expected duration with each stage and the disease itself.

BACKGROUND

Biology of Alzheimer's Disease

Alzheimer's disease (AD) is a continuous neurodegenerative disease in which dementia symptoms deliberately damage your past memories Tiraboschi et al. (2004), is written in the paper that Alzheimer disease is evolving by a collection of β-amyloid plaques as-well-as tau tangles. Luchsinger et al. (2019), hold that actual treatment is not available at present for preventing or reversing the disease. Social connections and regular mental activate can lower the risk of AD. But the reason behind these facts are not known to vide Stern et al. (2006) and Szekely et al. (2007), and Paradise et al. (2009) established that the neurogenesis arises from subventricular zone of the lateral ventricle as well as the subgranular zone of the hippocampus and progresses throughout life vide Ming and H. Song et al. (2005), Balu and Lucki et al. (2009). In the SGZ region, new cells are differentiated into both neurons and glial cells, as well as the new-born neurons, incorporate to the granule cell layer of the dentate gyrus vide Lledo et al. (2006), a growing body of clue hold the contribution of new born neurons to hippocampus-dependent memories vide Shors et al. (2001), Saxe et al. (2006). However, conflicting results have also been reported. For example, ablation of hippocampal neurogenesis has no effect on tasks including contextual fear memory and Morris water maze vide Shors et al. (2002), Snyder et al. (2005).

Classification Feature Extraction Approach

Classification feature extraction approach can be categorized by voxel method, vertex method and ROI method vide Zheng, et al. (2015). In the mid-1990s, Wright et al. (1995), started the study of the gray matter and the white matter voxel assessment. He used statistical methods. Voxel-based methods usually use statistics of voxel diffusion on large scale of brain tissues vide Vemuri et al. (2008), and Davatzikos et al. (2008), Fan et al. (2008), Kloeppel et al. (2008), Magnin et al. (2008), Leo Z et al., J Ye (2008), calculate the voxel importance histogram in large scale anatomical regions, which could be accessed by each of two image segmentation. Fan et al. (2007), Davatzikos C et al. (2007), Misra et al. (2009), proposed an additive parcellation method. In this method, the image space is apart into the better discriminative regions. Liu et al. (2015), suggested voxel-based morphometry (VBM). Currently, Liu et al. (2015), proposed a simulation method to predict the longitudinal brain morphological mutation in degenerative brains placed on VBM.

Clinical experiments lead to the conclusion that if we want to differentiate between MCI, NC, AD we require a volume of anatomical regions, as well as their vertex atrophy, vide Desikan RS et al. (2009), Querbes et al. (2009), Direct index of atrophy caused by dementia is defined by cortica thickness. Cortical thickness is measured by an elegant method given by Querbes et al. (2009), cortical thickness measurement helps in the cortical atrophy. Lerch et al. (2005), suggested a link between cortical atrophy and the changes examined by a microscope which observes the appearance of diseased cells in biological tissues. Desikan et al. (2006), divided the brain into parcels viz. neocortical and non-neocortical ROIs. He used the mean thickness and volume of each ROI as features. Methods based on ROI determine image features in major brain components e.g. corpus callosum, cingulum, fasciculus, and hippocampi. Neurodegeneration in AD starts in the medial temporal lobe and affects entorhinal cortex, hippocampi and limbic system. It extends to neocortical areas vide Braak et al. (1995), National Institutes of Health (NIH) (2005). Most of the researchers in this area hold the view that medical temporal atrophy is a sensitive AD biomarker vide Frisoni et al. (2010), CR et al. (2010). This is why in most of the studies use hippocampi as a marker of early AD vide Cuingnet et al. (2011).

CASE STUDY 1: AUTOMATED IMAGING MODALITIES OF DIAGNOSIS OF BIOMEDICAL ANALYSIS IN 3D IMAGES

Magnetic Resonance Imaging (MRI) is not an invasive test. It requires a powerful magnetic field as well as radio frequency pulses.

Brain MRI Mapping

The procedure is very simple, the patients to lay flat inside the MRI suite. And is provided with a cushion for your knees which will help in to take some pressure off from the back. The test is a bit noisy so patients are provided with some hearing protection gear. In this case, earplugs are given, there is also a call button facility which is required in case patient need to stop the test or want to talk with the technician. MRI is used to collect the brain image and therefore head is placed inside a head coil. The coil is nothing but a fancy antenna which uses to collect the MRI data. The table-like platform is raised and the head is placed in the center of the machine. Now, the rest of the body is still outside the MRI scanner. As per the Doctor's permission, the test proceeds, and contrast injection is injected. This procedure will normally take about half an hour and during this time the technologist will keep tracking your all date. Once the MRI is completed the technologists will re-enter the room and slide the table out of the machine, it will lower the table and take the head out from the coil. This is the whole scenario for the MRI scanning procedure.

Diagnosing Alzheimer's Disease

According to Cummings et al. (2007), diagnosis of Alzheimer diseases (AD) is conducted by the MRI. The magnetic field, as well as Radio Frequency Pulses, are used to build the virtual structure of all the internal parts of the brain. The soft tissues and detailed pictures of organs are used to predict the irregularity in brain condition which is associated with MCI to AD. In the prodromal stage of Alzheimer, the MRI examination of the brain is found to be normal. Basically, it affects the temporal and parietal lobes of the brain. The size of different areas of the brain may show a decrease during MRI scanning. Whether a person has Alzheimer's disease or not can be determined in a single test. According to Petersen et al. (2001), symptoms of Dementia help in the diagnosis of the disease. The Medical evaluation is conducted by using the medical history of the patient, mental status, physical and neurological exam, blood test and brain imaging. In the late '70s, most of the people develop a mild memory loss. According to neuroradiologist, it is a normal part of aging. A sign of dementia is the inability to recognize a person or the patient recognizes after some time. According to the Alzheimer's Association, 5.7 million Americans are suffering from Alzheimer's (AD). By 2050 this number is calculated to increase by nearly 14 million. More and more are people looking for the doctors for diagnosis? The doctors can only provide immediate reliefs while checking the MRI images. The neurologists cannot ensure that the patient is not suffering from cerebral infarction, stroke, old trauma, and unexpected brain tumor. But using advanced software for comparing the brain volume with a large database for predictions including gender and age for matching. The comparison can help doctors to know whether memory loss is related to Alzheimer's or not. Currently, the tremendous amount of research is going on in a country like the US, UK, India, etc. for the analysis of Alzheimer's (AD). Different medications are being developed to slow down the process of Alzheimer but there is no accurate diagnosis available to help the patient.

Advantages and Disadvantages of MRI

As with any form of medical measure, there are also a few "Pros" as well as "Cons" such as MRI is not an invasive imaging technique and doesn't involve exposure to ionizing radiation. The contrast material in some MRI has less probability to produce an allergic reaction when compared to the material based on iodine. However certain metal used in MRI examination cause problem. If a coil malfunction during the scan it causes serious damage to brain cells which cannot be recovered

fMRI (FUNCTIONAL MAGNETIC RESONANCE)

For a long period of time, we have not known anything about the brain. That's because it is extremely dense to measure the changes in electric signals during brain activity. In the year 1992, the invention of Functional magnetic resonance imaging (fMRI) done by a group of scientists in order to observe brain activity. Functional magnetic resonance (fMRI) imaging is also not an invasive approach to examining brain activity or in short it allows us to learn about what every single brain block.

Working Principle of fMRI

The fMRI is a magnetic field based imaging machine which is used to scan the brain block. It is a very powerful magnet, 10000 times stronger than the earth magnetic field. The brain is made up of neurons and these communicate with each other using electrical signals. Now a brain area becomes more progressive when the neurons inside that the brain area start sending more signals than before. For example, if you want to move your arm, the fMRI view that which brain area is lights up or become active so that you can know which brain area is mainly responsible for your arm movement. But it is not possible to measure electric signals directly from the scalp. To find the exact origin of the signal in the brain area by measuring the signal by overlaying signals that you actually want to measure. Now fMRI can solve the problem but it also involves three things:

- **Blood Neurons**: These have a pretty nifty trick after sleep. When they become active they need more oxygen which they get from red blood cells (RBC). So, what they do is that they actually widen the blood vessels surrounding them in order to attract more oxygenated blood. That means that a neuron becomes more active with oxygen concentration.

Table 1. Pros and cons

Modality	Advantages	Disadvantages
fMRI	• Spatial resolution is good • Not invasive • Easily available	• Almost low temporal resolution • It cannot trace neurotransmission-related PET

- **Water and Spins**: Our bodies are mainly made up of water and each water molecules has a spin orientation of hydrogen atom. The magnetic property is generated by the spin orientation of the molecules. Now we all know that how the compass always points to the north because it always aligns with Earth magnetic field. The same thing is done with water molecules but you need a much stronger magnet like fMRI machine. Our bodies are mainly made up of water. Each water molecule has something called a spin which gives its magnetic property. For example, the compass always points to the north because it wants to realign with the earth's magnetic field. The same thing holds for the water molecules but it needed a much stronger magnet like fMRI machine. Suppose, you want to align the water molecules in your strong magnetic field on same position and direction then you add a little bit of energy in the form of radio waves. You can actually force them for the alignment. If you want to stop sending radio waves all the molecules regained their original position. It shows that radio waves can add up small energy to strong signal for the alignment.

- **Magnetic Field Disturbances**: Small interference in the magnetic field cause a serious problem for the patient. Suppose that a magnetic field has a small disturbance that causes water molecules to desynchronize faster. For example, two coins are spinning on your desk and one of them constantly bumping into other objects then one will stop spinning earlier. Similarly, for water molecules also it turns out that deoxygenated blood causes such disturbances while oxygenated blood doesn't. Now we can put everything together, a brain area becomes more active, causes the blood vessels riding meaning more oxygenated blood flowing towards it. It means less magnetic field disturbances. The spins synchronizing for a longer period of time and the signal that we want to measure staying for a long duration of instant. In other words, what fMRI is doing is that it looks at a particular brain area and repeatedly measures how long the signals stay and when that signal start staying longer. We know there is more oxygen and we know that the brain area is becoming more active

Just twenty year ago we hardly knew anything about the brain but with fMRI, we are able to learn so many things. Every single brain area is responsible for movement in the body. The scientists are already looking at the next frontier and brain research. Now the current work is going on:

- How the brain areas are connected to each other?
- How they work together depending on the task goal?

The network of connections inside the brain would have tremendous value. One day one will be able to diagnose depression by just looking at how the brain map of patients differs from a healthy people's brain map. It could also help to explain how a tiny brain is capable of so many amazing things. Computer and Brain scientists are already working together to build new powerful computers that mimic the human brain. All these advancements and many more were largely made possible by fMRI (Functional Magnetic Resonance Imaging).

Advantages and Disadvantages of fMRI

PET (Positron Emission Tomography)

Positron emission tomography (PET) is used to represent images of diminutive changes in the body's Meta. The procedure for scanning is as follows: a PET scan will have restrictions on what a patient can eat or drink before the start of the procedure. Detailed information on diet is especially given by the technologist. Another precaution taken by the doctor does not bring any children or pregnant women inside the room. The technologist first checks the blood sugar and then the radioactive tracer called FDG is injected. The radiotracer is circulated with blood for about 45 minutes. After that, the PET scan is taken. After the examination, you will not feel anything. You have to body drink plenty of fluids to flush the radiotracer. A radiologist will review the report sent to the physician for thorough evaluation. The computed tomography images are used to allow the physicians to identify the correct locus size as well as the shape of the tissue or else tumor. PET scans are often used in to detect the cancer cell. Whereas, PET scan of the brain is used to evaluate the patients suffering from memory loss, seizure problems, or brain tumors. PET scans of the heart are used to check the blood flow inside the heart muscle and it also helps to evaluate the signs of the heart disease.

Workflow of PET Scan

A PET scan uses a radioactive tracer to make 3D images of the body. The radioactive tracers are administered to the body of the patient through intravenous injection. The tracer consist of molecules that are lightly bounded to an isotope. The molecules can interact with specific protein-sugar in the body. If a doctor suspect's the sign of cancer or wants to know cancer's cell growth. Then the molecule is FDG which is a modified form of glucose. When tissues absorb a lot of glucose it indicates a cancerous tumor. The isotope produces small particles called positrons. Positrons interact with surrounding electrons resulting in the complete annihilation of both particles which release two photons. The detectors in the PET scanner measures theses photons movements. It is used for creating an image.

Advantages and Disadvantages of PET

Advantages

- To study bodily function in biomedical processes, PET scan is able to detect disease easily before any sign and symptoms show through the biomedical process. Hence PET scan is more effective as compared to another medical imaging test.
- PET scan can easily find metabolic function and can also easily determine how far the disease has spread when compared to biopsy and other exploratory surgeries.
- PET scan is an effective biomedical tool that can help in to minimize the number of unnecessary surgeries.
- PET scan are very effective tools for easy detection of Alzheimer's, epilepsy and other mental illnesses.
- PET scan is exposed relatively very low radiation dosage as compared to other forms of CT scan.
- Through the infection from a medical procedure, people are scared. PET scan is the best options for analysis of the body.

Table 2. Comparison between MRI and PET

	MRI	PET
Patient Advantages Drawbacks	• The non – invasive method • Free Radiation combine with imaging • Consist of two possibly anatomical as well as biochemical information from MR spectroscopy. • Smaller patient bore due to the claustrophobia • Interior body contraindicated in patients for loose metal foreign bodies.	• Using PET scanners used for both anatomical as well as functional information • High acquisition scan • Direction by intervenes injection related to radiopharmaceutical compounds
Imaging Advantages Drawbacks	• Among good spatial resolution major soft tissue imaging. • Any oblique plane is the correct multiplanar capability to image • Distortion in MR image • Being dosimetry due to lack of electron density information • To make DDR (digitally reconstructed radiographs) due to lack of cortical bone information.	• Both functional as well as biological information. • Either conventional imaging may have diagnostic value. • Major increase asses locoreginal lymph node correctly than CT • Finite spatial resolution • Lesion detectability • Large interobserver variability • The variable result of thresholds
Machine Advantages Drawbacks	• Strength as well as positioning for RT, easier patient access for open MRI system • Shorter bore than CT(50cm) • Twisted table top	• Comparative high bore (70cm) • Smooth table top • Protecting to escape radiation risk

Disadvantages

- PET scan is not very good especially to pregnant ladies because of the radioactive elements used in the scanning process.
- PET is an expensive treatment compared to another form of medical imaging. The PET instrument (cyclotron) are attached to it which emits radioactive rays.
- To create radio-isotopes for radioactive rays is not good as well as a radioactive component at the time of scan are not long lasting. That's Why PET imaging is required a number of times again and again.

CASE STUDY 2: APPLICATION OF MACHINE LEARNING IN BIOMEDICAL IMAGE PROCESSING

Machine Learning Used in Medical Image Analysis

Analysis of medical image is being widely used in the modern system of disease diagnosis. With the increase of patient's data, we face new challenges and get a new opportunity for a different stage of the clinical routine. Use of machine learning helps in automatic analysis of patient's data. Modern techniques of Machine learning are used for automatic measurement of anatomy and anomalies. It can monitor disease progression semantic navigation and visualization. It can also develop a natural user interface for Doctor's, computer-aided diagnosis and personalized medicine. Here, we will talk about the analysis of radiological images which is used in medical science. But in many cases, patients undergo medical scans such as CT scans, Magnetic Resonance Scans (MRI) which is used for looking inside of your body. PET is another type of scan which uses the ultrasound for scanning. There are many ways of acquiring medical images. Applying modern machine learning technique to the automatic analysis of medical scans like CT scan of the patient it helps for computed tomography. With a patients scan image, you can see the different horizontal views and different side views of the patient. First of all, we want to automatically identify the spine parts of the patients. After that, it is important to identify as well as analyze whether there are broken vertebrae. Because the spine is a natural coordinate system for the patients. So, it is very helpful. They already have a good idea of where the spine is and not only have that you have an exact name for each of the vertebrae. So, any trained radiologist will able to identify the location. Using the machine learning technique we use the labeled data of patients. Using some machine learning algorithms is used to learn the model by using the labeled data of the patients. Three-dimensional (3D) and four-dimensional (4D) imaging play an important role in computer-aided diagnosis treatment. At the same time progress in (Supervised and unsupervised), machine learning techniques lead to the solution many old problems by computer-vision based machine learning.

Artificial Intelligence in Medical Image Classification

What is Artificial intelligence (AI)?

Artificial intelligence can be defined as vision, hope, and threat to the world. With the help of Artificial Intelligence image-based data analysis is used to extract more information for the diagnostic process. It also provides a way of treatment and decision support for any patient data. Artificial Intelligence can be used to detect various diseases. Using a simple body scan can provide enough data to detect any diseases. Doctors are trained for many years to do this type of diagnosis but the error rate is still higher. Artificial intelligence (AI) can diagnose disease better than any human being provided the datasets is correctly trained. This will lead to a considerable reduction in the rate of patient's death. Artificial intelligence thus is a powerful tool for the diagnosis of any disease. In the current scenario, artificial intelligence start-ups are growing very fast in the field of healthcare. The radiologist regular disagree on their respective interpretation of medical images but artificial intelligence can do many things. It is estimated that the results are 10% more accurate than any average radiologist. The accuracy gap will only be increased by using more computing power. It also gets cheaper and applied in many countless subfields. Doctors also have to understand the patients' medical records and it can be a very complex task. A Natural Language Processing is a sub-branch of artificial intelligence that helps in to understand human language. It used for evaluation of thousands of medical records in optimal time. The objective of artificial intelligence is the diagnosis of patients without any preconceived socio-economic notions which can produce disparities in care. Today Computer's algorithms are performing the unbelievable task with a high degree of exactness using superhuman intelligence. This intelligence of computer is known as Artificial Intelligence (AI). AI will make a profound impact on human lives in the future. In spite of this, we have to phase big challenges in detecting and diagnosing, many fractal diseases such as cancer as well as other bacterial, viral and genetic diseases. The only way to save their lives is to make only the detection and diagnosis of diseases. If a person is suspecting the above types of diseases. Some expensive medical test like CTs, MRIs, fluorescent imaging is necessary. After the collecting of images, another expert physician analyses those images and talks to the patient. Thus the process requires several resources viz expert physician, medical imaging technologies. This expensive process is not suitable for developing country like India. It is better to solve this problem by using new techniques of Artificial Intelligence (AI).In traditional Artificial Intelligence (AI) approaches we require tens of thousands of very expensive medical images which are sent to the expert physician for the analyses. Using these two information's one can train the system using a deep neural network. In the new approach of Artificial Intelligence (AI) we start with a single medical image. From this image one figure out a very clever way to extract billions of information packet. Thus one convert one image into billions of training data points viz colors, pixels, geometry, etc. One starts with standard white light photograph acquired either from a DSL camera or a mobile phone for the patient. Then one overlay the billions of information packets mentioned above. One to this image creating something called composite image. This one requires only fifty composite images to train one's algorithm to high efficiencies. We can see that in this new process. We can provide a diagnosis using a white light photograph from the patient instead of expensive medical imaging technology. Traditional Artificial Intelligence was reached in data but poor in application

CASE STUDY 3: AUTOMATED 3D TOOLS USED IN BIO-MEDICAL ANALYSIS

Case Study Cannabis User and Controls

In this paper, the author uses the Freesurfer software. It is an open source software suitable for processing and analyzing (human) brain MRI images. The 3D features extraction packages like Neuroimaging analysis software package. It fully characterizes the anatomy of cortex thickness, folding patterns, ROIs, subcortical structure boundaries and longitudinal. The Surface extraction like Inter-subject Registration and Multi-modal integration like fMRI (task, rest, and retinotopy) and DTI tractography.

Working of Freesurfer

Freesurfer is an analysis suite for brain image segmentation vide Muschelli et al. (2018), the vast majority of our work is on MRI and brain imaging. Freesurfer is a fully automated pipeline tool to characterize the anatomy of brain blocks. Each block is well labeled by using the Freesurfer. Every macroscopically visible piece of brain block is generated by using a reasonably good input image. To measures the brain anatomy the input data is very reasonable in quality. The procedure is pretty much automated. Sometimes it also faces the failure modes. So, for the precaution, we always advise to look through their data and make sure that the results are what they except. If you are doing some type of group study and you find an effective interest in the analysis. Here, we use Freesurfer to analyze the different models for brain cortex. The brain is divided into two parts functional organization and structural organization. The cortex is just like sheet whose thickness is half a millimeter. However, voxel has a certain issue such as one single voxel can encompass information from two anatomically distinct areas. For example, if a single voxel encompasses two distinct gyri, this can make localization of fMRI activation much less accurate. The voxels and volumetric data are much harder to estimate structural properties such as gray matter thickness and gray matter volume to address this problem. We are going to use Freesurfer a program that reconstructs the cortical surface from the 3D volume. The reconstruction process converts this volume from 3D voxels to 2D triangles. The points of the triangle are called vertices and the lines connecting them are called edges. Each vertex contains a number indicating gray matter volume, thickness, areas, curvature as well as another surface of the brain.

Datasets Description

We are using Freesurfer to analyze a dataset from open source (fmri.org). Dataset consists of both cannabis users and control subject. The datasets are collected from the website openneuro.org. According to L. Koenders et al. (2016), Data comprises of Heavy cannabis users (N = 20, age baseline M = 20.5, SD = 2.1) as well as non-cannabis working healthy controls (N = 22, age baseline M = 21.6, SD = 2.45) endured a full psychological valuation and a T1- structural MRI scan at baseline as well as 3-years follow-up. Entire structural MRI scans were collected by 3T MRI scanner (Intera, Philips Healthcare, Best, and The Netherlands) through a phased array SENSE eight-channel receiver head coil. For all participant, a T1-weighted structural MRI image was attained (T1 turbo field echo, TR 9.6 s, TE 4.6 s, 182 slices, slice thickness 1.2 mm, FOV 256x256 mm, in-plane resolution 256x256 mm, flip angle 8°).

Procedure

Here we are going to discuss a single subject data out of 42 samples data size. We use a single virtual machine to find out the whole brain reconstruction process. The correlation analysis is used for comparison between two individuals. The separate time point is baseline and a follow-up session is used for longitudinal analysis of brain. Since it contains one of two different groups which can be compared to individual difference measures which can be used for correlation analyses, and three two separate time point a baseline and a follow-up session this can be used for longitudinal. Let's take a look at the directory structure in Figure 4. Each subject directory contains a baseline anatomical and a follow-up anatomical for this analysis. We have compared baseline anatomical scans of the cannabis users with the baseline anatomical scans for the control subjects. Freesurfer analyzes individual subjects or several subjects simultaneously (represented in Figure 5). Here, we have to cover the batch mode and custom options.

Figure 4. Representation of sample data

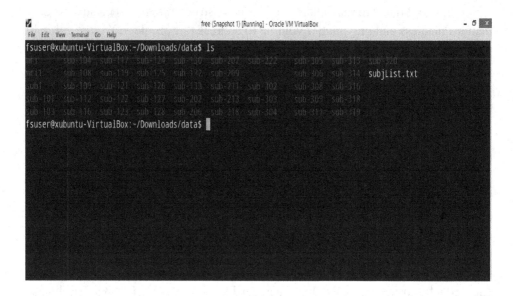

Figure 5. Representation of single set data

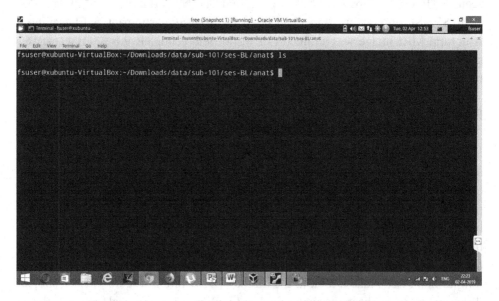

Figure 6, represents the individual difference within the data. Each subject directory contains a baseline directory anatomical and a follow-up anatomical. For this analysis, we compare the baseline anatomical scans of the cannabis users with baseline anatomical scans for the control subjects. Freesurfer can analyze

244

Figure 6. Reconstruction of brain 1

individual subjects or several subjects simultaneously. Here, we first create a text file of subject_list.txt by using the grep command. we then redirect to subject_list .txt, run the script to prepare the data for surf. Each subjects anatomical folder in the baseline session and then runs a recon-all command which is shown in Figure 6 and Figure 7. Here, 30 different reconstruction brain processing outputs are done if you notice that Freesurfer has not failed at any stage for reconstruction. For again the reconstruction of the result, you can go back and run a subset of those steps to save time. Note that all flag is omitted which will only convert the anatomical data set to (.mgz) format and then create subfolders for the Freesurfer analysis without any further pre-processing.

Here, we have implemented the segmentation process for one data sample. The same process is done for 42 different samples using Freesurfer 3D automated tool for reconstruction of the whole brain. The performance of Freesurfer is increased by using the high performance computing machine) or remote server. One major disadvantage regarding Freesurfer is its high computing time if using a single machine. It takes so long to analyse a single subject as shown above figure 6 and figure 7, that it might take 6 to 24 hours for single subject analysis. In the case of several subjects, processing can take weeks. This disadvantage can, however, be overcome using high performance computing machine.

Figure 7. Reconstruction of brain 2

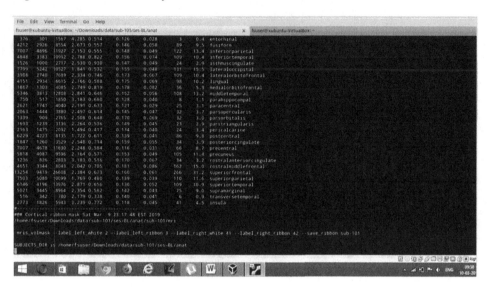

CONCLUSION

A brief introduction to Alzheimer's disease and its diagnosis by biomedical imaging has been presented. The last two sections aimed to provide the solutions and uses of biomedical imaging in the diagnosis of Alzheimer Diseases. The solutions are exhibited through three case studies. It evolves the machine learning technique to meet the challenges of modern health care system. Foremost diagnosis using biomedical imaging technology is a better track for prediction. The methods are used to quantify the value of care and it also evolves a shift from fee-for-service care to value-based care.

ACKNOWLEDGMENT

We are indebted to Prof. Mithilesh Kumar Singh, Dept. of Mathematics, Ranchi University for his valuable suggestions. And I would like to thanks Mr. Keshav Sinha, Dept. of Computer Science & Engg, for the valuable suggestion in technical parts of this book chapter.

REFERENCES

Balu, D. T., & Lucki, I. (2009). Adult hippocampal neurogenesis: Regulation, functional implications, and contribution to disease pathology. [PubMed]. *Neuroscience and Biobehavioral Reviews, 33*(3), 232–252. doi:10.1016/j.neubiorev.2008.08.007

Braak, H., & Braak, E. (1995). Staging of Alzheimer's disease-related neurofibrillary changes. *Neurobiology of Aging, 16*(3), 271–278.

Brookmeyer, R., Johnson, E., Ziegler-Graham, K., & Arrighi, H. M. (2007). Forecasting the global burden of Alzheimer's disease. [PubMed]. *Alzheimer's & Dementia, 3*(3), 186–191. doi:10.1016/j.jalz.2007.04.381

Cuingnet, R., Gerardin, E., Tessieras, J., Auzias, G., Lehéricy, S., & Habert, M. O. (2011). Automatic classification of patients with Alzheimer's disease from structural MRI: A comparison of ten methods using the ADNI database. *NeuroImage, 56*(2), 766–781.

Cummings, J. L., Doody, R., & Clark, C. (2007). Disease-modifying therapies for Alzheimer disease: Challenges to early intervention. [PubMed]. *Neurology, 69*(16), 1622–1634. doi:10.1212/01.wnl.0000295996.54210.69

Davatzikos, C., Resnick, S. M., Wu, X., Parmpi, P., & Clark, C. M. (2008). Individual patient diagnosis of AD and FTD via high-dimensional pattern classification of MRI. [PubMed]. *NeuroImage, 41*(4), 1220–1227. doi:10.1016/j.neuroimage.2008.03.050

Desikan, R. S., Cabral, H. J., Hess, C. P., Dillon, W. P., Glastonbury, C. M., Weiner, M. W., ... Fischl, B. (2009). Automated MRI measures identify individuals with mild cognitive impairment and Alzheimer's disease. [PubMed]. *Brain, 132*(8), 2048–2057. doi:10.1093/brain/awp123

Desikan, R. S., Ségonne, F., Fischl, B., Quinn, B. T., Dickerson, B. C., Blacker, D., ... Killiany, R. J. (2006). An automated labeling system for subdividing the human cerebral cortex on MRI scans into gyral based regions of interest. [PubMed]. *NeuroImage, 31*(3), 968–980. doi:10.1016/j.neuroimage.2006.01.021

Fan, Y., Batmanghelich, N., Clark, C. M., & Davatzikos, C. (2008). Spatial patterns of brain atrophy in MCI patients, identified via high-dimensional pattern classification, predict subsequent cognitive decline. [PubMed]. *NeuroImage, 39*(4), 1731–1743. doi:10.1016/j.neuroimage.2007.10.031

Fan, Y., Shen, D., Gur, R. C., Gur, R. E., & Davatzikos, C. (2007). COMPARE: Classification of Morphological Patterns Using Adaptive Regional Elements. [PubMed]. *IEEE Transactions on Medical Imaging, 26*(1), 93–105. doi:10.1109/TMI.2006.886812

Frisoni, G. B., Fox, N. C., Jack, C. R., Scheltens, P., & Thompson, P. M. (2010). The clinical use of structural MRI in Alzheimer disease. [PubMed]. *Nature Reviews. Neurology, 6*(2), 67–77. doi:10.1038/nrneurol.2009.215

Gauthier, S., Reisberg, B., Zaudig, M., Petersen, R. C., Ritchie, K., Broich, K., ... Winblad, B. (2006). Mild cognitive impairment. [PubMed]. *Lancet, 367*(9518), 1262–1270. doi:10.1016/S0140-6736(06)68542-5

Klöppel, S., Stonnington, C. M., Chu, C., Draganski, B., Scahill, R. I., Rohrer, J. D., ... Frackowiak, R. S. (2008). Automatic classification of MR scans in Alzheimer's disease. [PubMed]. *Brain, 131*(3), 681–689. doi:10.1093/brain/awm319

Koenders, L., Cousijn, J., Vingerhoets, W. A. M., van den Brink, W., Wiers, R. W., Meijer, C. J., ... de Haan, L. (2016). Grey Matter Changes Associated with Heavy Cannabis Use: A Longitudinal sMRI Study. [PubMed]. *PLoS One, 11*(5), e0152482. doi:10.1371/journal.pone.0152482

Lerch, J. P., Pruessner, J. C., Zijdenbos, A., Hampel, H., Teipel, S. J., & Evans, A. C. (2004). Focal decline of cortical thickness in Alzheimer's disease identified by computational neuroanatomy. [PubMed]. *Cerebral Cortex, 15*(7), 995–1001. doi:10.1093/cercor/bhh200

Liu, S., Liu, S., Zhang, F., Cai, W., Pujol, S., Kikinis, R., & Feng, D. (2015). Longitudinal brain MR retrieval with diffeomorphic demons registration: What happened to those patients with similar changes? 2015 IEEE 12th International Symposium on Biomedical Imaging (ISBI). doi:10.1109/isbi.2015.7163942

Lledo, P.-M., Alonso, M., & Grubb, M. S. (2006). Adult neurogenesis and functional plasticity in neuronal circuits. [PubMed]. *Nature Reviews. Neuroscience, 7*(3), 179–193. doi:10.1038/nrn1867

Luchsinger José, A., & Mayeux, R. (2019). Dietary factors and Alzheimer's disease. [PubMed]. *Lancet Neurology, 3*(10), 579–587. doi:10.1016/S1474-4422(04)00878-6

Magnin, B., Mesrob, L., Kinkingnéhun, S., Pélégrini-Issac, M., Colliot, O., Sarazin, M., ... Benali, H. (2008). Support vector machine-based classification of Alzheimer's disease from whole-brain anatomical MRI. [PubMed]. *Neuroradiology, 51*(2), 73–83. doi:10.100700234-008-0463-x

Ming, G., & Song, H. (2005). Adult Neurogenesis in the Mammalian Central Nervous System. [PubMed]. *Annual Review of Neuroscience, 28*(1), 223–250. doi:10.1146/annurev.neuro.28.051804.101459

Misra, C., Fan, Y., & Davatzikos, C. (2009). Baseline and longitudinal patterns of brain atrophy in MCI patients, and their use in prediction of short-term conversion to AD: Results from ADNI☆. [PubMed]. *NeuroImage, 44*(4), 1415–1422. doi:10.1016/j.neuroimage.2008.10.031

Muschelli, J., Sweeney, E., & Crainiceanu, C. M. (2018). freesurfer: Connecting the Freesurfer software with R. [PubMed]. *F1000 Research, 7*, 599. doi:10.12688/f1000research.14361.1

National Institutes of Health (NIH). (2005). Progress Report on Alzheimer's Disease 2004–2005. NIH Publication Number: 05-5724, Nov 2005.

Ng, J., Aguilar, M.-I., & Small, D. H. (2007). Amyloid Toxicity, Synaptic Dysfunction, and the Biochemistry of Neurodegeneration in Alzheimer's disease. Abeta Peptide and Alzheimer's Disease, 93–101. doi:10.1007/978-1-84628-440-3_6

Paradise, M., Cooper, C., & Livingston, G. (2009). Systematic review of the effect of education on survival in Alzheimer's disease. [PubMed]. *International Psychogeriatrics, 21*(1), 25–32. doi:10.1017/S1041610208008053

Querbes, O., Aubry, F., Pariente, J., Lotterie, J. A., Démonet, J. F., Duret, V., ... Celsis, P. (2009). Early diagnosis of Alzheimer's disease using cortical thickness: Impact of cognitive reserve. [PubMed]. *Brain, 132*(8), 2036–2047. doi:10.1093/brain/awp105

Reisberg, B., Ferris, S. H., de Leon, M. J., & Crook, T. (1982). The Global Deterioration Scale for assessment of primary degenerative dementia. [PubMed]. *The American Journal of Psychiatry, 139*(9), 1136–1139. doi:10.1176/ajp.139.9.1136

Saxe, M. D., Battaglia, F., Wang, J.-W., Malleret, G., David, D. J., Monckton, J. E., ... Drew, M. R. (2006). Ablation of hippocampal neurogenesis impairs contextual fear conditioning and synaptic plasticity in the dentate gyrus. [PubMed]. *Proceedings of the National Academy of Sciences of the United States of America, 103*(46), 17501–17506. doi:10.1073/pnas.0607207103

Shors, T. J., Miesegaes, G., Beylin, A., Zhao, M., Rydel, T., & Gould, E. (2001). Neurogenesis in the adult is involved in the formation of trace memories. [PubMed]. *Nature*, *410*(6826), 372–376. doi:10.1038/35066584

Shors, T. J., Townsend, D. A., Zhao, M., Kozorovitskiy, Y., & Gould, E. (2002). Neurogenesis may relate to some but not all types of hippocampal-dependent learning. [PubMed]. *Hippocampus*, *12*(5), 578–584. doi:10.1002/hipo.10103

Snyder, J. S., Hong, N. S., McDonald, R. J., & Wojtowicz, J. M. (2005). A role for adult neurogenesis in spatial long-term memory. [PubMed]. *Neuroscience*, *130*(4), 843–852. doi:10.1016/j.neuroscience.2004.10.009

Stern, Y. (2006). Cognitive Reserve and Alzheimer Disease. [PubMed]. *Alzheimer Disease and Associated Disorders*, *20*(2), 112–117. doi:10.1097/01. wad.0000213815.20177.19

Szekely, C. A., Breitner, J. C. S., & Zandi, P. P. (2007). Prevention of Alzheimer's disease. [PubMed]. *International Review of Psychiatry (Abingdon, England)*, *19*(6), 693–706. doi:10.1080/09540260701797944

Tiraboschi, P., Hansen, L. A., Thal, L. J., & Corey-Bloom, J. (2004). The importance of neuritic plaques and tangles to the development and evolution of AD. [PubMed]. *Neurology*, *62*(11), 1984–1989. doi:10.1212/01.WNL.0000129697.01779.0A

Tobin, A. J. (1987). Alzheimer disease: Enter molecular biology. [PubMed]. *Alzheimer Disease and Associated Disorders*, *1*(2), 69–71. doi:10.1097/00002093-198701020-00001

Van Cauwenberghe, C., Van Broeckhoven, C., & Sleegers, K. (2015). The genetic landscape of Alzheimer disease: Clinical implications and perspectives. [PubMed]. *Genetics in Medicine*, *18*(5), 421–430. doi:10.1038/gim.2015.117

Vemuri, P., Gunter, J. L., Senjem, M. L., Whitwell, J. L., Kantarci, K., Knopman, D. S., ... Jack, C. R. Jr. (2008). Alzheimer's disease diagnosis in individual subjects using structural MR images: Validation studies. [PubMed]. *NeuroImage*, *39*(3), 1186–1197. doi:10.1016/j.neuroimage.2007.09.073

Wright, I. C., McGuire, P. K., Poline, J.-B., Travere, J. M., Murray, R. M., Frith, C. D., ... Friston, K. J. (1995). A Voxel-Based Method for the Statistical Analysis of Gray and White Matter Density Applied to Schizophrenia. [PubMed]. *NeuroImage*, *2*(4), 244–252. doi:10.1006/nimg.1995.1032

Ye, J., Chen, K., Wu, T., Li, J., Zhao, Z., Patel, R., ... Reiman, E. (2008, August). Heterogeneous data fusion for alzheimer's disease study. In *Proceedings of the 14th ACM SIGKDD international conference on Knowledge discovery and data mining* (pp. 1025-1033). ACM. doi:10.1145/1401890.1402012

Zheng, C., Xia, Y., Pan, Y., & Chen, J. (2015). Automated identification of dementia using medical imaging: A survey from a pattern classification perspective. [PubMed]. *Brain Informatics*, *3*(1), 17–27. doi:10.100740708-015-0027-x

Chapter 13

An Algorithmic Approach Based on CMS Edge Detection Technique for the Processing of Digital Images

Kalyan Kumar Jena
Parala Maharaja Engineering College, India

Sasmita Mishra
Indira Gandhi Institute of Technology, India

Sarojananda Mishra
Indira Gandhi Institute of Technology, India

ABSTRACT

Research in the field of digital image processing (DIP) has increased in the current scenario. Edge detection of digital images is considered as an important area of research in DIP. Detecting edges in different digital images accurately is a challenging work in DIP. Different methods have been introduced by different researchers to detect the edges of images. However, no method works well under all conditions. In this chapter, an edge detection method is proposed to detect the edges of gray scale and color images. This method focuses on the combination of Canny, mathematical morphological, and Sobel (CMS) edge detection operators. The output of the proposed method is produced using matrix laboratory (MATLAB) R2015b and compared with Sobel, Prewitt, Roberts, Laplacian of Gaussian (LoG), Canny, and mathematical morphological edge detection operators. The experimental results show that the proposed method works better as compared to other existing methods in detecting the edges of images.

DOI: 10.4018/978-1-7998-0066-8.ch013

INTRODUCTION

DIP is an eminent area of research for different researchers. It is widely applied in many fields and can be considered as one of the rapidly growing technologies in the current scenario. Several concepts, techniques as well as applications of image processing are provided by Niblack (1986), Gonzalez et al. (1987), Green (1989), Jain (1989), Baxes (1994), Klette et al. (1996), Pitas (2000), Gonzalez et al. (2004), Annadurai (2007), Gonzalez et al.(2007), Petrou et al. (2010), Bhabatosh (2011), Solomon et al. (2011), Ekstrom (2012), Nayak et al. (2015), Burger et al. (2016), Nayak et al. (2016), Joshi (2018), Vyas et al.(2018), Majumder et al.(2018) and Bechtel et al.(2018), Nayak et al. (2018a), Nayak et al. (2018b), Nayak et al. (2018c), Nayak et al. (2018d), Nayak et al. (2018e), Nayak et al. (2018f), Nayak et al. (2018g), Nayak et al. (2019). In DIP, computer algorithms are used to perform processing on images (digital). Digital image is an image or picture which is represented digitally that means in group of combination of bits (0 or 1) or specifically called pixels. The digital image can be classified as gray scale, color and multispectral. JPEG, GIF, TIFF, PNG, BMP, etc. are the file types of digital image. DIP technologies can be used for manipulating the pixels in order to improve the quality of image, to draw out information digitally from the image, using computer algorithms. Pictorial information can be improved for human interpretation and the image data can be processed for storage, transmission as well as representation for autonomous machine perception by using DIP mechanism. Different techniques such as image edge detection, image preprocessing, image classification, image enhancement, image segmentation, feature extraction, pattern recognition, image projection, anisotropic diffusion, image editing, image filtering, image compression, etc. are used in DIP. Different applications of DIP includes image sharpening, image restoration, remote sensing, machine vision, color processing, pattern recognition, video processing, computer graphics arts, image encoding, forensic studies, etc. DIP can be applied in medical field, military applications, textiles industry, printing industry, film industry, etc. for several purposes. It can also be applied in radar and sonar. Different issues and challenges such as image edge detection, image segmentation, object recognition, image steganography, image enhancement, image restoration, image acquisition, image enhancement, image compression, image security, etc. are associated with DIP. This chapter is focused on the edge detection of digital images as it plays an important role in real world scenario. Edge detection is considered as an important technique of DIP to detect the edges of digital images. It is used to identify the sudden modification in pixels values relating to the adjacent pixels values in an image. Different concepts or techniques are provided by Scharcanski et al. (1997), Giannarou et al. (2005), Yu-qian et al. (2006), Xin et al. (2012), Goel et al. (2013), Gupta et al. (2013), Katiyar et al. (2014), Shanmugavadivu et al. (2014), Chaple et al. (2014), Wang et al. (2016), Othman et al. (2017), Kumar et al. (2017), Avots et al. (2018), Lahani et al. (2018), Alshorman et al. (2018), Hemalatha et al. (2018), Agrawal et al. (2018), Podder et al. (2018) and Halder et al. (2019) related to edge detection and processing of several images. It is a very challenging work for the DIP researchers to detect the edges in several images (digital) accurately. Different edge detection methods or operators such as Sobel, Prewitt, Roberts, LoG, Canny, etc. are used for detecting the edges in different images. However, no method works well under all conditions. In this chapter, an algorithmic approach is proposed to process the gray scale as well as color images for detecting the edges.

The main contribution in this chapter is stated as follows:

1. A hybrid edge detection scheme is proposed in order to detect the edges of color and gray scale digital images using the quantitative combination of Canny, Morphological and Sobel edge detection operators.
2. At first, Canny edge detection operator is applied in the original image. Afterwards, Morphological operator is applied and then Sobel edge detection operator is used to obtain the resultant image.
3. The results of the proposed edge detection method are produced using MATLAB R2015b and compared with Sobel, Prewitt, Roberts, LoG, Canny and Mathematical Morphological edge detection methods.

RELATED WORKS

Different methods or techniques are proposed by different researchers for the detection of edges as well as for the processing of several images. Some methods have focused in this section. Gupta et al. (2013) presents an improved Sobel edge detection algorithm for detecting the edges of image. The Sobel edge detection technique generally uses a 3x3 convolution mask on an image. This mask is elongated to a 5×5 convolution mask. However, the gradient approximation produced by this may be inaccurate due to which broken, thick as well as false edges may exist in the output image. Goel et al. (2013) proposed a method based on GA implementation by using local contrast enhancement method to enhance the natural contrast of an image. Local standard deviation, local mean and extended range of parameter values are used in this method which may provide better results. Gray level enhancement can be performed to emphasize less dynamic regions in image by using GA. The presented method may provide better image contrast enhancement. However, this method may not work for images that contain large amount of edge details. Katiyar et al. (2014) focuses on a comparative examination of familiar edge detection techniques. The edge detection method such as Sobel, Prewitt, Canny and Laplacian are compared. This paper presents that the Canny edge detection may perform better and the detection of false edges may less as compared to other methods. However, these techniques may not suppress the broken and false edges. Wang et al. (2016) proposed an enhanced Canny edge detection algorithm for dealing with existing problems in conventional algorithms. At first, the anisotropic filter is used to denoise initial gray scale images. This technique suppresses the noise and preserves the edge feature effectively. Furthermore, the low and high thresholds carried out in Canny operator is optimized using genetic algorithm (GA) on the basis of Otsu evaluation function for avoiding human factors. The presented algorithm may lower the false negative and may enhance the detection accuracy than traditional operators. The experiment explores that this algorithm may be strong in pedestrian identification. This work enhances the edge detection performance considerably, however there are some places which need additional enhancement and more suitable criterion of GA can be determined in edge detection process through experiments. Nayak et al. (2016) presents an enhanced differential box counting technique to improve the accuracy by focusing on less fit error and to provide several fractal dimension at a time by focusing on least regression line and fractal dimension at every corresponding size of box. The presented method may be able to accurately capture the roughness and may provide better results consistently than other traditional methods. Avots et al. (2018) proposed a new set of kernels to detect the edge by the help of ratio of image singular values that outputs in more particularized edge detection in origination image. The criterion, that are the essential features of mask matrices and the threshold value used to provide binary image after convolving the masks with the image of presented method, are optimized for achieving more particularized image edge detection. This paper focuses on more experiments on thresholds and its optimization as well as the study of denoising effect before edge detection mechanism. The experimental outputs explore that more particularized edges may be identified by the presented method than existing edge detection methods. However, the images are not liable to be subjected to noise. Nayak et al. (2018c) presents an improved differential box counting Algorithm by segmenting the box of grid into two patterns (asymmetric) in order to get greater precision box count and to estimate fractal dimension accurately by focusing on less computational time and less fit error than existing methods such as differential box counting, relative differential box counting, improved box counting and improved differential box counting. Nayak et al. (2018e) presents a new color fractal dimension estimation algorithm by the extension of original differential box counting algorithm and the implementation of maximum color Euclidean distance from every box block (non overlapping) of RGB components. The presented algorithm may capture the RGB color image surface roughness efficiently and the computational time of the presented method is comparatively less than the existing algorithms. This method may be more precise and more reliable method for color images. Nayak et al. (2018f) attempts to estimate the fractal dimension of RGB color images by the extension of differential box counting algorithm into a domain (color). Gradient images with known fractal dimension are generated with controlled images (experimentally) for validating this approach. The presented method may be more precise and efficient, and may take less time. Nayak et al. (2019) focuses on box counting mechanism and the improved algorithms associated with this mechanism, its working principle and the applications in medical image processing. Fractal dimension plays an important role for characterizing the irritated or complex objects available in nature. Classical Euclidian geometry may not able to analyze such complex objects accurately. Fractal dimension mechanism can work on self similarity theory. Fractal geometry can be applied in medical images for detecting the cancer cells in human body can also be applied in brain imaging to detect tumor, ECG signal, etc. Most of the researchers focus on box counting method for analyzing such complex structures. Halder et al. (2019) proposed an approach for detecting edge based on Richardson's extrapolation method. This technique is used to compute the edge strength. This approach proximate the second order derivative by the help of Richardson's extrapolation method that is carried out to proximate the Taylor series. This approach is applied to several gray scale images and a threshold is applied in order to get the final image as a binary image that means edge or no edge. The presented approach may obtain promising results for edge detection as compared to other techniques such as Sobel, Prewitt, Roberts, statistical approach, a novel edge detection method.

PROPOSED METHODOLY

In this work, Canny, Morphological and Sobel edge detection operators are used for detecting the edges of several images. These operators are described as follows:

Canny Edge Detection Operator

The concepts of Canny edge detection operator are described by Xin et al. (2012), Shanmugavadivu et al. (2014), Wang et al. (2016), Othman et al. (2017), Lahani et al. (2018) and Podder et al. (2018). This operator is considered as an optimal edge detection operator. This operator deals with multi stage processing mechanism. At first, Gaussian filter can be used to smoothen the image. Afterwards, a two dimensional first derivative edge detector such as Sobel is applied in the image (smoothed) to focus the areas with high first spatial derivatives of the image. Canny edge detection algorithm deals with the following steps:

Step 1: Noise of image is filtered out using a Gaussian filter.

Step 2: Edge strength is determined by considering the gradient of the image. Sobel operator masks (mentioned in Figure 1) can be used for such purpose.

Step 3: Edge direction can be calculated using the formula $\theta = \tan^{-1} (S_Y / S_X)$, where S_Y and S_X are the Sobel edge detection operator masks for vertical computation and horizontal computation respectively.

Step 4: Non maxima suppression is performed for gaining thin line of edges in the images.

Step 5: Hysteresis thresholding is performed for eliminating streaking.

Mathematical Morphological Edge Detection Operator

The idea of mathematical morphology is described by Yu-qian et al. (2006). It is considered as a technique for detecting the edges of several images. Mathematical morphological operator is used to analyze and process geometrical structures which are based on topology, lattice theory, set theory and random functions. It is commonly applied in digital images. It is considered as the base of morphological image processing and it deals with a group of operators which alter images as per the specified features. Topological as well as geometrical continuous space approaches

Figure 1. Sobel operator masks

-1	0	+1
-2	0	+2
-1	0	+1

S_X

+1	+2	+1
0	0	0
-1	-2	-1

S_Y

such as shape, size, connectivity, convexity, geodesic distance, etc. can be initiated by this operator on both discrete as well as continuous spaces. It takes a major role in detecting the edges in images. It is used to process images based on shapes. Pixel value in the output focuses on a comparison of the pixel (corresponding) in the input image with its vicinity pixels.

Erosion, dilation, opening and closing are considered as the fundamental morphological operators. Erosion operator is generally represented by $\ominus$. It is used to remove pixels on the object borderlines. The number of pixels added or taken out from the objects in an image normally relies upon the shape and size of the structuring elements which are used for image processing mechanism. Dilation operator is generally represented by $\oplus$. It uses a structuring element to probe and expand the shapes contained in the image (input). It is used to add pixels to the object boundaries in an image. Opening is represented by o. It is used to discard mini objects from the forefront of an image, establishing them in the background. Closing is represented by ●. It can be used to remove mini holes in the forefront, altering mini islands of background into forefront. Generally, opening is used for removing small objects where as closing is used for removing small holes.

Opening the dilation of the erosion of a set X by an element (structuring) Y can be depicted as $XoY = (X \ominus Y) \oplus Y$, where $\ominus$ represents erosion and $\oplus$ represents dilation. Closing of a set X by a structuring aspect Y is the erosion of the dilation of that set can be represented as $X \bullet Y = (X \oplus Y) \ominus Y$, where $\oplus$ represents dilation and $\ominus$ represents erosion. Generally, dilation and closing can make the image shape big but erosion and opening can make the image shape reasonable small. These can be used to find the several edges. Let k: A->B be a gray scale image, mapping points from Euclidean space or discrete grid (A) into real line (B), and c is a gray scale structuring aspect, then the morphological gradient MG of k is represented as $MG(k) = k \oplus c - k \ominus c$. An internal gradient GM_i can be depicted as $GM_i(k) = k - k \ominus c$ and an external gradient GM_e can be depicted as $GM_e = k \oplus c - k$.

Sobel Edge Detection Operator

The Sobel edge detection operator is described by Gupta et al. (2013), Chaple et al. (2014), Alshorman et al. (2018) and Agrawal et al. (2018). It is a gradient based edge detection operator. This edge detection operator carries out a two dimensional spatial gradient computation on the image and hence focuses the areas with extreme spatial frequency that lead to edges. Generally, it is carried to compute the approximate absolute gradient magnitude at every point in an image (input). This edge detection operator generally comprises of two 3×3 convolution masks S_x and S_y as mentioned in Figure 1.

These masks are used separately for separate computation of the gradient component in horizontal and vertical orientations. S_x is used for horizontal computation and S_y is used for vertical computation. Then, the computed values are combined to calculate the gradient magnitude (absolute) at every point as well as such gradient orientation. The magnitude of gradient G can be computed as G= $((S_x)^2+(S_y)^2)^{1/2}$ and the approximate magnitude can be computed as $|S_x| + |S_y|$.

PROPOSED ALGORITHM

```
1. If(image I is grayscale)
2. I=imread('image');
3. G=rgb2gray(I);
4. [m,n]=size(G);
% Canny (C) of I is found
5. C=edge(G,'canny');
6. imshow(C);
% Black and White (BW) of I is found
7. BW = im2bw(G,0.4);
8. imshow(BW);
% Morphing (M) of BW image
9. M = bwmorph(BW,'remove');
10.imshow(M)
% Sobel (S) of I is found

11.S=edge(G,'sobel');
12.imshow(S);
% Prewitt (P) of I is found
13.P=edge(G,'prewitt');
14.imshow(P);
% Roberts (R) of I is found
15.R=edge(G,'Roberts');
16.imshow(R);
% LoG (LG) of I is found
17.LG=edge(G,'log');
18.imshow(LG);
% Generation of final C-M-S image
```

```
19. for i=1:m
20.     for j=1:n
21.         if C(i,j)==1
22.             CMSfinal(i,j)=C(i,j);
23.         else if M(i,j)==1
24.             CMSfinal(i,j)=M(i,j);
25.         else if S(i,j)==1
26.             CMSfinal(i,j)=S(i,j);
27.         else
28.             CMSfinal(i,j)=0;
29.         end
30.     end
31. end

32. else (for color image I)
% Canny (C) of I is found
33. C=edge(I,'canny');
34. imshow(C);
% Black and White (BW) of I is found
35. BW = im2bw(G,0.4);
36. imshow(BW);
% Morphing (M) of BW image
37. M = bwmorph(BW,'remove');
38. imshow(M)
% Sobel (S) of I is found
39. S=edge(G,'sobel');
40. imshow(S);
% Prewitt (P) of I is found
41. P=edge(G,'prewitt');
42. imshow(P);
% Roberts (R) of I is found
43. R=edge(G,'Roberts');
44. imshow(R);
% LoG (LG) of I is found

45. LG=edge(G,'log');
```

```
46. imshow(LG);
% Generation of final C-M-S image
47. for i=1:m
48.     for j=1:n
49.         if C(i,j)==1
50.             CMSfinal(i,j)=C(i,j);
51.         else if M(i,j)==1
52.             CMSfinal(i,j)=M(i,j);
53.         else if S(i,j)==1
54.             CMSfinal(i,j)=S(i,j);
55.         else
56.             CMSfinal(i,j)=0;
57.         end
58.     end
59. end
60. imshow(CMSfinal)
```

RESULTS AND DISCUSSION

MATLAB R2015b is used to analyze the performance of the proposed method. In this chapter, MATLAB toolbox images (gray scale and color) such as mandi, office_6, trees, spine and mri are taken for processing using the proposed method. The results of the proposed method are compared with the results of Sobel, Prewitt, Roberts, LoG, Canny and mathematical morphological edge detection methods. The experimental outputs are mentioned in Figure 2 to Figure 6.

Figure 2 to Figure 6 shows the outputs of Sobel, Prewitt, Roberts, LoG, Canny, mathematical morphological and the proposed method in (b), (c), (d), (e), (f), (g) and (h) respectively. From the results, it is observed (subjective method) that the proposed method shows edges prominently as compared to Sobel, Prewitt, Roberts, LoG, Canny, and mathematical morphological edge detection methods and the edges are thicker in some locations.

Figure 2. (a) Original spine image with 490×367 pixels. (b) Result by applying Sobel edge detection operator. (c) Result by applying Prewitt edge detection operator. (d) Result by applying Roberts edge detection operator. (e) Result by applying LOG edge detection operator. (f) Result by applying Canny edge detection operator. (g) Result by applying Morphological operator. (h) Result by applying Proposed method.

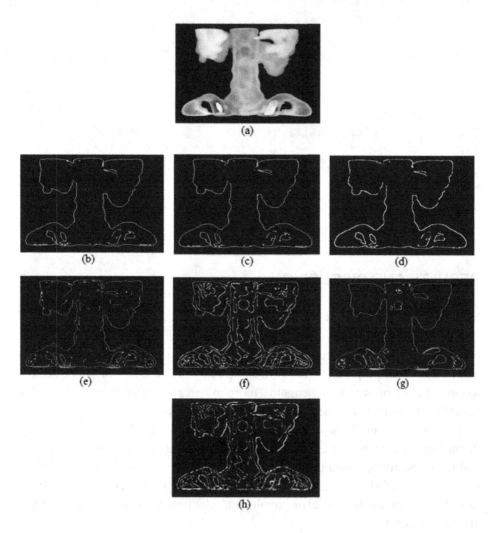

Figure 3. (a) Original office_6 image with 903×600 pixels. (b) Result by applying Sobel edge detection operator. (c) Result by applying Prewitt edge detection operator. (d) Result by applying Roberts edge detection operator. (e) Result by applying LOG edge detection operator. (f) Result by applying Canny edge detection operator. (g) Result by applying Morphological operator. (h) Result by applying Proposed method.

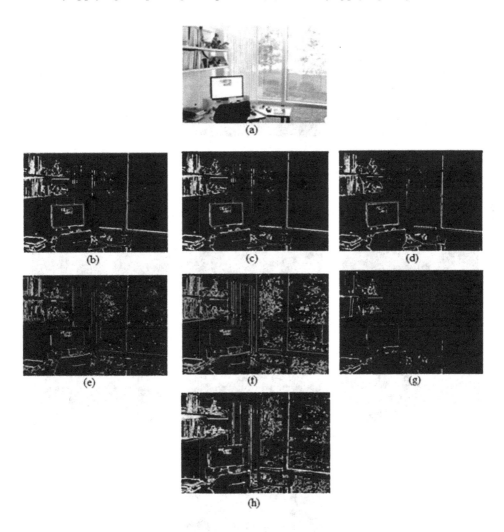

FUTURE RESEARCH DIRECTIONS

In this chapter, several MATLAB toolbox images (gray scale and color) are taken for processing using the proposed method. The results of proposed method are compared with Sobel, Prewitt, Roberts, LoG, Canny, mathematical morphological

Figure 4. (a) Original trees image with 350×258 pixels. (b) Result by applying Sobel edge detection operator. (c) Result by applying Prewitt edge detection operator. (d) Result by applying Roberts edge detection operator. (e) Result by applying LOG edge detection operator. (f) Result by applying Canny edge detection operator. (g) Result by applying Morphological operator. (h) Result by applying Proposed method.

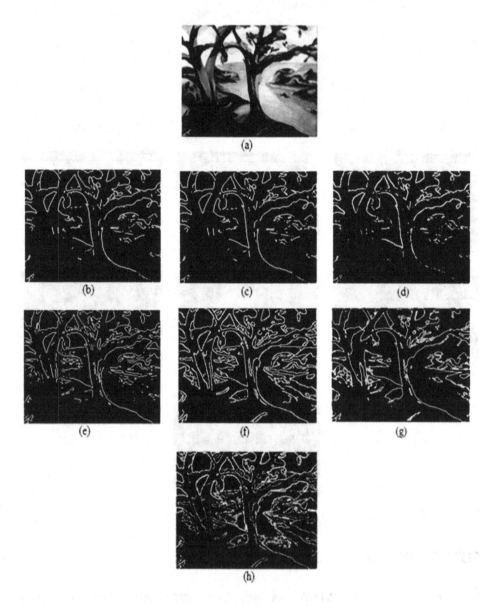

Figure 5. (a) Original mandi image with 3039×2014 pixels. (b) Result by applying Sobel edge detection operator. (c) Result by applying Prewitt edge detection operator. (d) Result by applying Roberts edge detection operator. (e) Result by applying LOG edge detection operator. (f) Result by applying Canny edge detection operator. (g) Result by applying Morphological operator. (h) Result by applying Proposed method.

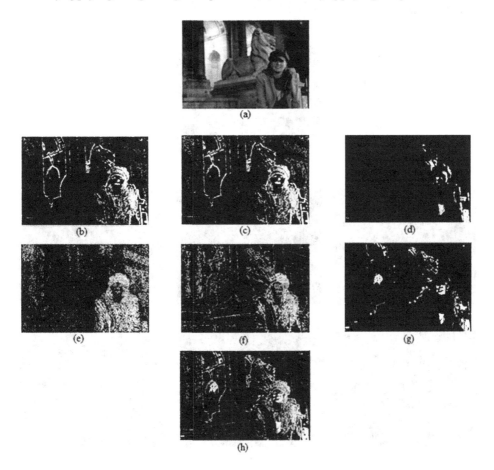

edge detection methods. We will carry our future research for reducing the thickness of edges in output images by using improved edge detection method.

CONCLUSION

The method presented in this chapter uses a hybrid edge detection approach for detecting the edges of several images. For detecting the edges the combination of Canny, mathematical morphological and Sobel edge detectors are used. This method

Figure 6. (a) Original mri image with 128×128 pixels. (b) Result by applying Sobel edge detection operator. (c) Result by applying Prewitt edge detection operator. (d) Result by applying Roberts edge detection operator. (e) Result by applying LOG edge detection operator. (f) Result by applying Canny edge detection operator. (g) Result by applying mathematical morphological operator. (h) Result by applying Proposed method.

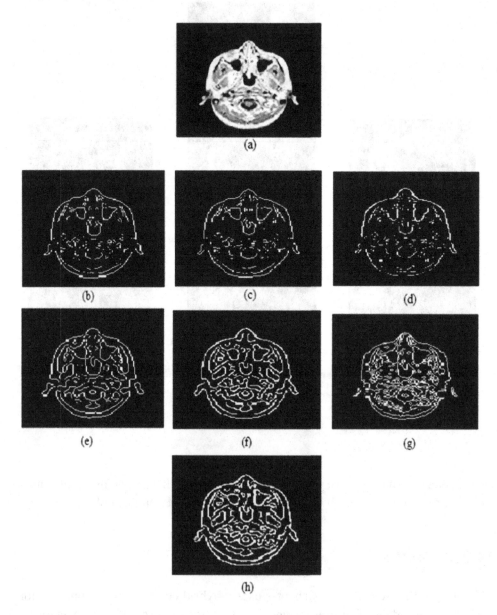

is easily implemented and is used for gray scale as well as color images. From the analysis (subjective method) of the experimental results mentioned in Figure 2 to Figure 6, it is concluded that the proposed method provides better results (edges) for both gray scale and color images as compared to Sobel, Prewitt, Roberts, LoG, Canny, mathematical morphological edge detection methods. This method can be considered as a suitable edge detection method for both gray scale and color images.

ACKNOWLEDGMENT

We owe our deep gratitude to the department of Computer Science Engineering and Applications, Indira Gandhi Institute of Technology, Sarang (nodal centre of Utkal University, Bhubaneswar) for providing better research environment for the completion of our research work successfully.

REFERENCES

Agrawal, A., & Bhogal, R. K. (2018). Edge Detection Techniques in Dental Radiographs (Sobel, T1FLS & IT2FLS). In *International Conference on Communication, Networks and Computing* (pp. 411-421). Springer.

Alshorman, M. A., Junoh, A. K., Muhamad, W. Z. A. W., Zakaria, M. H., & Desa, A. M. (2018). Leukaemia's Cells Pattern Tracking Via Multi-phases Edge Detection Techniques. Journal of Telecommunication, Electronic and Computer Engineering, 10(1-15), 33-37.

Avots, E., Arslan, H. S., Valgma, L., Gorbova, J., & Anbarjafari, G. (2018). A new kernel development algorithm for edge detection using singular value ratios. *Signal, Image and Video Processing*, 1–9.

Chaple, G., & Daruwala, R. D. (2014). Design of Sobel operator based image edge detection algorithm on FPGA. In Communications and Signal Processing (ICCSP), 2014 International Conference on (pp. 788-792). IEEE. doi:10.1109/ICCSP.2014.6949951

Giannarou, S., & Stathaki, T. (2005). Edge detection using quantitative combination of multiple operators. In Signal Processing Systems Design and Implementation, 2005. IEEE Workshop on (pp. 359-364). IEEE. doi:10.1109/SIPS.2005.1579893

Goel, S., Verma, A., & Kumar, N. (2013). Gray level enhancement to emphasize less dynamic region within image using genetic algorithm. In Advance Computing Conference (IACC), 2013 IEEE 3rd International (pp. 1171-1176). IEEE.

Gupta, S., & Mazumdar, S. G. (2013). Sobel edge detection algorithm. *International Journal of Computer Science and Management Research*, 2(2), 1578–1583.

Halder, A., Bhattacharya, P., & Kundu, A. (2019). Edge Detection Method Using Richardson's Extrapolation Formula. In *Soft Computing in Data Analytics* (pp. 727–733). Singapore: Springer; doi:10.1007/978-981-13-0514-6_69

Hemalatha, K., & Rani, K. U. (2018). Feature Extraction of Cervical Pap Smear Images Using Fuzzy Edge Detection Method. In *Data Engineering and Intelligent Computing* (pp. 83–90). Singapore: Springer; doi:10.1007/978-981-10-3223-3_8

Katiyar, S. K., & Arun, P. V. (2014). Comparative analysis of common edge detection techniques in context of object extraction. arXiv preprint arXiv:1405.6132

Kumar, S., Saxena, R., & Singh, K. (2017). Fractional Fourier transform and fractional-order calculus-based image edge detection. *Circuits, Systems, and Signal Processing*, *36*(4), 1493–1513. doi:10.100700034-016-0364-x

Lahani, J., Sulaiman, H. A., Muniandy, R. K., & Bade, A. (2018). An Enhanced Edge Detection Method Based on Integration of Entropy—Canny Technique. *Advanced Science Letters*, *24*(3), 1575–1578. doi:10.1166/asl.2018.11112

Nayak, S., Khandual, A., & Mishra, J. (2018g). Ground truth study on fractal dimension of color images of similar texture. *Journal of the Textile Institute*, *109*(9), 1159–1167. doi:10.1080/00405000.2017.1418710

Nayak, S. R., & Mishra, J. (2018a). A modified triangle box-counting with precision in error fit. *Journal of Information and Optimization Sciences*, *39*(1), 113–128. do i:10.1080/02522667.2017.1372155

Nayak, S. R., & Mishra, J. (2019). Analysis of Medical Images Using Fractal Geometry. In *Histopathological Image Analysis in Medical Decision Making* (pp. 181–201). IGI Global; doi:10.4018/978-1-5225-6316-7.ch008

Nayak, S. R., Mishra, J., & Jena, P. M. (2018b). Fractal Dimension of GrayScale Images. In Progress in Computing, Analytics and Networking (pp. 225-234). Springer. doi:10.1007/978-981-10-7871-2_22

Nayak, S. R., Mishra, J., Khandual, A., & Palai, G. (2018f). Fractal dimension of RGB color images. *Optik (Stuttgart)*, *162*, 196–205. doi:10.1016/j.ijleo.2018.02.066

Nayak, S. R., Mishra, J., & Padhy, R. (2016). An improved algorithm to estimate the fractal dimension of gray scale images. In *2016 International Conference on Signal Processing, Communication, Power and Embedded System (SCOPES)* (pp. 1109-1114). IEEE. doi:10.1109/SCOPES.2016.7955614

Nayak, S. R., Mishra, J., & Padhy, R. (2018c). A New Extended Differential Box-Counting Method by Adopting Unequal Partitioning of Grid for Estimation of Fractal Dimension of Grayscale Images. In *Computational Signal Processing and Analysis* (pp. 45–57). Singapore: Springer; doi:10.1007/978-981-10-8354-9_5

Nayak, S. R., Mishra, J., & Palai, G. (2018d). A modified approach to estimate fractal dimension of gray scale images. *Optik (Stuttgart)*, *161*, 136–145. doi:10.1016/j. ijleo.2018.02.024

Nayak, S. R., Mishra, J., & Palai, G. (2018e). An extended DBC approach by using maximum Euclidian distance for fractal dimension of color images. *Optik (Stuttgart)*, *166*, 110–115. doi:10.1016/j.ijleo.2018.03.106

Nayak, S. R., Ranganath, A., & Mishra, J. (2015). Analysing fractal dimension of color images. In *2015 International Conference on Computational Intelligence and Networks* (pp. 156-159). IEEE. doi:10.1109/CINE.2015.37

Othman, Z., & Abdullah, A. (2017). An Adaptive Threshold Based On Multiple Resolution Levels for Canny Edge Detection. In *International Conference of Reliable Information and Communication Technology* (pp. 316-323). Springer.

Podder, P., Parvez, A. M. S., Yeasmin, M. N., & Khalil, M. I. (2018). Relative Performance Analysis of Edge Detection Techniques in Iris Recognition System. In *2018 International Conference on Current Trends towards Converging Technologies (ICCTCT)* (pp. 1-6). IEEE. doi:10.1109/ICCTCT.2018.8551023

Scharcanski, J., & Venetsanopoulos, A. N. (1997). Edge detection of color images using directional operators. *IEEE Transactions on Circuits and Systems for Video Technology*, *7*(2), 397–401. doi:10.1109/76.564116

Shanmugavadivu, P., & Kumar, A. (2014). Modified eight-directional canny for robust edge detection. In Contemporary Computing and Informatics (IC3I), 2014 International Conference on (pp. 751-756). IEEE. doi:10.1109/IC3I.2014.7019768

Wang, M., Jin, J. S., Jing, Y., Han, X., Gao, L., & Xiao, L. (2016). The Improved Canny Edge Detection Algorithm Based on an Anisotropic and Genetic Algorithm. In *Chinese Conference on Image and Graphics Technologies* (pp. 115-124). Springer. doi:10.1007/978-981-10-2260-9_14

Xin, G., Ke, C., & Xiaoguang, H. (2012). An improved Canny edge detection algorithm for color image. In Industrial Informatics (INDIN), 2012 10th IEEE International Conference on (pp. 113-117). IEEE. doi:10.1109/INDIN.2012.6301061

Yu-qian, Z., Wei-hua, G., Zhen-cheng, C., Jing-tian, T., & Ling-Yun, L. (2006). Medical images edge detection based on mathematical morphology. In Engineering in Medicine and Biology Society, 2005. IEEE-EMBS 2005. 27th Annual International Conference of the (pp. 6492-6495). IEEE.

ADDITIONAL READING

Annadurai, S. (2007). *Fundamentals of digital image processing*. Pearson Education India.

Bechtel, J. H., Andrus, J. C., & Sherman, T. B. (2018). U.S. Patent No. 9,866,805. Washington, DC: U.S. Patent and Trademark Office.

Bhabatosh, C. (2011). *Digital image processing and analysis*. PHI Learning Pvt. Ltd.

Burger, W., & Burge, M. J. (2016). *Digital image processing: an algorithmic introduction using Java*. Springer; doi:10.1007/978-1-4471-6684-9

Ekstrom, M. P. (2012). *Digital image processing techniques* (Vol. 2). Academic Press.

Gonzales, R. C., & Wintz, P. (1987). *Digital image processing*. Addison-Wesley.

Gonzalez, R. C., & Woods, R. E. (2007). Image processing. Digital image processing, 2.

Gonzalez, R. C., Woods, R. E., & Eddins, S. L. (2004). *Digital image processing using MATLAB* (Vol. 624). Upper Saddle River: Pearson-Prentice-Hall.

Green, W. B. (1989). *Digital image processing: a systems approach* (pp. 69–72). New York: Van Nostrand Reinhold.

Jain, A. K. (1989). *Fundamentals of digital image processing*. Englewood Cliffs, NJ: Prentice Hall.

Joshi, M. A. (2018). *Digital image processing: An algorithmic approach*. PHI Learning Pvt. Ltd.

Klette, R., Zamperoni, P., Schimke, W., & Oppermann, K. (1996). *Handbook of image processing operators* (pp. I–IX). New York: Wiley.

Majumder, A., & Gopi, M. (2018). *Introduction to Visual Computing: Core Concepts in Computer Vision, Graphics, and Image Processing*. CRC Press; doi:10.1201/9781315372846

Niblack, W. (1986). *An introduction to digital image processing* (Vol. 34). Englewood Cliffs: Prentice-Hall.

Petrou, M., & Petrou, C. (2010). *Image processing: the fundamentals*. John Wiley & Sons; doi:10.1002/9781119994398

Pitas, I. (2000). *Digital image processing algorithms and applications*. John Wiley & Sons.

Solomon, C., & Breckon, T. (2011). *Fundamentals of Digital Image Processing: A practical approach with examples in Matlab*. John Wiley & Sons.

Vyas, A., Yu, S., & Paik, J. (2018). Fundamentals of Digital Image Processing. In *Multiscale Transforms with Application to Image Processing* (pp. 3–11). Singapore: Springer; doi:10.1007/978-981-10-7272-7_1

KEY TERMS AND DEFINITIONS

Canny Operator: An edge detection operator that focuses on multistage algorithm for detecting edges in several images.

CMS: Canny, mathematical morphological, and Sobel.

Digital Image Processing: Application of computer algorithms for performing image processing on several digital images.

Edge Detection: An image processing technique to find the objects boundaries within images.

LoG Operator: An edge detection operator that focuses on zero crossings points in several images.

Mathematical Morphology: A technique to analyze and process geometrical structures.

Prewitt Operator: An edge detection operator that focuses on the computation of gradient approximation of the image intensity function.

Roberts Operator: An edge detection operator that focuses on approximation of image gradient using discrete differentiation operation.

Sobel Operator: An edge detection operator that focuses on two dimensional gradient measurements on several images and highlights the high spatial frequency regions which correspond to edges.

Compilation of References

Abd-El-Hafiz, S. K., Radwan, A. G., Haleem, S. H. A., & Barakat, M. L. (2014). A fractal-based image encryption system. *IET Image Processing*, *8*(12), 742–752.

Abtahi, S., Omidyeganeh, M., Shirmohammadi, S., & Hariri, B. (2014). YawDD: A Yawning Detection Dataset. *Proc. ACM Multimedia Systems*. 10.1145/2557642.2563678

Agarwal, S. (2017). Image encryption techniques using fractal function: A review. *International Journal of Computer Science and Information Technology*, *9*(2), 53–68. doi:10.5121/ijcsit.2017.9205

Agarwal, S. (2017). Symmetric key encryption using iterated fractal functions. *International Journal of Computer Network and Information Security*, *9*(4), 1–9. doi:10.5815/ijcnis.2017.04.01

Agarwal, S. (2018). Secure Image Transmission Using Fractal and 2D-Chaotic Map. *Journal of Imaging*, *4*(1), 17.

Agrawal, A., & Bhogal, R. K. (2018). Edge Detection Techniques in Dental Radiographs (Sobel, T1FLS & IT2FLS). In *International Conference on Communication, Networks and Computing* (pp. 411-421). Springer.

Alsafasfeh, Q. H., & Arfoa, A. A. (2011). Image encryption based on the general approach for multiple chaotic systems. *J. Signal and Information Processing*, *2*(3), 238–244. doi:10.4236/jsip.2011.23033

Alshorman, M. A., Junoh, A. K., Muhamad, W. Z. A. W., Zakaria, M. H., & Desa, A. M. (2018). Leukaemia's Cells Pattern Tracking Via Multi-phases Edge Detection Techniques. *Journal of Telecommunication, Electronic and Computer Engineering (JTEC)*, *10*(1-15), 33-37.

Alshorman, M. A., Junoh, A. K., Muhamad, W. Z. A. W., Zakaria, M. H., & Desa, A. M. (2018). Leukaemia's Cells Pattern Tracking Via Multi-phases Edge Detection Techniques. Journal of Telecommunication, Electronic and Computer Engineering, 10(1-15), 33-37.

Anandkumar, R., & Kalpana, R. (2018, August). Analyzing of Chaos based Encryption with Lorenz and Henon Map. In *2018 2nd International Conference on I-SMAC (IoT in Social, Mobile, Analytics and Cloud)(I-SMAC) I-SMAC (IoT in Social, Mobile, Analytics and Cloud)(I-SMAC), 2018 2nd International Conference on* (pp. 204-208). IEEE.

Anandkumar, R., & Kalpana, R. (2019). A Survey on Chaos Based Encryption Technique. In *Enabling Technologies and Architectures for Next-Generation Networking Capabilities* (pp. 147–165). IGI Global. doi:10.4018/978-1-5225-6023-4.ch007

Ancuti, C., & Ancuti, C. (2013). Single image dehazing by multi-scale fusion. *IEEE Transactions on Image Processing, 22*(8), 3271–3282. doi:10.1109/TIP.2013.2262284 PMID:23674449

Ancuti, C., Ancuti, C. O., Haber, T., & Bekaert, P. (2012). EnhancingUnderwater Images and Videos by Fusion. In *Conference on Computer Vision and Pattern Recognition (ICCVPR 2012)* (pp. 81-88). IEEE. 10.1109/CVPR.2012.6247661

Antonini, M., Barlaud, M., Mathieu, P., & Daubechies, I. (1992). Image Coding Using Wavelet Transform. *IEEE Transactions on Image Processing, 1*(2), 205–220. doi:10.1109/83.136597 PMID:18296155

Antony, J., McGuinness, K., Connor, N. E. O., & Moran, K. (2016). *Quantifying radiographic knee osteoarthritis severity using deep convolutional neural networks.* arxiv:1609.02469

Ashraf, M., Gardner, L., & Nethercot, D. A. (2006). Compression strength of stainless steel cross-sections. *Journal of Constructional Steel Research, 62*(1), 105–115. doi:10.1016/j.jcsr.2005.04.010

Avots, E., Arslan, H. S., Valgma, L., Gorbova, J., & Anbarjafari, G. (2018). A new kernel development algorithm for edge detection using singular value ratios. *Signal, Image and Video Processing, 1*–9.

Azim, T. (2009). *Automatic fatigue detection of drivers through Yawning analysis.* Signal Processing, Image Processing and Pattern Recognition. Springer Berlin Heidelberg. doi:10.1007/978-3-642-10546-3_16

Balu, D. T., & Lucki, I. (2009). Adult hippocampal neurogenesis: Regulation, functional implications, and contribution to disease pathology. [PubMed]. *Neuroscience and Biobehavioral Reviews, 33*(3), 232–252. doi:10.1016/j.neubiorev.2008.08.007

Bao, Z. L., & Ming, Z. (2003). ROI Coding Research Based on Residual Image. *Journal of Opto-Electronics Laser, 14*(1), 75–78.

Barbu, A., Lu, L., Roth, H., Seff, A., & Summers, R. M. (2016). *An analysis of robust cost functions for CNN in computer-aided diagnosis Comput.* Methods Biomech. Biomed. Eng. Imag. Visual.

Barlaud, M., Sole, P., Gaidon, T., Antonini, M., & Mathieu, P. (1993). Elliptical codebook for lattice vector quantization. *Proceedings of IEEE International Conference on Acoustics, Speech and Signal Processing,* 590-593. 10.1109/ICASSP.1993.319880

Compilation of References

Barnsley, M. (1989). *Fractals Everywhere*. San Diego, CA: Academic Press.

Barnsley, M. F., & Hurd, L. P. (1992). *Fractal Image Compression*. Wellesley, MA: AK Peters Ltd.

Bharti, P., Gupta, S., & Bhatia, R. K. (2009). Comparative Analysis of Image Compression Techniques: A Case Study on Medical Images. *2009 International Conference on Advances in Recent Technologies in Communication and Computing*, 820–822. Retrieved from https://ieeexplore.ieee.org/document/5328178

Bhatnagar, G., & Wu, Q. J. (2019). A fractal dimension based framework for night vision fusion. *IEEE/CAA Journal of Automatica Sinica, 6*(1), 220-227.

Bhowmik, T. K., Parui, S. K., Bhattacharya, U., & Shaw, B. (2006, December). An HMM based recognition scheme for handwritten Oriya numerals. In *9th International Conference on Information Technology (ICIT'06)* (pp. 105-110). IEEE.

Braak, H., & Braak, E. (1995). Staging of Alzheimer's disease-related neurofibrillary changes. *Neurobiology of Aging, 16*(3), 271–278.

Bradski, G. R. (1998). Real Time Face and Object Tracking as a Component of a Perceptual User Interface. In *Fourth IEEE Workshop on Applications of Computer Vision WACV '98* (pp. 214-219). IEEE. 10.1109/ACV.1998.732882

Brookmeyer, R., Johnson, E., Ziegler-Graham, K., & Arrighi, H. M. (2007). Forecasting the global burden of Alzheimer's disease. [PubMed]. *Alzheimer's & Dementia, 3*(3), 186–191. doi:10.1016/j.jalz.2007.04.381

Brown, M., & Lowe, D. (2002). Invariant features from interest point groups. BMVC02. doi:10.5244/C.16.23

Carreira, J., & Sminchisescu, C. (2012). Cpmc: Automatic object segmentation using constrained parametric min-cuts. *IEEE Transactions on Pattern Analysis and Machine Intelligence, 34*(7), 1312–1328. doi:10.1109/TPAMI.2011.231 PMID:22144523

Catte, E., Lions, P. I., Morel, J. M., & Coll, T. (1992). Image selective smoothing and edge detection by nonlinear diffusion. *SIAM Journal on Numerical Analysis, 29*(1), 182–193. doi:10.1137/0729012

Cech, J., & Soukupova, T. (2016). *Real-Time Eye Blink Detection using Facial Landmarks. 21st Comput*. Vis. Winter Work.

Cederberg, J. N. (2001). Chaos to Symmetry: An Introduction to Fractal Geometry. In *A Course in Modern Geometries* (pp. 315–387). New York, NY: Springer. doi:10.1007/978-1-4757-3490-4_5

Chang, C. C. (2011). LIBSVM: a library for support vector machines. *ACM Transactions on Intelligent Systems and Technology, 2*. Retrieved from http://www. csie. ntu. edu.tw/~cjlin/libsvm

Chao, S. M., & Tsai, D. M. (2006). Astronomical image restoration using an improved anisotropic diffusion. *Pattern Recognition Letters, 27*(5), 335–344. doi:10.1016/j.patrec.2005.08.021

Chao, S. M., & Tsai, D. M. (2008). An anisotropic diffusion-based defect detection for low-contrast glass substrates. *Image and Vision Computing*, 26(2), 187–200. doi:10.1016/j.imavis.2007.03.003

Chao, S. M., & Tsai, D. M. (2010). An improved anisotropic diffusion model for detail- and edge-preserving smoothing. *Pattern Recognition Letters*, 31(13), 2012–2023. doi:10.1016/j.patrec.2010.06.004

Chaple, G., & Daruwala, R. D. (2014). Design of Sobel operator based image edge detection algorithm on FPGA. In *Communications and Signal Processing (ICCSP), 2014 International Conference on* (pp. 788-792). IEEE. 10.1109/ICCSP.2014.6949951

Chaudhuri, B. B., Pal, U., & Mitra, M. (2002). Automatic recognition of printed Oriya script. *Sadhana*, 27(1), 23–34. doi:10.1007/BF02703310

Chen, Y. T., Tseng, D. C., & Chang, P. C. (2006). Wavelet-Based Image Compression with Polygon-Shaped Region of Interest. *LNCS 4319*, 878–887. Retrieved from https://link.springer.com/chapter/10.1007/11949534_88

Cheng, N. T., & Kingsbury, N. G. (1992). The erpc: An efficient error resilient technique for encoding positional information or sparse data. *IEEE Transactions on Communications*, 40(1), 140–148. doi:10.1109/26.126715

Chen, Y.-Y. (2007). Medical image compression using DCT-based subband decomposition and modified SPIHT data organization. *International Journal of Medical Informatics*, 76(10), 717–725. doi:10.1016/j.ijmedinf.2006.07.002 PMID:16931130

Choong, M-K., Logeswaran, R., & Bister, M. (2007). Cost-effective handling of digital medical images in the telemedicine environment. *International Journal of Medical Informatics*, 76(9), 646-654.

Chowdhury, M. M. H., & Khatun, A. (2012). Image Compression Using Discrete Wavelet Transform. *International Journal of Computer Science Issues*, 9(1).

Coleman, S. A., Scotney, B. W., & Herron, M. G. (2004). A systematic design procedure for scalable near-circular Laplacian of Gaussian operators. In *Pattern Recognition, 2004. ICPR 2004. Proceedings of the 17th International Conference on* (Vol. 1, pp. 700-703). IEEE. 10.1109/ICPR.2004.1334275

Cosman, P. C., Gray, R. M., & Olshen, R. A. (1994). Evaluating quality of compressed medical images SNR, subjective rating, and diagnostic accuracy. *Proceedings of the IEEE*, 82(6), 919 – 932. 10.1109/5.286196

Cosman, P. C., Gray, R. M., & Vetterli, M. (1996). Vector quantization of image sub-bands: A review. *IEEE Transactions on Image Processing*, 5(2), 202–225. doi:10.1109/83.480760 PMID:18285108

Cruz, D. S., Ebrahimi, T., Larsson, M., Askelof, J., & Christopoulos, C. A. (1999). *Region of Interest Coding in JPEG 2000 for Interactive Client/Server Applications. In IEEE 3rd Workshop on Multimedia Signal Processing* (pp. 389–394). Copenhagen, Denmark: MMSP. Retrieved from https://ieeexplore.ieee.org/document/793870

Cuingnet, R., Gerardin, E., Tessieras, J., Auzias, G., Lehéricy, S., & Habert, M. O. (2011). Automatic classification of patients with Alzheimer's disease from structural MRI: A comparison of ten methods using the ADNI database. *NeuroImage, 56*(2), 766–781.

Cummings, J. L., Doody, R., & Clark, C. (2007). Disease-modifying therapies for Alzheimer disease: Challenges to early intervention. [PubMed]. *Neurology, 69*(16), 1622–1634. doi:10.1212/01. wnl.0000295996.54210.69

Dalal, N., & Triggs, B. (2005, June). Histograms of oriented gradients for human detection. In *International Conference on computer vision & Pattern Recognition (CVPR'05)* (Vol. 1, pp. 886-893). IEEE Computer Society. 10.1109/CVPR.2005.177

Dalal, N., Triggs, B., & Schmid, C. (2006). Human detection using oriented histograms of flow and appearance. In *European conference on computer vision*, (pp. 428–441). Springer. 10.1007/11744047_33

Danisman, T. (2010). Drowsy driver detection system using eye blink patterns. In *Machine and Web Intelligence (ICMWI), 2010 International Conference on*. IEEE. 10.1109/ICMWI.2010.5648121

Dasa, Ghosha, Palb, Maitib, & Chakraborty. (2013). Machine learning approach for automated screening of malaria parasite using light microscopic images. *Micron (Oxford, England), 45*(February), 97–106. PMID:23218914

Dash, K. S., Puhan, N. B., & Panda, G. (2015). Handwritten numeral recognition using non-redundant Stockwell transform and bio-inspired optimal zoning. *IET Image Processing, 9*(10), 874–882. doi:10.1049/iet-ipr.2015.0146

Dash, K. S., Puhan, N. B., & Panda, G. (2016). BESAC: Binary External Symmetry Axis Constellation for unconstrained handwritten character recognition. *Pattern Recognition Letters, 83*, 413–422. doi:10.1016/j.patrec.2016.05.031

Daubechics, I. (1992). *Ten Lectures on Wavelets*. Society for Industrial and Applied Mathematics Philadelphia. doi:10.1137/1.9781611970104

Daubechies, I. (1990). The wavelet transform time-frequency localization and signal analysis. *IEEE Transformation and Information Theory, 36*(5), 961-1005. Retrieved from https://ieeexplore. ieee.org/document/57199

Davatzikos, C., Resnick, S. M., Wu, X., Parmpi, P., & Clark, C. M. (2008). Individual patient diagnosis of AD and FTD via high-dimensional pattern classification of MRI. [PubMed]. *NeuroImage, 41*(4), 1220–1227. doi:10.1016/j.neuroimage.2008.03.050

Davis, L., & Aggarwal, J. (1979). Texture analysis using generalized co-occurrence matrices. *IEEE Transactions on Pattern Analysis and Machine Intelligence, PAMI-1*(3), 251–259. doi:10.1109/TPAMI.1979.4766921 PMID:21868856

De, K., & v, M. (2013). A new no-reference image quality measure for blurred images in spatial domain. *J. of Image and Graphics, 1*(1), 39–42. doi:10.12720/joig.1.1.39-42

Deshlahra, A. (2013). *A Thesis on Analysis of Image Compression Methods Based On Transform and Fractal Coding*. Rourkela.

Desikan, R. S., Cabral, H. J., Hess, C. P., Dillon, W. P., Glastonbury, C. M., Weiner, M. W., ... Fischl, B. (2009). Automated MRI measures identify individuals with mild cognitive impairment and Alzheimer's disease. [PubMed]. *Brain, 132*(8), 2048–2057. doi:10.1093/brain/awp123

Desikan, R. S., Ségonne, F., Fischl, B., Quinn, B. T., Dickerson, B. C., Blacker, D., ... Killiany, R. J. (2006). An automated labeling system for subdividing the human cerebral cortex on MRI scans into gyral based regions of interest. [PubMed]. *NeuroImage, 31*(3), 968–980. doi:10.1016/j.neuroimage.2006.01.021

Dong, Y., Liu, J., Zhu, C., & Wang, Y. (2010, July). Image encryption algorithm based on chaotic mapping. In *2010 3rd International Conference on Computer Science and Information Technology* (Vol. 1, pp. 289-291). IEEE.

Dragan. (2009). An approach to DICOM extension for medical image streaming. DAAAM international scientific book, 25-35.

Economopoulos, T. L., Asvestas, P. A., & Matsopoulos, G. K. (2010). Contrast enhancement of images using partitioned iterated function systems. *Image and Vision Computing, 28*(1), 45–54. doi:10.1016/j.imavis.2009.04.011

Erickson, B. J., Manduca, A., Palisson, P., Persons, K. R., Earnest, F. IV, Savcenko, V., & Hangiandreou, N. J. (1998). Wavelet compression of medical images. *Radiology, 206*(3), 599–607. doi:10.1148/radiology.206.3.9494473 PMID:9494473

Ester, M., Kriegel, H. P., Sander, J., & Xu, X. (1996). A density-based algorithm for discovering clusters in large spatial databases with noise. In *KDD'96 Proceedings of the Second International Conference on Knowledge Discovery and Data Mining* (pp. 226-231). ACM.

Fabio, G. D., González, A., & Romero, E. (2009, April). A semi-automatic method for quantification and classification of erythrocytes infected with malaria parasites in microscopic images. *Journal of Biomedical Informatics Volume, 42*(2), 296–307. doi:10.1016/j.jbi.2008.11.005 PMID:19166974

Fadhel, S., Shafry, M., & Farook, O. (2017). Chaos Image Encryption Methods: A Survey Study. *Bulletin of Electrical Engineering and Informatics, 6*(1), 99–104.

Fan, Y., Batmanghelich, N., Clark, C. M., & Davatzikos, C. (2008). Spatial patterns of brain atrophy in MCI patients, identified via high-dimensional pattern classification, predict subsequent cognitive decline. [PubMed]. *NeuroImage*, *39*(4), 1731–1743. doi:10.1016/j.neuroimage.2007.10.031

Fan, Y., Shen, D., Gur, R. C., Gur, R. E., & Davatzikos, C. (2007). COMPARE: Classification of Morphological Patterns Using Adaptive Regional Elements. [PubMed]. *IEEE Transactions on Medical Imaging*, *26*(1), 93–105. doi:10.1109/TMI.2006.886812

Farbman, Z., Fattal, R., Lischinski, D., & Szeliski, R. (2008). Edge-preserving decompositions for multi-scale tone and detail manipulation. *ACM Transaction on Graphics, 27*(3), 67:1-67:10.

Fattal, R. (2014). Dehazing using color-lines. *ACM Transactions on Graphics*, *34*(1), 1–4. doi:10.1145/2651362

Fei, P., Qiu, S. S., & Min, L. (2005, May). An image encryption algorithm based on mixed chaotic dynamic systems and external keys. In *Proceedings. 2005 International Conference on Communications, Circuits and Systems* (Vol. 2). IEEE.

Felzenszwalb, P. F., Girshick, R. B., McAllester, D., & Ramanan, D. (2010). Object detection with discriminatively trained part-based models. *IEEE Transactions on Pattern Analysis and Machine Intelligence*, *32*(9), 1627–1645. doi:10.1109/TPAMI.2009.167 PMID:20634557

Findlay, J. M. (1980). The Visual Stimulus for Saccadic Eye Movements in Human Observers. *Perception*, *9*(1), 7–21. doi:10.1068/p090007 PMID:7360616

Fisher, Y. (1992). A Discussion of Fractal Image Compression. In chaos and fractals. New York: Springer-Verlag.

Fisher, Y. (1992). *Fractal Image Compression.* Siggraph 92 course notes.

Fisher, T. R., Marcellin, M. W., & Wang, M. (1991). Trellis-coded vector quantization. *IEEE Transactions on Information Theory*, *37*(6), 1551–1566. doi:10.1109/18.104316

Fouhey, D. F., Gupta, A., & Hebert, M. (2014). Unfolding an indoor origami world. In *ECCV: European Conference on Computer Vision* (Vol. 8694, pp. 687–702). Springer. 10.1007/978-3-319-10599-4_44

Frisoni, G. B., Fox, N. C., Jack, C. R., Scheltens, P., & Thompson, P. M. (2010). The clinical use of structural MRI in Alzheimer disease. [PubMed]. *Nature Reviews. Neurology*, *6*(2), 67–77. doi:10.1038/nrneurol.2009.215

Gauthier, S., Reisberg, B., Zaudig, M., Petersen, R. C., Ritchie, K., Broich, K., ... Winblad, B. (2006). Mild cognitive impairment. [PubMed]. *Lancet*, *367*(9518), 1262–1270. doi:10.1016/S0140-6736(06)68542-5

Geiger, A., Wojek, C., & Urtasun, R. (2011). Joint 3d estimation of objects and scene layout. *Neural Information Processing Systems 24 (NIPS 2011).*

Gerhard, D. B., & Kinsner, W. (1996). Lossy Compression of Head and Shoulder Images Using Zero-tree of Wavelet Coefficients. *IEEE Conference on Electrical and Computer Engineering*, 433-437. Retrieved from https://ieeexplore.ieee.org/document/548129

Gersho, R., & Gray, R. M. (1992). *Vector quantization and signal compression*. Boston: Kluwer Academic Publishers. doi:10.1007/978-1-4615-3626-0

Giannarou, S., & Stathaki, T. (2005). Edge detection using quantitative combination of multiple operators. In Signal Processing Systems Design and Implementation, 2005. IEEE Workshop on (pp. 359-364). IEEE. doi:10.1109/SIPS.2005.1579893

Giguet, D., Karam, L. J., & Abousleman, G. P. (2001). Very Low Bit-Rate Target Based Image Coding. *Proc. Asilomar Conf. on Signals, Systems, and Computers*, 778-782. 10.1109/ACSSC.2001.987030

Goel, S., Verma, A., & Kumar, N. (2013). Gray level enhancement to emphasize less dynamic region within image using genetic algorithm. In Advance Computing Conference (IACC), 2013 IEEE 3rd International (pp. 1171-1176). IEEE.

Goel, S., Verma, A., & Kumar, N. (2013). Gray level enhancement to emphasize less dynamic region within image using genetic algorithm. In *Advance Computing Conference (IACC), 2013 IEEE 3rd International* (pp. 1171-1176). IEEE.

Goldberg, M. A., Pivovarov, M., Mayo-Smith, W. W., Bhalla, M. P., Blickman, J. G., Bramson, R. T., ... Halpern, E. (1994). Applicationof wavelet compression to digitized radiographs. *AJR. American Journal of Roentgenology*, *163*(2), 463–468. doi:10.2214/ajr.163.2.8037051 PMID:8037051

Gonzalez, R. & Eugene, R. (2008). *Digital Image Processing*. Academic Press.

Govindan, V. K., & Shivaprasad, A. P. (1990). Character recognition—A review. *Pattern Recognition*, *23*(7), 671–683. doi:10.1016/0031-3203(90)90091-X

Gross, R., Matthews, I., Cohn, J., Kanade, T., & Baker, S. (2010). Multi-pie. *Image and Vision Computing*, *28*(5), 807–813. doi:10.1016/j.imavis.2009.08.002 PMID:20490373

Guan, Z. H., Huang, F., & Guan, W. (2005). Chaos-based image encryption algorithm. *Physics Letters. [Part A]*, *346*(1-3), 153–157. doi:10.1016/j.physleta.2005.08.006

Guo, Z., Sun, J., Zhang, D., & Wu, B. (2012). Adaptive perona-malik model based on the variable exponent for image denoising. *IEEE Transactions on Image Processing*, *21*(3), 958–967. doi:10.1109/TIP.2011.2169272 PMID:21947525

Gupta, S., & Mazumdar, S. G. (2013). Sobel edge detection algorithm. *International Journal of Computer Science and Management Research, 2*(2), 1578-1583.

Gupta, S., & Mazumdar, S. G. (2013). Sobel edge detection algorithm. *International Journal of Computer Science and Management Research, 2*(2), 1578–1583.

Halder, A., Bhattacharya, P., & Kundu, A. (2019). Edge Detection Method Using Richardson's Extrapolation Formula. In *Soft Computing in Data Analytics* (pp. 727–733). Singapore: Springer. doi:10.1007/978-981-13-0514-6_69

Hartl, D. (2004). The origin of malaria: Mixed messages from genetic diversity. *Nature Reviews. Microbiology*, *2*(1), 15–22. doi:10.1038/nrmicro795 PMID:15035005

Hemalatha, K., & Rani, K. U. (2018). Feature Extraction of Cervical Pap Smear Images Using Fuzzy Edge Detection Method. In *Data Engineering and Intelligent Computing* (pp. 83–90). Singapore: Springer. doi:10.1007/978-981-10-3223-3_8

Hou, W., Gray, D. J., Weidemann, A. D., Fournier, G. R., & Forand, J. L. (2007) Automated Underwater Image Restoration and Retrieval of Related Optical Properties. In *International Symposium of Geoscience and Remote Sensing (ISGRS 2007)* (pp. 1889-1892). IEEE. 10.1109/IGARSS.2007.4423193

Huang, R. Berg, & Learned-Miller. (2007). *Labeled faces in the wild: A database for studying face recognition in unconstrained environments* (Tech. Rep. 07-49). University of Massachusetts, Amherst.

Huang, R., Wang, Y., & Guo, L. (2018, October). P-FDCN Based Eye State Analysis for Fatigue Detection. In *2018 IEEE 18th International Conference on Communication Technology (ICCT)* (pp. 1174-1178). IEEE. 10.1109/ICCT.2018.8599947

Huertas, A., & Medioni, G. (1986). Detection of intensity changes with subpixel accuracy using Laplacian-Gaussian masks. *IEEE Transactions on Pattern Analysis and Machine Intelligence*, *PAMI-8*(5), 651–664. doi:10.1109/TPAMI.1986.4767838 PMID:21869362

Huffman, D. A. (1952). A Method for the Construction of Minimum-Redundancy Codes. *Proceedings of the IRE*, 40, 1098-1101. 10.1109/JRPROC.1952.273898

Hunter, R., & Robinson, A. H. (1980). International Digital facsimile Standards. *Proceedings of the IEEE*, *68*(7), 854–867. doi:10.1109/PROC.1980.11751

Hutchinson, J. E. (1981). Fractals and Self Similarity. *Indiana University Mathematics Journal*, *35*(5), 713. doi:10.1512/iumj.1981.30.30055

Imtiyaz, A., & Arun, K. (2017). Vision enhancement through single image fog removal. *Engineering Science and Technology, 20*, 1075-1083.

Ishigaki, Sakuma, Ikeda, Itoh, Suzuki, & Iwa. (1990). Clinical evaluation of irreversible image compression: analysis of chest imaging with computed radiography. *Journal of Radiology, 175*(3).

Jacquin, A. (1989). *Fractal Theory of Iterated Markov Operators with applications to Digital Image Coding* (Doctoral Thesis). Georgia Institute of Technology.

Jacquin, E. (1992). Image Coding Based on a Fractal Theory of Iterated Contractive Image Transformation. *IEEE Transactions on Image Processing*, *1*(1), 18–30. doi:10.1109/83.128028 PMID:18296137

Jindal, M. K., Sharma, R. K., & Lehal, G. S. (2007). Segmentation of horizontally overlapping lines in printed Indian scripts. *International Journal of Computational Intelligence Research*, *3*(4), 277–286. doi:10.5019/j.ijcir.2007.109

Joardar, S., Sanyal, A., Sen, D., Sen, D., & Chatterjee, A. (2019). An Enhanced Fractal Dimension Based Feature Extraction for Thermal Face Recognition. In *Decision Science in Action* (pp. 217–226). Singapore: Springer. doi:10.1007/978-981-13-0860-4_16

Joshi, M., Agarwal, A. K., & Gupta, B. (2019). Fractal Image Compression and Its Techniques: A Review. In *Soft Computing: Theories and Applications* (pp. 235–243). Singapore: Springer. doi:10.1007/978-981-13-0589-4_22

Jugessur, D., & Dudek, D. (2000). Local appearance for robust object recognition. In Computer Vision and Pattern Recognition (ICCVPR 2000) (pp. 834-840). IEEE. doi:10.1109/CVPR.2000.855907

Kadam, S., & Rathod, V. R. (2019). Medical Image Compression Using Wavelet-Based Fractal Quad Tree Combined with Huffman Coding. In *Third International Congress on Information and Communication Technology* (pp. 929-936). Springer.

Kaiming, H., Jian, S., & Xiaoou, T. (2011). Single image haze removal using dark channel prior. *IEEE Transactions on Pattern Analysis and Machine Intelligence*, *33*(12), 2341–2353. doi:10.1109/TPAMI.2010.168 PMID:20820075

Kale, K. V., Deshmukh, P. D., Chavan, S. V., Kazi, M. M., & Rode, Y. S. (2013, October). Zernike moment feature extraction for handwritten Devanagari compound character recognition. In *2013 Science and Information Conference* (pp. 459-466). IEEE.

Kalyanpur, A., Neklesa, V. P., Taylor, C. R., Daftary, A. R., & Brink, J. A. (2000). Evaluation of JPEG and Wavelet Compression of Body CT Images for Direct Digital Teleradiologic Transmission 1. *Radiology*, *217*(3), 772–779. doi:10.1148/radiology.217.3.r00nv22772 PMID:11110942

Kamencay, Jelsovka, & Zachariasova. (2011). The impact of segmentation on face recognition using the principal component analysis (PCA). *Signal Processing Algorithms, Architectures, Arrangements, and Applications Conference Proceedings (SPA)*. IEEE.

Kamencay, P. (2012). Improved face recognition method based on segmentation algorithm using SIFT-PCA. *Telecommunications and Signal Processing (TSP), 2012 35th International Conference on*. IEEE. 10.1109/TSP.2012.6256399

Kanth, S. S. (2013). *Compression Efficiency for Combining Different Embedded Image Compression Techniques with Huffman Encoding. In 2013.* Melmaruvathur, India: International Conference on Communication and Signal Processing. Retrieved from https://ieeexplore.ieee.org/document/6577170

Karim, T. F. (2010). Face recognition using PCA-based method. In *Advanced Management Science (ICAMS), 2010 IEEE International Conference on., 3.* IEEE.

Katiyar, S. K., & Arun, P. V. (2014). Comparative analysis of common edge detection techniques in context of object extraction. arXiv preprint arXiv:1405.6132

Kavitha, V., & Easwarakumar, K. S. (2008). Enhancing Privacy in Arithmetic Coding. *ICGST-AIML Journal, 8*(1).

Kazemi & Josephine. (2014). One millisecond face alignment with an ensemble of regression trees. In *27th IEEE Conference on Computer Vision and Pattern Recognition, CVPR 2014* (pp. 1867–1874). IEEE Computer Society.

Kim, T. (1988). New finite-state vector quantizer for images. *IEEE International Conference on Acoustics, Speech and Signal Processing*, 1180-1183.

Kimura, F., Wakabayashi, T., Tsuruoka, S., & Miyake, Y. (1997). Improvement of handwritten Japanese character recognition using weighted direction code histogram. *Pattern Recognition, 30*(8), 1329–1337. doi:10.1016/S0031-3203(96)00153-7

Kim, W. J., Kim, S. D., & Kim, K. (2005). Fast Algorithms for Binary Dilation and Erosion Using Run-Length Encoding. *ETRI Journal, 27*(6), 814–817. doi:10.4218/etrij.05.0205.0013

King, D. E. (2009). Dlib-ml: A Machine Learning Toolkit. *Journal of Machine Learning Research, 10*, 1755–1758. doi:10.1145/1577069.1755843

Klöppel, S., Stonnington, C. M., Chu, C., Draganski, B., Scahill, R. I., Rohrer, J. D., ... Frackowiak, R. S. (2008). Automatic classification of MR scans in Alzheimer's disease. [PubMed]. *Brain, 131*(3), 681–689. doi:10.1093/brain/awm319

Koenders, L., Cousijn, J., Vingerhoets, W. A. M., van den Brink, W., Wiers, R. W., Meijer, C. J., ... de Haan, L. (2016). Grey Matter Changes Associated with Heavy Cannabis Use: A Longitudinal sMRI Study. [PubMed]. *PLoS One, 11*(5), e0152482. doi:10.1371/journal.pone.0152482

Kumar, S. (2011). *Thesis on Image compression based on improved SPIHT and region of interest.* Thapar University.

Kumar, T. M. P. R., & Latte, M. V. (2011). ROI Based Encoding of Medical Images: An Effective Scheme Using Lifting Wavelets and SPIHT for Telemedicine. *International Journal of Computer Theory and Engineering, 3*(3), 338-346. Doi:10.7763/IJCTE.2011.V3.329

Kumari, M., Gupta, S., & Sardana, P. (2017). A Survey of Image Encryption Algorithms. *3D Research, 8*(4), 37.

Kumar, K. (2012). Morphology based facial feature extraction and facial expression recognition for driver vigilance. *International Journal of Computers and Applications*, *51*(2), 17–24. doi:10.5120/8578-2317

Kumar, S., Saxena, R., & Singh, K. (2017). Fractional Fourier transform and fractional-order calculus-based image edge detection. *Circuits, Systems, and Signal Processing*, *36*(4), 1493–1513. doi:10.100700034-016-0364-x

Kundu, A., He, Y., & Chen, M. Y. (1998). Alternatives to variable duration HMM in handwriting recognition. *IEEE Transactions on Pattern Analysis and Machine Intelligence*, *20*(11), 1275–1280. doi:10.1109/34.730561

Lagendijk, R., Biemond, J., & Boekee, D. E. (1988). Regularized iterative image restoration with ringing reduction. *IEEE Transactions on Acoustics, Speech, and Signal Processing*, *36*(12), 1874–1888. doi:10.1109/29.9032

Lahani, J., Sulaiman, H. A., Muniandy, R. K., & Bade, A. (2018). An Enhanced Edge Detection Method Based on Integration of Entropy—Canny Technique. *Advanced Science Letters*, *24*(3), 1575–1578. doi:10.1166/asl.2018.11112

Langdon, G. G. (1984). An introduction to arithmetic coding. *IBM Journal of Research and Development*, *28*(2), 135–149. doi:10.1147/rd.282.0135

Lee, H., Kim, Y., Rowberg, A., & Riskin, E. A. (1993). Statistical distributions of DCT coefficients and their application to an interframe compression algorithm for 3-D medical images. *IEEE Transactions on Medical Imaging*, *12*(3), 478–485. doi:10.1109/42.241875 PMID:18218440

Lee, J. W., Lim, B. R., Park, R.-H., Kim, J.-S., & Ahn, W. (2006). Two-stage false contour detection using directional contrast features and its application to adaptive false contour reduction. *IEEE Transactions on Consumer Electronics*, *52*, 179–188.

Lerch, J. P., Pruessner, J. C., Zijdenbos, A., Hampel, H., Teipel, S. J., & Evans, A. C. (2004). Focal decline of cortical thickness in Alzheimer's disease identified by computational neuroanatomy. [PubMed]. *Cerebral Cortex*, *15*(7), 995–1001. doi:10.1093/cercor/bhh200

Levin, A., Lischinski, D., & Weiss, Y. (2008). A closed-form solution to natural image matting. *IEEE Transactions on Pattern Analysis and Machine Intelligence*, *30*(2), 228–242. doi:10.1109/TPAMI.2007.1177 PMID:18084055

Lewis, A. S., & Knowles, G. (1992). Image compression using the 2- D wavelet transform. *IEEE Transactions on Image Processing*, *1*(2), 244–250. doi:10.1109/83.136601 PMID:18296159

Li, J. H., Cheng, Y., & Shi, H. (2013). Passport Photo Compression Technique with JPEG2000. *Proceedings of 2013 IEEE International Conference on Mechatronics and Automation*. Retrieved from https://ieeexplore.ieee.org/document/6618116

Liu, S., Liu, S., Zhang, F., Cai, W., Pujol, S., Kikinis, R., & Feng, D. (2015). Longitudinal brain MR retrieval with diffeomorphic demons registration: What happened to those patients with similar changes? 2015 IEEE 12th International Symposium on Biomedical Imaging (ISBI). doi:10.1109/isbi.2015.7163942

Liu, Y., Li, H., & Wang, M. (2017). Single image dehazing via large sky region segmentation and multiscale opening dark channel model. *IEEE Access: Practical Innovations, Open Solutions*, 5, 8890–8903. doi:10.1109/ACCESS.2017.2710305

Li, X. X., Tian, D., He, C. H., & He, J. H. (2019). A fractal modification of the surface coverage model for an electrochemical arsenic sensor. *Electrochimica Acta*, 296, 491–493. doi:10.1016/j. electacta.2018.11.042

Lledo, P.-M., Alonso, M., & Grubb, M. S. (2006). Adult neurogenesis and functional plasticity in neuronal circuits. [PubMed]. *Nature Reviews. Neuroscience*, 7(3), 179–193. doi:10.1038/nrn1867

Lowe, D. G. (2004). Distinctive image features from scale-invariant key points. *International Journal of Computer Vision*, 60(2), 91–110. doi:10.1023/B:VISI.0000029664.99615.94

Luchsinger José, A., & Mayeux, R. (2019). Dietary factors and Alzheimer's disease. [PubMed]. *Lancet Neurology*, 3(10), 579–587. doi:10.1016/S1474-4422(04)00878-6

Mackworth, N. H., & Morandi, A. J. (1967). The Gaze Selects Informative Details Within Pictures. *Perception & Psychophysics*, 2(11), 547–552. doi:10.3758/BF03210264

MacMahon, H. (1991). *Radiology, Data compression: effect on diagnostic accuracy in digital chest radiography*. Academic Press.

Magnin, B., Mesrob, L., Kinkingnéhun, S., Pélégrini-Issac, M., Colliot, O., Sarazin, M., ... Benali, H. (2008). Support vector machine-based classification of Alzheimer's disease from whole-brain anatomical MRI. [PubMed]. *Neuroradiology*, 51(2), 73–83. doi:10.100700234-008-0463-x

Maiseli, B. J., & Gao, H. (2016). Robust edge detector based on anisotropic diffusion-driven process. *Information Processing Letters*, 116(5), 373–378. doi:10.1016/j.ipl.2015.12.003

Mallat, S. G. (1989). A Theory of multi-resolution Signal Decomposition: The Wavelet Representation. *IEEE Transactions on Pattern Analysis and Machine Intelligence*, 11(7), 674–693. doi:10.1109/34.192463

Mandelbrot, B. B. (1993). *The Fractal Geometry of Nature*. W.H. Freeman and Company.

Mantas, J. (1986). An overview of character recognition methodologies. *Pattern Recognition*, 19(6), 425–430. doi:10.1016/0031-3203(86)90040-3

Manu, B. N. (2017). Facial features monitoring for real time drowsiness detection. *Proc. 2016 12th Int. Conf. Innov. Inf. Technol. IIT 2016*, 78–81.

Martin, M. B. (1999). *Applications of Multi-wavelets to Image Compression*. M.S. Thesis.

Meyer. (1993). Wavelets: their past and their future. *Progress in Wavelet Analysis and its Applications*, 9-18.

Ming, G., & Song, H. (2005). Adult Neurogenesis in the Mammalian Central Nervous System. [PubMed]. *Annual Review of Neuroscience*, *28*(1), 223–250. doi:10.1146/annurev. neuro.28.051804.101459

Mishra, T. K., Majhi, B., Sa, P. K., & Panda, S. (2014). Model based odia numeral recognition using fuzzy aggregated features. *Frontiers of Computer Science*, *8*(6), 916–922. doi:10.100711704-014-3354-9

Misra, C., Fan, Y., & Davatzikos, C. (2009). Baseline and longitudinal patterns of brain atrophy in MCI patients, and their use in prediction of short-term conversion to AD: Results from ADNI☆. [PubMed]. *NeuroImage*, *44*(4), 1415–1422. doi:10.1016/j.neuroimage.2008.10.031

Mitiku, K., Mengistu, G., & Gelaw, B. (2000). The reliability of blood film examination for malaria at the peripheral health unit. *Tropical Medicine & International Health*, *5*, 3–8. PMID:10672199

Mitra, C., & Pujari, A. K. (2013). Directional decomposition for odia character recognition. In *Mining Intelligence and Knowledge Exploration* (pp. 270–278). Cham: Springer. doi:10.1007/978-3-319-03844-5_28

Mitra, S. K., Murthy, C. A., & Kundu, M. K. (1998). Technique for Fractal Image compression Using Genetic Algorithm. *IEEE Transactions on Image Processing*, *7*(4), 586–593. doi:10.1109/83.663505 PMID:18276275

Mohammed, U. S., & Abd-Elhafiez, W. M. (2011). New Approaches for DCT Based Image Compression Using Region of Interest Scheme. *Applied Mathematics & Information Sciences*, *5*(1), 29–43.

Mohan, J., Krishnaveni, V., & Guo, Y. (2014). A survey on the magnetic resonance image denoising methods. *Biomedical Signal Processing and Control*, *9*, 56–69. doi:10.1016/j.bspc.2013.10.007

Moulin, P. (1995). A multi-scale relaxation algorithm for SNR maximization in non-orthogonal sub-band coding. *IEEE Transactions on Image Processing*, *4*(9), 1269–1281. doi:10.1109/83.413171 PMID:18292023

Muschelli, J., Sweeney, E., & Crainiceanu, C. M. (2018). freesurfer: Connecting the Freesurfer software with R. [PubMed]. *F1000 Research*, *7*, 599. doi:10.12688/f1000research.14361.1

Nagamani, K., & Ananth, A. G. (2011). EZW and SPIHT Image Compression Techniques for High Resolution Satellite Imageries. *International Journal of Advanced Engineering Technology Computer Application*, *2*(2), 82-86.

Nasrabadi, N. M. (2007). Pattern recognition and machine learning. *Journal of Electronic Imaging*, *16*(4), 049901. doi:10.1117/1.2819119

Nasrabadi, N. M., & King, R. A. (1988). Image coding using vector quantization: A review. *IEEE Transactions on Communications*, *36*(8), 957–971. doi:10.1109/26.3776

National Institutes of Health (NIH). (2005). Progress Report on Alzheimer's Disease 2004–2005. NIH Publication Number: 05-5724, Nov 2005.

Nayak, S. R., Mishra, J., & Jena, P. M. (2018b). Fractal Dimension of GrayScale Images. In Progress in Computing, Analytics and Networking (pp. 225-234). Springer. doi:10.1007/978-981-10-7871-2_22

Nayak, S. R., & Mishra, J. (2018a). A modified triangle box-counting with precision in error fit. *Journal of Information and Optimization Sciences*, *39*(1), 113–128. doi:10.1080/02522667 .2017.1372155

Nayak, S. R., & Mishra, J. (2019). Analysis of Medical Images Using Fractal Geometry. In *Histopathological Image Analysis in Medical Decision Making* (pp. 181–201). IGI Global. doi:10.4018/978-1-5225-6316-7.ch008

Nayak, S. R., Mishra, J., Khandual, A., & Palai, G. (2018f). Fractal dimension of RGB color images. *Optik (Stuttgart)*, *162*, 196–205. doi:10.1016/j.ijleo.2018.02.066

Nayak, S. R., Mishra, J., & Padhy, R. (2016). An improved algorithm to estimate the fractal dimension of gray scale images. In *2016 International Conference on Signal Processing, Communication, Power and Embedded System (SCOPES)* (pp. 1109-1114). IEEE. 10.1109/SCOPES.2016.7955614

Nayak, S. R., Mishra, J., & Padhy, R. (2018c). A New Extended Differential Box-Counting Method by Adopting Unequal Partitioning of Grid for Estimation of Fractal Dimension of Grayscale Images. In *Computational Signal Processing and Analysis* (pp. 45–57). Singapore: Springer. doi:10.1007/978-981-10-8354-9_5

Nayak, S. R., Mishra, J., & Palai, G. (2018d). A modified approach to estimate fractal dimension of gray scale images. *Optik (Stuttgart)*, *161*, 136–145. doi:10.1016/j.ijleo.2018.02.024

Nayak, S. R., Mishra, J., & Palai, G. (2018e). An extended DBC approach by using maximum Euclidian distance for fractal dimension of color images. *Optik (Stuttgart)*, *166*, 110–115. doi:10.1016/j.ijleo.2018.03.106

Nayak, S. R., Ranganath, A., & Mishra, J. (2015). Analysing fractal dimension of color images. In *2015 International Conference on Computational Intelligence and Networks* (pp. 156-159). IEEE. 10.1109/CINE.2015.37

Nayak, S., Khandual, A., & Mishra, J. (2018g). Ground truth study on fractal dimension of color images of similar texture. *Journal of the Textile Institute*, *109*(9), 1159–1167. doi:10.1080/004 05000.2017.1418710

Ng, J., Aguilar, M.-I., & Small, D. H. (2007). Amyloid Toxicity, Synaptic Dysfunction, and the Biochemistry of Neurodegeneration in Alzheimer's disease. Abeta Peptide and Alzheimer's Disease, 93–101. doi:10.1007/978-1-84628-440-3_6

O'Hanen, B., & Wisan M. (2005). *JPEG Compression*. Academic Press.

Olkkonen, H. (2011). *Discrete Wavelet Transforms- Bio-Medical Applications*. doi:10.5772/1818

Omidyeganeh, M., Javadtalab, A., & Shirmohammadi, S. (2011). Intelligent driver drowsiness detection through fusion of yawning and eye closure. In *Virtual Environments Human-Computer Interfaces and Measurement Systems (VECIMS), 2011 IEEE International Conference on*. IEEE. 10.1109/VECIMS.2011.6053857

Othman, Z., & Abdullah, A. (2017). An Adaptive Threshold Based On Multiple Resolution Levels for Canny Edge Detection. In *International Conference of Reliable Information and Communication Technology* (pp. 316-323). Springer.

Padmavati, S., & Meshram, V. (2019). A Hardware Implementation of Fractal Quadtree Compression for Medical Images. In *Integrated Intelligent Computing, Communication and Security* (pp. 547–555). Singapore: Springer. doi:10.1007/978-981-10-8797-4_55

Pal, U., & Chaudhuri, B. B. (2004). Indian script character recognition: a survey. *Pattern Recognition, 37*(9), 1887-1899.

Pal, U., Wakabayashi, T., & Kimura, F. (2007, December). A system for off-line Oriya handwritten character recognition using curvature feature. In *10th international conference on information technology (ICIT 2007)* (pp. 227-229). IEEE. 10.1109/ICIT.2007.63

Palanisamy, G., & Samukutti, A. (2008). Medical image compression using a novel embedded set partitioning significant and zero block coding. *The International Arab Journal of Information Technology, 5*(2), 132–139.

Pal, C., Chakrabarti, A., & Ghosh, R. (2015). A brief survey of recent edge-preserving smoothing algorithms on digital images. *Procedia Computer Science*, 1–40.

Pal, U., & Chaudhuri, B. B. (2001). Machine-printed and hand-written text lines identification. *Pattern Recognition Letters, 22*(3-4), 431–441. doi:10.1016/S0167-8655(00)00126-4

Pal, U., Jayadevan, R., & Sharma, N. (2012). Handwriting recognition in indian regional scripts: A survey of offline techniques. *ACM Transactions on Asian Language Information Processing, 11*(1), 1–35. doi:10.1145/2090176.2090177

Paradise, M., Cooper, C., & Livingston, G. (2009). Systematic review of the effect of education on survival in Alzheimer's disease. [PubMed]. *International Psychogeriatrics, 21*(1), 25–32. doi:10.1017/S1041610208008053

Pasco, R. (1976). *Source Coding Algorithms for Fast Data Compression* (Ph.D. thesis). Stanford University.

Patel, J., Patwardhan, J., Sankhe, K., & Kumbhare, R. (2011). Fuzzy inference based edge detection system using Sobel and Laplacian of Gaussian operators. In *Proceedings of the International Conference & Workshop on Emerging Trends in Technology* (pp. 694-697). ACM. 10.1145/1980022.1980171

Patra, P. K., Nayak, M., Nayak, S. K., & Gobbak, N. K. (2002). Probabilistic neural network for pattern classification. In *Proceedings of the 2002 International Joint Conference on Neural Networks. IJCNN'02 (Cat. No. 02CH37290)* (Vol. 2, pp. 1200-1205). IEEE.

Penebaker, W., & Mitchell, J. (1993). *JPEG Still Image Data Compression Standard.* Van Nostrand.

Perlmutter, S. M., Cosman, P. C., Gray, R. M., Olshen, R. A., Ikeda, D., Adams, C. N., ... Daniel, B. L. (1997). Image quality in lossy compressed digital mammograms. *Signal Processing, 59*(2), 189–210. doi:10.1016/S0165-1684(97)00046-7

Perona, P., & Malik, J. (1990). Scale-Space and Edge Detection Using Anisotropic Diffusion. *IEEE Transactions on Pattern Analysis and Machine Intelligence, 12*(7), 629–639. doi:10.1109/34.56205

Persons all People, Among Young. (2000). A Report of the Surgeon General.

Plamondon, R., & Srihari, S. N. (2000). Online and off-line handwriting recognition: A comprehensive survey. *IEEE Transactions on Pattern Analysis and Machine Intelligence, 22*(1), 63–84. doi:10.1109/34.824821

Podder, P., Parvez, A. M. S., Yeasmin, M. N., & Khalil, M. I. (2018). Relative Performance Analysis of Edge Detection Techniques in Iris Recognition System. In *2018 International Conference on Current Trends towards Converging Technologies (ICCTCT)* (pp. 1-6). IEEE. 10.1109/ICCTCT.2018.8551023

Pratt, W. K. (1978). *Digital Image Processing.* New York: Wiley.

Qian, J. (2011). Face detection and recognition method based on skin color and depth information. In *Consumer Electronics, Communications and Networks (CECNet), 2011 International Conference on.* IEEE. 10.1109/CECNET.2011.5768500

Querbes, O., Aubry, F., Pariente, J., Lotterie, J. A., Démonet, J. F., Duret, V., ... Celsis, P. (2009). Early diagnosis of Alzheimer's disease using cortical thickness: Impact of cognitive reserve. [PubMed]. *Brain, 132*(8), 2036–2047. doi:10.1093/brain/awp105

Radwan, A. G., AbdElHaleem, S. H., & Abd-El-Hafiz, S. K. (2016). Symmetric encryption algorithms using chaotic and non-chaotic generators: A review. *Journal of Advanced Research, 7*(2), 193–208. doi:10.1016/j.jare.2015.07.002 PMID:26966561

Raja, S. P., & Suruliandi, A. (2010). Performance Evaluation on EZW & WDR Image Compression Techniques. In 2010 international conference on communication control and computing technologies. Ramanathapuram, India: Academic Press. Retrieved from https://ieeexplore.ieee.org/abstract/document/5670757

Rana, R., Chauhan, Y. S., & Negi, A. (2011). Generation of New Fractals for Sin Function. *Int. J. Comp. Tech. Appl., 2*(6), 1747–1754.

Rani & Bansal, R K. (2009). Comparison of JPEG and SPIHT image compression algorithms using objective quality measures. In *Proc. IEEE International Multimedia Signal Processing and Communication Technologies*, (pp. 90-93). IEEE.

Rao, K., & Hwang, J. (1996). *Techniques and Standards for Image, Video and Audio Coding.* Prentice-Hall.

Reisberg, B., Ferris, S. H., de Leon, M. J., & Crook, T. (1982). The Global Deterioration Scale for assessment of primary degenerative dementia. [PubMed]. *The American Journal of Psychiatry, 139*(9), 1136–1139. doi:10.1176/ajp.139.9.1136

Rezaee, K. (2013). Real-time intelligent alarm system of driver fatigue based on video sequences. In *Robotics and Mechatronics (ICRoM), 2013 First RSI/ISM International Conference on.* IEEE. 10.1109/ICRoM.2013.6510137

Rioul, O., & Vetterli, M. (1991). Wavelets and Signal Processing. *IEEE Transactions on Signal Processing, 8*(4), 14–38. doi:10.1109/79.91217

Risa. (n.d.). Retrieved from: http://risa.is.tokushima-u.ac.jp/~tetsushi/chen

Rissanen, J. J. (1976). Generalized Kraft Inequality and Arithmetic Coding. *IBM Journal of Research and Development, 20*(3), 198–203. doi:10.1147/rd.203.0198

Rissanen, J. J., & Langdon, G. G. (1979). Arithmetic Coding. *IBM Journal of Research and Development, 23*(2), 146–162. doi:10.1147/rd.232.0149

Ruberto, C. D., Dempster, A., Khan, S., & Jarra, B. (2002). Analysis of infected blood cell images using morphological operators. *Image and Vision Computing, 20*(2), 133–146. doi:10.1016/S0262-8856(01)00092-0

Rudin, L. I., Osher, S., & Fatemi, E. (1992). Nonlinear total variation based noise removal algorithms, Phys. *D Nonlinear Phenom., 60*(1-4), 259–268. doi:10.1016/0167-2789(92)90242-F

Saffor, E., Ramli, A., & Kh, N. (2001). A comparative study of image compression between JPEG and wavelet. *Malaysian Journal of Computer Science, 14*, 39–45.

Sagonas, C., Tzimiropoulos, G., Zafeiriou, S., & Pantic, M. (2013). 300 faces in-the-wild challenge: The first facial landmark localization challenge. In *Computer Vision Workshops (ICCVW), 2013 IEEE International Conference on*, (pp. 397–403). IEEE.

Saha, S. (2001). *Image Compression from DCT to Wavelet: A Review.* Retrieved from http://www.acm.org/crossroads/xrds6-3/sahaimgcoding.html

Said, A., & Pearlman, W. A. (1996). A new fast and efficient image codec based on Set Partitioning in Hierarchical Trees. *IEEE Transcation Circuits System Video Tech., 6*(3), 1–16.

Said, A., & Pearlman, W. A. (1996). A new, fast, and efficient image codec based on set partitioning in hierarchical trees. *IEEE Transactions on Circuits and Systems for Video Technology*, 6(3), 243–250. https://ieeexplore.ieee.org/document/499834. doi:10.1109/76.499834

Saxe, M. D., Battaglia, F., Wang, J.-W., Malleret, G., David, D. J., Monckton, J. E., ... Drew, M. R. (2006). Ablation of hippocampal neurogenesis impairs contextual fear conditioning and synaptic plasticity in the dentate gyrus. [PubMed]. *Proceedings of the National Academy of Sciences of the United States of America*, 103(46), 17501–17506. doi:10.1073/pnas.0607207103

Sayed, U. (2005). Image Coding Technique Based on Object-Feature Extraction. *Proceedings of (NRSC'2005)*.

Scharcanski, J., & Venetsanopoulos, A. N. (1997). Edge detection of color images using directional operators. *IEEE Transactions on Circuits and Systems for Video Technology*, 7(2), 397–401. doi:10.1109/76.564116

Schelkens, P., Munteanu, A., & Cornelis, J. (1999). Wavelet-based compression of medical images: Protocols to improve resolution and quality scalability and region-of-interest coding. *Future Generation Computer Systems*, 15(2), 171–184. doi:10.1016/S0167-739X(98)00061-2

Seeram, E. (2006). Irreversible compression in digital radiology. A literature review. *Radiography*, 12(1), 45–59. doi:10.1016/j.radi.2005.04.002

Senapati, D., Rout, S., & Nayak, M. (2012, July). A novel approach to text line and word segmentation on odia printed documents. In *2012 Third International Conference on Computing, Communication and Networking Technologies (ICCCNT'12)* (pp. 1-6). IEEE. 10.1109/ICCCNT.2012.6396063

Senoo, T., & Girod, B. (1992). Vector quantization for entropy coding of image sub-bands. *IEEE Transactions on Image Processing*, 1(4), 526–533. doi:10.1109/83.199923 PMID:18296186

Sethi, I. K., & Chatterjee, B. (1977). Machine recognition of constrained hand printed Devanagari. *Pattern Recognition*, 9(2), 69–75. doi:10.1016/0031-3203(77)90017-6

Sethy, A., Patra, P. K., & Nayak, D. R. (2018). Off-Line Handwritten Odia Character Recognition Using DWT and PCA. In Progress in Advanced Computing and Intelligent Engineering (pp. 187-195). Springer. doi:10.1007/978-981-10-6872-0_18

Shanmugavadivu, P., & Kumar, A. (2014). Modified eight-directional canny for robust edge detection. In *Contemporary Computing and Informatics (IC3I), 2014 International Conference on* (pp. 751-756). IEEE. 10.1109/IC3I.2014.7019768

Sharma, M. (2010). Compression Using Huffman Coding. *International Journal of Computer Science and Network Security*, 10(5).

Sharma, N., Pal, U., Kimura, F., & Pal, S. (2006). Recognition of off-line handwritten devnagari characters using quadratic classifier. In *Computer Vision, Graphics and Image Processing* (pp. 805–816). Berlin: Springer. doi:10.1007/11949619_72

Shi, Y. Q., & Sun, H. (2000). *Image and Video Compression for Multimedia Engineering: Fundamentals, Algorithms, and Standards* (1st ed.). Boca Raton, FL: CRC Press LLC.

Shors, T. J., Miesegaes, G., Beylin, A., Zhao, M., Rydel, T., & Gould, E. (2001). Neurogenesis in the adult is involved in the formation of trace memories. [PubMed]. *Nature, 410*(6826), 372–376. doi:10.1038/35066584

Shors, T. J., Townsend, D. A., Zhao, M., Kozorovitskiy, Y., & Gould, E. (2002). Neurogenesis may relate to some but not all types of hippocampal-dependent learning. [PubMed]. *Hippocampus, 12*(5), 578–584. doi:10.1002/hipo.10103

Sifuzzaman, M., Islam, M. R., & Ali, M. Z. (2009). Application of Wavelet Transform and its Advantages Compared to Fourier Transform. *Journal of Physical Sciences, 13*, 121-134.

Singh, P. N., Gupta, D., & Sharma, S. (2012). Performance Analysis of Embedded Zero Tree and Set Partitioning In Hierarchical Tree. *International Journal of Computer Technology & Applications, 3*, 572-577.

Singh, P., & Duhan, M., & Priyanka. (2006). Enhancing LZW Algorithm to Increase Overall Performance. *Annual IEEE Indian Conference*, 1-4. 10.1109/INDCON.2006.302770

Singh, P., & Singh, P. (2011). Design and Implementation of EZW & SPIHT Image Coder for Virtual Image. *International Journal of Computer Science and Security, Kuala Lumpur, Malaysia, 5*(5), 433–442.

Singh, S., & Verma, H. K. (2007). DWT–DCT hybrid scheme for medical image compression. *Journal of Medical Engineering & Technology, 31*(2), 109–122. doi:10.1080/03091900500412650 PMID:17365435

Sinha, R. M. K., & Mahabala, H. N. (1979). Machine recognition of Devanagari script. *IEEE Transactions on Systems, Man, and Cybernetics, 9*(8), 435–441. doi:10.1109/TSMC.1979.4310256

Slone, R. M., Foos, D. H., Whiting, B. R., Muka, E., Rubin, D. A., Pilgram, T. K., ... Hendrickson, D. D. (2000). Assessment of Visually Lossless Irreversible Image Compression:Comparison of Three Methods by Using an Image-Comparison Workstation 1. *Radiology, 215*(2), 543–553. doi:10.1148/radiology.215.2.r00ap47543 PMID:10796938

Smith, M. J. T., & Eddins, S. L. (1990). Analysis/synthesis techniques for sub-band image coding. *IEEE Trans. Acoustic, Speech, Signal Processing*, 1446–1456. Retrieved from https://ieeexplore.ieee.org/abstract/document/57579/similar#similar

Smutek, D. (2005). Quality measurement of lossy compression in medical imaging. *Prague Medical Report, 106*(1), 5–26. PMID:16007906

Snyder, J. S., Hong, N. S., McDonald, R. J., & Wojtowicz, J. M. (2005). A role for adult neurogenesis in spatial long-term memory. [PubMed]. *Neuroscience, 130*(4), 843–852. doi:10.1016/j.neuroscience.2004.10.009

Song. (2014). Eyes closeness detection from still images with multi-scale histograms of principal oriented gradients. *Pattern Recognition, 47*(9).

Song, C. (2002). ROI Image Coding methods in JPEG2000. *TV Engineering, 5*, 15–18.

Soumya, R. N., & Mishra, J. (2018c). Analysis of Medical images using Fractal Geometry. In Histopathological Image Analysis in Medical Decision Making, (pp. 181-201). Academic Press.

Soumya, R. N., Mishra, J., & Palai, G. (2018). A modified approach to estimate fractal dimension of gray scale Images. International Journal for Light and Electron Optics, 161, 136-145.

Srljan, N., Grgic, S., & Grgic, M. (2005). Modified SPIHT algorithm for wavelet packet image coding. *Real-Time Imaging, 11*(5-6), 378–388. doi:10.1016/j.rti.2005.06.009

Sridhar, K. V. (2008). *Implementation of Prioritised ROI Coding for Medical Image Archiving using JPEG2000.* International Conference on Signals and Electronic Systems. Retrieved from https://ieeexplore.ieee.org/document/4673403

Sriram, B., & Thiyagarajans, S. (2012). Hybrid Transformation technique for image compression. *Journal of Theoretical and Applied Information Technology, 41*(2), 175-180.

Stark, L., Yamashita, I., Tharp, G., & Ngo, H. X. (1993). Search Patterns and Search Paths in Human Visual Search. In D. Brogan, A. Gale, & K. Carr (Eds.), *Visual Search 2* (pp. 37–58). London: Taylor and Francis.

Stelmach, L. B., Tam, W. J., & Hearty, P. J. (1991). Static and Dynamic Spatial Resolution in Image Coding: An Investigation of Eye Movements. *Proc. SPIE Human Vision, Visual Processing and Digital Display II, 1453*, 147-152. 10.1117/12.44351

Stern, Y. (2006). Cognitive Reserve and Alzheimer Disease. [PubMed]. *Alzheimer Disease and Associated Disorders, 20*(2), 112–117. doi:10.1097/01.wad.0000213815.20177.19

Stough, T. M., & Brodley, C. E. (2001). Focusing Attention on Objects of Interest Using Multiple Matched Filters. *IEEE Transactions on Image Processing, 10*(3), 419–426. doi:10.1109/83.908516 PMID:18249631

Strang, G., & Nguyen, T. (1996). *Wavelets and Filter Banks.* Wellesley, MA: Wellesley Cambridge Press.

Szekely, C. A., Breitner, J. C. S., & Zandi, P. P. (2007). Prevention of Alzheimer's disease. [PubMed]. *International Review of Psychiatry (Abingdon, England), 19*(6), 693–706. doi:10.1080/09540260701797944

Tang, C., & Wang, B. (2016). A no-reference adaptive blockiness measure for JPEG compressed images. *PLoS One, 11*(11), 1–12. doi:10.1371/journal.pone.0165664 PMID:27832092

Tao, M., Hempel, M., Dongming, P., & Sharif, H. (2013). A survey of energy-efficient compression and communication techniques for multimedia in resource-constrained systems. *IEEE Communications Surveys and Tutorials*, *15*(3), 963–972. doi:10.1109/SURV.2012.060912.00149

Tarel, J. P., & Hautiere, N. (2009). Fast visibility restoration from a single color or gray level image. In *12th International Conference on Computer Vision (ICCV 2009)* (pp. 2201-2208). IEEE. 10.1109/ICCV.2009.5459251

Tarel, J., & Hautiere, N. (2008). Fast visibility restoration from a single color or gray level image. In *Conference on Computer Vision and Pattern Recognition (ICCVPR 2008)* (pp. 2201-2208). IEEE.

Tian, H., Cai, H., Lai, J. H., & Xu, X. (2011). Effective image noise removal based on difference eigenvalue. *18th IEEE Int. Conf. Image Process*, 3357–3360. 10.1109/ICIP.2011.6116392

Tiesheng, P. (2005). Yawning detection for determining driver drowsiness. *VLSI Design and Video Technology, 2005. Proceedings of 2005 IEEE International Workshop*, 373 – 376.

Timo, K., Pasi, F., & Olli, N. (1996). Empirical study on subjective quality evaluation of compressed images. *Proceedings of the Society for Photo-Instrumentation Engineers*, 78–87.

Tiraboschi, P., Hansen, L. A., Thal, L. J., & Corey-Bloom, J. (2004). The importance of neuritic plaques and tangles to the development and evolution of AD. [PubMed]. *Neurology*, *62*(11), 1984–1989. doi:10.1212/01.WNL.0000129697.01779.0A

Tobin, A. J. (1987). Alzheimer disease: Enter molecular biology. [PubMed]. *Alzheimer Disease and Associated Disorders*, *1*(2), 69–71. doi:10.1097/00002093-198701020-00001

Tripathi, A. K., & Mukhopadhyay, S. (2012). Single image fog removal using anisotropic diffusion. *IET Image Processing*, *6*(7), 966–975. doi:10.1049/iet-ipr.2011.0472

Tripathy, N., & Pal, U. (2006). Handwriting segmentation of unconstrained Oriya text. *Sadhana*, *31*(6), 755–769. doi:10.1007/BF02716894

Tropf, A., & Chai, D. (2005). Region Segmentation for Facial Image Compression. *Proc. IEEE Communications and Signal Processing,* 1556-1560. Retrieved from https://ieeexplore.ieee.org/document/1689320

Tsai, D. M., & Chao, S. M. (2005). An anisotropic diffusion-based defect detection for sputtered surfaces with inhomogeneous textures. *Image and Vision Computing*, *23*(3), 325–338. doi:10.1016/j.imavis.2004.09.003

Uemura, K., Toyama, H., Baba, S., Kimura, Y., Senda, M., & Uchiyama, A. (2000). Generation of fractal dimension images and its application to automatic edge detection in brain MRI. *Computerized Medical Imaging and Graphics*, *24*(2), 73–85. doi:10.1016/S0895-6111(99)00045-2 PMID:10767587

Usevitch, B. E. (2001). A Tutorial on Modern Lossy Wavelet Image Compression: Foundations of JPEG 2000. *IEEE Signal Processing Magazine*, *18*(5), 22–35. doi:10.1109/79.952803

Compilation of References

Vaidyanathan, P. (1993). *Multirate Systems and Filter Banks*. Prentice-Hall.

Van Cauwenberghe, C., Van Broeckhoven, C., & Sleegers, K. (2015). The genetic landscape of Alzheimer disease: Clinical implications and perspectives. [PubMed]. *Genetics in Medicine*, *18*(5), 421–430. doi:10.1038/gim.2015.117

Vemuri, P., Gunter, J. L., Senjem, M. L., Whitwell, J. L., Kantarci, K., Knopman, D. S., ... Jack, C. R. Jr. (2008). Alzheimer's disease diagnosis in individual subjects using structural MR images: Validation studies. [PubMed]. *NeuroImage*, *39*(3), 1186–1197. doi:10.1016/j.neuroimage.2007.09.073

Vetterli, M., & Herley, C. (1992). Wavelets and filter banks: Theory and design. *IEEE Transactions on Signal Processing*, *40*(9), pp2207–pp2232. doi:10.1109/78.157221

Videla, L.S., & Ashok Kumar, M. (2018, March). Modified Feature Extraction Using Viola Jones Algorithm. *Journal of Advanced Research in Dynamical & Control Systems, 10*(3), 528-538.

Viola & Jones. (2001). Rapid Object Detection using a Boosted Cascade of Simple Features. *Proceedings of the 2001 IEEE Computer Society Conference on Computer Vision and Pattern Recognition (CVPR 2001)*.

Viola, P., & Jones, M. J. (2004). Robust real-time face detection. *International Journal of Computer Vision*, *57*(2), 137–154. doi:10.1023/B:VISI.0000013087.49260.fb

Wallace, G. K. (1991). The JPEG Still Picture Compression Standard. *Conference of the ACM*, *34*, 30–44.

Wallace, G. K. (1992). The JPEG Still Picture Compression Standard. *IEEE Transactions on Consumer Electronics*, *38*(1), 18–34. doi:10.1109/30.125072

Wang, L., Ye, Q., Xiao, Y., Zou, Y., & Zhang, B. (2008, May). An image encryption scheme based on cross chaotic map. In 2008 Congress on Image and Signal Processing (Vol. 3, pp. 22-26). IEEE. doi:10.1109/CISP.2008.129

Wang, M., Jin, J. S., Jing, Y., Han, X., Gao, L., & Xiao, L. (2016). The Improved Canny Edge Detection Algorithm Based on an Anisotropic and Genetic Algorithm. In *Chinese Conference on Image and Graphics Technologies* (pp. 115-124). Springer. 10.1007/978-981-10-2260-9_14

Wang, W., Yuan, X., Wu, X., & Liu, Y. (2017). Fast image dehazing method based on linear transformation. *IEEE Transactions on Multimedia*.

Wang, X. (2007). Laplacian operator-based edge detectors. *IEEE Transactions on Pattern Analysis and Machine Intelligence*, *29*(5), 886–890. doi:10.1109/TPAMI.2007.1027 PMID:17356206

Wang, Y. Q., Guo, J., Chen, W., & Zhang, W. (2013). Image denoising using modified Perona-Malik model based on directional Laplacian. *Signal Processing*, *93*(9), 2548–2558. doi:10.1016/j.sigpro.2013.02.020

Wang, Y., & Fan, C. (2014). Single image defogging by multi-scale depth fusion. *IEEE Transactions on Image Processing*, *23*(11), 4826–4837. doi:10.1109/TIP.2014.2358076 PMID:25248180

Wang, Z., Bovik, A. C., Sheikh, H. R., & Simonelli, E. P. (2004). Image Quality Assessment: From Error Visibility to Structural Similarity. *IEEE Transactions on Image Processing*, *13*(4), 600–612. doi:10.1109/TIP.2003.819861 PMID:15376593

Wan, J., He, X., & Shi, P. (2007). *An Iris Image Quality Assessment Method Based on Laplacian of Gaussian Operation*. MVA.

Wei-Bin, C., & Xin, Z. (2009, April). Image encryption algorithm based on Henon chaotic system. In *2009 International Conference on Image Analysis and Signal Processing* (pp. 94-97). IEEE. 10.1109/IASP.2009.5054653

Welch, T. A. (1984). A technique for high-performance data compression. *IEEE Computer*, *17*(6), 8–19. doi:10.1109/MC.1984.1659158

Westerink, P., Biemond, J., Boekee, D., & Woods, J. W. (1988). Subband coding of images using vector quantization. *IEEE Transactions on Communications*, *36*(6), 713–719. doi:10.1109/26.2791

Whittaker, E. T. (1915). On the Functions which are Represented by the Expansions of Interpolation Theory. *Proceedings of the Royal Society of Edinburgh*, *35*, 181–194. doi:10.1017/S0370164600017806

Wise, J. (1984). *Eye Movements While Viewing Commercial NTSC Format Television*. White Paper, SMPTE Psychophysics Committee.

Witten, R. (1987). *Arithmetic coding revisited in Data Compression. DCC '95 Proceedings*.

Woods, J., & ONeil, S.D. (1986). Sub-band coding of images. *IEEE Transactions on Acoustics, Speech and Signal Processing, 34*(5), 1278-1288, https://ieeexplore.ieee.org/document/1164962

Wright, I. C., McGuire, P. K., Poline, J.-B., Travere, J. M., Murray, R. M., Frith, C. D., ... Friston, K. J. (1995). A Voxel-Based Method for the Statistical Analysis of Gray and White Matter Density Applied to Schizophrenia. [PubMed]. *NeuroImage*, *2*(4), 244–252. doi:10.1006/nimg.1995.1032

Xie, Y., Chen, K., & Murphey, Y. L. (2018, November). Real-time and Robust Driver Yawning Detection with Deep Neural Networks. In *2018 IEEE Symposium Series on Computational Intelligence (SSCI)* (pp. 532-538). IEEE.

Xin, G., Ke, C., & Xiaoguang, H. (2012). An improved Canny edge detection algorithm for color image. In *Industrial Informatics (INDIN), 2012 10th IEEE International Conference on* (pp. 113-117). IEEE. 10.1109/INDIN.2012.6301061

Xin, L. (2001). Edge-directed prediction for lossless compression of natural images. *IEEE Transactions on Image Processing*, *10*(6), 813–817. doi:10.1109/83.923277

Yang, S., Hu, Y. H., Nguyen, T. Q., & Tull, D. L. (2001). Maximum-Likelihood Parameter Estimation for Image Ringing Artifact Removal. *IEEE Transactions on Circuits and Systems for Video Technology, 11*(8).

Ye, J., Chen, K., Wu, T., Li, J., Zhao, Z., Patel, R., ... Reiman, E. (2008, August). Heterogeneous data fusion for alzheimer's disease study. In *Proceedings of the 14th ACM SIGKDD international conference on Knowledge discovery and data mining* (pp. 1025-1033). ACM. doi:10.1145/1401890.1402012

Yin, L., Li, X., Zheng, W., Yin, Z., Song, L., Ge, L., & Zeng, Q. (2019). Fractal dimension analysis for seismicity spatial and temporal distribution in the circum-Pacific seismic belt. *Journal of Earth System Science, 128*(1), 22. doi:10.100712040-018-1040-2

Yu-qian, Z., Wei-hua, G., Zhen-cheng, C., Jing-tian, T., & Ling-Yun, L. (2006). Medical images edge detection based on mathematical morphology. In *Engineering in Medicine and Biology Society, 2005. IEEE-EMBS 2005. 27th Annual International Conference of the* (pp. 6492-6495). IEEE.

Zahran, O., Kasban, H., El-Kordy, M., & El-Samie, F. E. A. (2013). Automatic weld defect identification from radiographic images. *NDT & E International, 57*, 26–35. doi:10.1016/j.ndteint.2012.11.005

Zhang, F., Su, J., Geng, L., & Xiao, Z. (2017). Driver fatigue detection based on eye state recognition. *Proc. - 2017 Int. Conf. Mach. Vis. Inf. Technol. C. 2017*, 105–110. 10.1109/CMVIT.2017.25

Zhao, J. H., Sun, W. J., Meng, Z., & Hao, Z. H. (2004). Wavelet transform characteristics and compression coding of remote sensing images. *Optics and Precision Engineering, 12*(2), 205–210.

Zheng, C., Xia, Y., Pan, Y., & Chen, J. (2015). Automated identification of dementia using medical imaging: A survey from a pattern classification perspective. [PubMed]. *Brain Informatics, 3*(1), 17–27. doi:10.100740708-015-0027-x

Ziv, J., & Lempel, A. (1977). A Universal Algorithm for Sequential Data Compression. *IEEE Transactions on Information Theory, 23*(3), 337–342. doi:10.1109/TIT.1977.1055714

Zmura, M. D. (1991). Color in Visual Search. *Vision Research, 31*(6), 951–966. doi:10.1016/0042-6989(91)90203-H PMID:1858326

About the Contributors

Soumya Ranjan Nayak was born in Odisha in 1984. He received the B.Tech and M.Tech degree in computer science and engineering from Biju Patnaik University of Technology, Odisha, India in 2009 and 2012, respectively. After he join as full time Research Scholar under the fellowship of MHRD Govt. of India (TEQIP-II) at from 2013-2017 at College of Engineering and Technology, Govt. Autonomous Engineering College, Bhubaneswar. He currently is working as an Assistant Professor at Chitkara University Institute of Engineering and Technology, Chitkara University, Punjab, India. He has published more than 40 articles in prestigious international journal and conferences in the area of Fractal Graphics, Pattern Recognition and Color and Texture Analysis. His currently focus on fundamental color image processing. His research interest includes image analysis by means of fractal geometry, color and texture.

Jibitesh Mishra has more than 25 years of teaching and research experience in the field of Computer Science and Information Technology. He has published many papers and books with publishers of repute. His research interests are fractal graphics, mobile computing and web engineering.

* * *

M. Tariq Banday was born in Srinagar, India. He obtained his M.Sc., M. Phil. and Ph. D. degrees in Electronics (Network Security) from the Department of Electronics and Instrumentation Technology, University of Kashmir, Srinagar, India in 1996, 2008, and 2010 respectively. At present, he is working as Associate Professor in the same department. He is a senior member of IEEE, ACM, and CSI. He currently investigates a few government-sponsored research projects in network security. He has to his credit over 100 research publications in reputed journals and conference proceedings. His teaching and research interests include microprocessors & microcontrollers: architecture, programming, and interfacing; programming and problem solving, computer organization, design & architecture, network, internet, e-mail and web security, Internet of Things, data structures and database management systems.

Zeelan Basha is working as assistant professor in department of CSE in KL University. His research area is Image processing. He has published several papers in area of image processing. He is having around 10 years of experience in teaching. Area of interest in subjects are Image processing, data mining and data ware housing, data structures, python programming, OOPS through Java, etc.

Koustav Dutta is a student at KIIT Deemed to be University.

Kalyan Kumar Jena received B. Tech. and M.Tech. degrees in Computer Science & Engineering from BPUT, Odisha. He is continuing his Ph. D. in Utkal University, Bhubaneswar, India (Nodal Centre- IGIT, Sarang). He is working as an Assistant Professor in the dept. of CSE, PMEC, Berhampur. His publications comprise more than 30 papers in national and international journals. His research interests are image processing, WSN, IOT and parallel algorithms. He has more than 4 years of research as well as teaching experience. He acts as an editorial board member of various national and international journals and different professional bodies. He has acted as supervisor of B.Tech. and M.Tech. students.

Ashimananda Khandual is a professor at College of Engineering and Technology.

Azmira Krishna is working as assistant professor in department of CSE in KL University. His research area is Image processing. He has published several papers in area of image processing. He is having around 3 years of experience in teaching. Area of interest in subjects are image processing, data mining and data ware housing, data structures, python programming, OOPS through Java, etc.

Rashmi Kumari is a Ph.D. student in Computer Science & Engineering Department, Birla Institute of Technology, Jharkhand (Ranchi), India. She received her M.Tech. From BIT Mesra, India in 2016. Her research area of interest is machine learning, deep learning, data mining, and BioMedical Image Processing.

Rasmita Lenka is a professor at School of Electronics Engineering at KIIT University.

Muthukumaran Malarvel received his Master of Computer Applications and Master of Technology degree in Computer Science and Engineering. He received his Doctor of Philosophy degree in Digital Image Processing from SASTRA Deemed University, India. From 2014 to 2017, he got fellowship as a senior research fellow under Board of Research in Nuclear Sciences (BRNS), India. He is currently working as Associate Professor in Chitkara University Institute of Engineering and Technology, Chitkara University, Punjab, India. His research interests include: image enhancement, image segmentation, statistical analysis & feature extraction, and machine learning in digital images. He is also interested in developing scientific software applications.

Sarojananda Mishra received MCA from S.U. and M. Tech. degree in Computer Science& Engineering from IIT, Delhi. He received his Ph. D. degree from Utkal University, Bhubaneswar, Odisha. He is working as an Professor & HOD in the dept. of CSEA, IGIT, Sarang. His publications comprise more than 50 papers in national and international journals and conferences. His research interests are Image Processing, Fractals and Graphics, System Dynamics, MIS, Operation Research, Networking, Computer Programming. He has more than 26 years of research as well as teaching experience. He acts as an editorial board member of various national &international journals and member of several national & international professional bodies. He has acted as supervisor of 12 Ph.D. students.

Sasmita Mishra received MCA and ME degree in Computer Science& Engineering from REC, Rourkela. She received her Ph. D. degree from Utkal University, Bhubaneswar, Odisha. She is working as an Associate Professor in the dept. of CSEA, IGIT, Sarang. Her publications comprise more than 40 papers in national and international journals and conferences. Her research interests are RDBMS, Analysis & Design of algorithms and Image Processing. She has more than 23 years of research as well as teaching experience. She acts as an editorial board member of various national &international journals and member of several national & international professional bodies. She has acted as supervisor of 6 Ph.D. students.

Shashank Pushkar is Assistant Professor in the Department of Computer Science and Engineering, Birla Institute of Technology, Mesra, Ranchi, India. He completed his Ph.D. in the Department of Computer Applications from National Institute of

Technology, Jamshedpur, India in the year 2012. He has published many research articles in reputed international Journals. His Current fields of Interest are Software Cost Estimation Using Heuristic Optimization, Data Mining, Privacy-Preserving Data Mining, Urban Computing, Heuristics for Combinatorial Optimization Problems.

R. Pandian has graduated from Madras University, Chennai in 1999 with Bachelor's Degree in Electrical and Electronics Engineering. He has obtained his M.E degree in Applied Electronics from Anna University, Chennai 2007. He has obtained his PhD from Sathyabama Institute of Science and Technology. He has gained a teaching experience of more than 16 years. Presently he is working as an Associate Professor in the Department of Electronics and Instrumentation Engineering, Sathyabama Institute of Science and Technology, Chennai. His research interests are Image Processing and Neural network. He has published papers more than twenty five papers in Sci and Scopus journals.

Anandkumar R. received his both B.Tech and M.Tech Degree from Pondicherry University. Currently he is pursuing full time research in Pondicherry Engineering College. His Research Interest includes Networks, Digital Image Security and Cryptography.

Abhisek Sethy is currently working as Assistant Professor in the department of CSE at Koneru Lakshmaiah Education Foundation, Guntur, Andhra Pradesh, India. My research are interest area are Pattern Recognition, Image Processing, Machine Learning.

Tawheed Jan Shah was born in Srinagar, India. She obtained her M.Sc. and M. Phil. degrees in Electronics (Image Processing) from the Department of Electronics and Instrumentation Technology, University of Kashmir, Srinagar, India in 2010 and 2015 respectively. She also achieved her B. Ed degree through Distance mode from the University of Kashmir, Srinagar, India in 2012. She has a gold medal in her Master of Electronics from University of Kashmir. At present, she is pursuing her Ph. D in the same department. Her research interests include Image Compression, Digital Image Forensics.

Lakshmi Sarvani Videla received her M. Tech degree in Computer Science and Engineering from Velagapudi Ramakrishna Siddhartha Engineering College (affiliated to JNTUK) in 2014. She is currently pursuing Ph. D (CSE) in Koneru Lakshmaiah Education Foundation (KLEF). She is working as Assistant professor in KLEF since 2016. Her main areas of research interest are machine learning, image processing and data mining. She has expertise in MATLAB, Python,C++, Java, and Android.

Index

A

accuracy 3, 5, 40, 53, 63, 85, 129, 161, 166-167, 171-172, 183-184, 197-199, 205, 241, 255

Adaptively Scanned Wavelet Difference Reduction (ASWDR) 43, 56

Alzheimer's disease (AD) 225, 228-230, 232

anisotropic diffusion 100, 102-104, 110, 118, 253

Antigen 160, 169

article 188-189

Artificial intelligence (AI) 240-241

B

Bits per Pixels (BPP) 39, 44, 56, 75, 78-82, 86-93, 99

blockiness 101, 103, 116, 118

blurriness 101, 103, 114-115, 118

C

Canny Operator 21, 255, 272

Chaos Mapping 37

Chaos theory 30, 37

chaotic 2, 23, 25-27, 29, 32-33, 35, 37

CLS 1, 21

cluttered scene 189-191

CMS 252, 272

color correction 211-212, 215, 217-218, 220-221, 223

compression ratio 38-40, 43, 50, 52, 56-57, 74-75, 99, 123, 157

Compression Ratio (CR) 38-40, 43-44, 50, 52-53, 56-57, 74-75, 78-79, 83, 85-86, 88-94, 99, 123, 125-127, 131, 140, 149, 152-153, 157, 233

Computed Tomography (CT) 38-39, 41-42, 49, 52-53, 56, 237, 240

Convolution 159, 161-162, 169, 179, 190-191, 254, 258

convolutional neural networks 158

CR 39, 44, 53, 56-57, 74-75, 78-79, 83, 85-86, 88-94, 99, 123, 125-127, 131, 140, 149, 152-153, 157, 233

Cryptography 23, 37

CWT 59, 61, 99

D

DCT 40-42, 56, 69, 128, 146-147, 149-152, 157

decryption 23, 25, 30, 37

dehazing model 211, 218-219, 223

dementia 225, 227-228, 230, 232-234

denoising 100-104, 110, 117-118, 255

DFT 146, 157

digital image processing 102, 158-159, 252, 272

DIP 252-254

Discrete cosine Transform (DCT) 40-42, 56, 69, 121, 128, 146-147, 149-152, 157

Dlib facial landmark detector 180-181

DWT 42, 56, 63-67, 74-75, 79, 86, 93, 99, 128, 146, 157

DWT - Discrete Wavelet Transform 56

Ensure Quality Research is Introduced to the Academic Community

Become an IGI Global Reviewer for Authored Book Projects

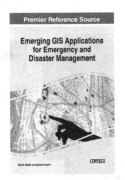
Premier Reference Source

Emerging GIS Applications for Emergency and Disaster Management

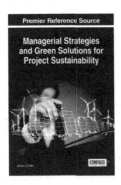
Premier Reference Source

Managerial Strategies and Green Solutions for Project Sustainability

Premier Reference Source

Comparative Approaches to Using R and Python for Statistical Data Analysis

Premier Reference Source

Solutions for High-Touch Communications in a High-Tech World

The overall success of an authored book project is dependent on quality and timely reviews.

In this competitive age of scholarly publishing, constructive and timely feedback significantly expedites the turnaround time of manuscripts from submission to acceptance, allowing the publication and discovery of forward-thinking research at a much more expeditious rate. Several IGI Global authored book projects are currently seeking highly-qualified experts in the field to fill vacancies on their respective editorial review boards:

Applications and Inquiries may be sent to:
development@igi-global.com

Applicants must have a doctorate (or an equivalent degree) as well as publishing and reviewing experience. Reviewers are asked to complete the open-ended evaluation questions with as much detail as possible in a timely, collegial, and constructive manner. All reviewers' tenures run for one-year terms on the editorial review boards and are expected to complete at least three reviews per term. Upon successful completion of this term, reviewers can be considered for an additional term.

If you have a colleague that may be interested in this opportunity, we encourage you to share this information with them.

Printed in the United States
By Bookmasters